PUBLIC SPEAKING

PUBLIC SPEAKING

SECOND EDITION

LINDA AND DICK HEUN

Northeast Missouri State University, Emeritus

WEST PUBLISHING COMPANY

St. Paul ▪ *New York* ▪ *Los Angeles* ▪ *San Francisco*

Copy Editor: Judith Peacock
Illustrations: Jim Kiehne
Composition: Janet Hansen Associates

PHOTO CREDITS

Cover (top) Hanson Carroll/FPG International (middle) Dick Luria/FPG International (bottom) Helena Frost/Frost Publishing Group **Page ii** (top left) Peter Southwick/Stock, Boston (top right) Billy E. Barnes/Jeroboam (bottom) Jean-Claude Lejeune/Stock, Boston **xiv** David S. Strickler/Monkmeyer Press **7** Ellis Herwig/Stock, Boston **11** The Bettmann Archive **14** Robert V. Eckert, Jr./Stock, Boston **18** Jeffrey Grosscup **26** Mary Regan **32** Owen Franken/Stock, Boston **38** Rick Smolan/Stock, Boston **46** G. C. Owen/Black Star **52** Jeffrey Grosscup **61** Peter Southwick/Stock, Boston **64** Jeff Dunn/Stock, Boston **70** Jill Cannefax/EKM-Nepenthe **95** Owen Franken/Stock, Boston **98** Howard Dratch/Black Star **108** Elizabeth Crews/Stock, Boston **115** Robert Pacheco/EKM-Nepenthe **124** UPI/Bettmann Newsphotos **130** Frank Siteman/EKM-Nepenthe **139** Christopher Morrow/Stock, Boston **148** Dennis Brack/Black Star **158** Elizabeth Hamlin/Stock, Boston **164** UPI/Bettmann Newsphotos **176** Cindy Charles/Gamma-Liaison **180** Jeff Albertson/Stock, Boston **187** Peter Menzel/Stock, Boston **195** Robert V. Eckert, Jr./EKM-Nepenthe **206** George Bellerose/Stock, Boston **213** Hazel Hankin/Stock, Boston **217** Barbara Alper/Stock, Boston **222** Edinger/Liaison **229** Mary Regan **240** Robert V. Eckert, Jr./EKM-Nepenthe **244** David Hurn/Magnum **249** Stuart Rosner/Stock, Boston **256** Howard Dratch/Black Star **260** Ellis Herwig/Stock, Boston **268** George Bellerose/Stock, Boston **273** UPI/Bettmann Newsphotos **280** Frank Siteman/EKM-Nepenthe **292** Howard Dratch/Black Star **295** Jeffrey Grosscup

Library of Congress Cataloging-in-Publication Data

Heun, Richard E.
    Public speaking.

    Includes index.
    1. Public speaking.   I. Heun, Linda R.   II. Title.
PN4121.H3485 1986   808.5'1   85-20230
ISBN 0-314-93187-2

To our parents—

    for their continuing love, support, and motivation to grow

CONTENTS

TO THE STUDENT

In this second edition of *Public Speaking* we've used the input of many, many students and colleagues to provide even better answers to a key question faced by public speaking students: "How do I get from the assignment to my speech?" This is the same question faced by speakers outside of a classroom situation and by your instructor as he or she decides the order in which you will work on the skills necessary to accomplish a specific speech purpose. There are two reasons for this uncertainty. The first is that the skills involved in public speaking are so interrelated that it actually seems that you need all skills to be developed before you can get "to the speech." The second reason is that the order in which a skilled speaker would actually use the skills to prepare a speech might not be the best order in which to develop them. This is because some of the skills involve higher level thinking and analysis than others and it is possible for you to give some kinds of speeches without them.

We wanted you to be able to begin speaking in this class as soon as possible, so we wrestled with the question, "What do they need to know and when do they need to know it?" The ordering of the units of study in this book, as listed below, reflects our answers.

- Self-assessment of public speaking skills
- Dealing with communication anxiety
- Developing listening skills
- Choosing a speech topic
- Developing a specific purpose and main points
- Analyzing your audience
- Identifying options for developing, supporting and clarifying materials
- Researching for speech materials
- Planning for visual aids
- Organizing the body of your message
- Developing introductions, conclusions and transitions
- Involving your audience through emotional appeals
- Developing reasoned arguments

- Choosing effective language
- Informing an audience about new ideas
- Developing effective delivery skills
- Persuading an audience to change an attitude or behavior
- Developing skills for special occasion speaking

The ordering is based on our development of skill hierarchies, which are a way to determine the major and component skills involved in preparing for a speaking situation. We introduced listening skills early because of their extensive use and importance in the process of skill development involved in classroom learning as well as in your everyday life. This is not the only way these units could be ordered. Because your instructor knows you and your current speaking skills better than we do, he or she may decide to reorder the chapters in some way.

You may not have realized that public speaking involved the use of such a variety of thinking and communication skills. Developing these skills will be a challenge, but worth the time you spend on your own and with your instructor and other class members. We've chosen a format for this book which we believe will help you reach this important goal. The format is based on a well-known study method called the SQ3R method. Essentially, that method suggests that efficient and effective learning occurs when you: Survey-Question-Read-Recite-Review. Here's how this text uses that basic format to assist your learning:

- The text helps you to SURVEY the learning you are about to do with
  — an introductory list of the skills you will work toward by Understanding, Interacting, and Speaking;
  — an Outline which summarizes the chapter content; and
  — a Preview which provides an orientation and overview of the chapter content.
- The text poses QUESTIONS about the learning you are about to do with a question-answer format. The questions are ones commonly asked by people working on public speaking skills.
- The text provides READING materials which contain information and examples to help you gain the background for skill development.
- The text helps you RECITE by providing frequent opportunities to check your understanding through Learning by Understanding sections and to check and develop skills through Learning by Interacting experiences.
- The text helps you REVIEW the learning you have done with
  — Internal Lists and Charts which summarize reading material for a quick review; and
  — Final Chapter Reviews which summarize the chapter content.

We think the combination of these procedures and the carefully revised and supplemented written materials, including seven sample speeches, result in a text that you'll really get involved with—because it is a valuable aid in your development of the important skills of public speaking.

ACKNOWLEDGMENTS

We would like to indicate our sincere appreciation to the many, many students and colleagues whose suggestions, enthusiasm, and overall support were vital to the improvements which appear in this second edition of *Public Speaking*. Special thanks for the continuing friendship of Bob, Anna Mae, and Elsie who always bring us back on target with caring and zest.

We were impressed and stimulated by the fine student finalists (and their coaches) at the 1985 American Forensic Association National Individual Events Tournament who willingly allowed us to use their excellent speeches as samples in our text: Judith J. Barton, University of Iowa; John C. Deeth, University of Wisconsin–Eau Claire; Randy Larsen, Humboldt State University; Mary Nielsen, Northern Illinois University; and Michael D. Stolts, University of Wisconsin–Eau Claire. We also appreciated the willingness of G. J. Tankersley, Chairman and Chief Executive Officer of Consolidated Natural Gas Company, to allow us to use his excellent speech in our text.

Reviewers whose ideas influenced the content of this revision through their insightful and constructive critiques were Elizabeth Coughlin, Northern Virginia Community College; Marion Couvillion, Mississippi State University; James Gibson, University of Missouri; Ralph Hillman, Middle Tennessee State University; David Mrizek, San Antonio College; Mary Anne Rhodes, Catonsville Community College; Charles Romero, Los Angeles City College; Enid Waldhart, University of Kentucky; Larry Winn, Western Kentucky University; Dennis White, Arkansas State University. Their time and effort greatly improved the materials.

Finally, our thanks to the people at West Publishing Company, whose professional skills were invaluable throughout the entire rethinking and preparation of this revision: J. B. Yowell, our insightful and sensitive editor; Tad Bornhoft, production editor; Lucinda Gatch, promotion manager.

PUBLIC SPEAKING

1

UNDERSTANDING PUBLIC SPEAKING

In this chapter, you'll be . . .

LEARNING BY UNDERSTANDING

- The importance of public speaking skills
- Seven basic elements of communication
- Two characteristics of public speaking that distinguish it from other levels of communication
- Three main types of audience response
- Classical contributions to the study of public speaking
- Modern contributions to the study of public speaking
- Five areas in which public speakers make choices
- The components of an audience's frame of reference
- How audience choices are influenced by their frame of reference
- Two bases for ethical choices in public speaking

LEARNING BY INTERACTING

- Developing a model of public speaking

LEARNING BY SPEAKING

- An informative speech to share the results of your interview with a practicing professional in your chosen occupation regarding his or her use of public speaking skills.

CHAPTER OUTLINE

(NOTE: As we explained in "To The Student," we have prepared detailed Chapter Outlines for your use. You might benefit from carefully reading through the Chapter Outline to *preview* the material in the chapter. This might be helpful to orient your thinking to enable you to skip over parts of the chapter you already know. Other students have found these Chapter Outlines most helpful as a *review* after they have read the chapter. Try using these outlines!)

I. Public speaking skills are important to success in many professional fields.
   A. Public speaking helps you share your ideas with others.
   B. Public speaking involves a variety of thinking, language, and behavioral skills.
   C. Public speaking is often a factor in hiring and promotion.

II. Public speaking is a level of human communication.
   A. The process of communication involves seven basic elements.
      1. The sender in the communication process is the person who sends the message.
      2. The message represents the meanings the sender wants to share with the receiver.
         a. The message consists of symbols chosen by the speaker to communicate intended meanings.
         b. The main symbol system used in human communication is the verbal symbol system.
      3. The channel is the means by which the message is sent.
      4. The receiver is the person receiving the sender's message.
      5. Feedback is the response messages sent by the receiver during and/or after the message is received and understood.
      6. Barriers are internal and external factors which interfere in accurate sending and receiving of messages.
      7. The communication situation includes the physical aspects of the speech setting and the relationship between speaker and listener.
   B. Human communication functions on three basic levels.
      1. Intrapersonal communication refers to the communication you have with yourself.
      2. Interpersonal communication refers to communication you have with one person or a group of people in which the roles of sender and receiver change often.
      3. Public speaking refers to the communication of a continuous message by one person to call up a response within a specific group of people called an audience.
   C. Public speaking differs from the other levels in two ways.
      1. In public speaking, the message is called a speech and is a continuous oral statement from the speaker.
      2. In public speaking, the audience's attention focuses on the speaker.
   D. Public speaking involves speaker and audience choice making.
      1. Speakers choose appropriate speech content to achieve their speech purpose.
      2. Audiences make choices depending on their listening goals.

    E. Public speeches can be classified in terms of the desired audience response.
        1. With informative speech, the speaker's purpose is to have the audience understand something new.
        2. With persuasive speech, the speaker's purpose is to have the audience believe or do something new.
        3. With entertaining speech, the speaker's purpose is to have members of the audience enjoy themselves.

III. Students of public speaking can learn from classical sources.
    A. Aristotle described most of the five basic areas for speaker choice making.
        1. Invention is the process of research and thinking that determines the content of the speech.
        2. Organization is the process of ordering the parts of the speech.
        3. Style refers to the process of selecting words to make the speech vivid, appropriate, and clear.
        4. Memory is the process of a speaker's memorizing the overall order of her or his speech and specific parts of the speech, which may be delivered without notes.
        5. Delivery is a process, involving both vocal and bodily action, of presenting a speech.
    B. Aristotle provided the basis for audience analysis by urging a consideration of audience emotions before making choices.

IV. Students of public speaking also can learn from modern sources.
    A. Modern research helps us understand an audience's frame of reference.
        1. A frame of reference combines an audience's attitudes, interests, and knowledge about a particular topic.
        2. An audience's frame of reference is composed of many factors—information the members already know about the speaker and the topic, attitudes they have formed about the speaker and the topic, interests, feelings they have about themselves, and degree of openness.
        3. An audience's frame of reference is the filter through which a speech is understood.
    B. Modern research helps us understand the process of audience listening.
        1. People process information and ideas in terms of what they already know, believe, and do.
        2. People process new information and ideas to fit into their current frame of reference.

V. Students of public speaking should consider the ethics of their choice making.
    A. Speakers should consider the end or results which they desire for the audience.
    B. Speakers should consider the means they choose to get the desired results.

1

UNDERSTANDING PUBLIC SPEAKING

If all my talents and powers were to be taken from me by some inscrutable Providence, and I had my choice of keeping but one, I would unhesitatingly ask to be allowed to keep the Power of Speaking, for through it, I would quickly recover all the rest.   —Daniel Webster

PREVIEW

Did you know that effective speaking skills are one of the most important factors employers will look for during job interviews and performance evaluations? This is because so many of the thinking, language, and behavioral skills involved in public speaking are important in a variety of professions. The time you spend developing your public speaking skills in this class will have significant payoffs for you in your personal and professional life.

This chapter will provide an overall framework for your public speaking skill development. You will consider public speaking as a process of speaker and audience choice making and discover how both classical and modern sources can aid you in your skill development.

How Will Public Speaking Skills Help Me?

Public speaking is a powerful communication tool by which you can share and/or sell your ideas to others. Because it is a form of human communication that calls for a variety of thinking, language, and behavioral skills, it is often considered the mark of a successful person. Employers who interview graduates for jobs frequently state that communication skills are vital in their fields.[1] Let's consider some of the situations in which you might make a public speech. You might use public speaking skills to teach employees or students a new procedure, to persuade customers with a sales presentation, to urge a jury to decide in favor of your client, to entertain guests at a retirement dinner, or to inspire others with a sermon or memorial speech. As an active citizen in a community, you might give a campaign speech to run for the local school board, express concern about an issue to the chamber of commerce, tell a local Girl Scout troop about an area of your expertise, or lead a lay group at your church. Consider recent campus activities, and you probably can make a similar list of the uses of public speaking skills at your school.

Organizations also seem to be returning to public speakers as a program source for their meetings. *Business Week* reports that "lecturing is now so popular and profitable that droves of celebrities are available for oratory and dozens of lecture bureaus have sprung up to serve them."[2] Carl Terzian, a consultant who trains executives in public speaking skills, reports, "The platform has become so popular in America—more than 80,000 audiences congregate daily in my native state of California alone."[3]

Your choice to develop your public speaking skills is important in terms of your professional preparation and employability. For example, Pamela M. Birchoff, a counselor at Ramapo College, writes that the ways of increasing a graduate's employability include "helping students to acquire well-developed communication skills, research capabilities, and analytical abilities . . . and the ability to complete independent research projects."[4]

Following is data from professionals in a sampling of areas which indicate the importance of the skills you are about to work on.

Robert E. Allen, president of the Chesapeake and Potomac Telephone Companies, in a speech entitled, "Effective Preparation for Career Opportunities within the Corporate World," indicated that a "very important characteristic we look for is evidence of good communication skills." He also referred to surveys of corporate recruiters and chief executive officers in which the "majority ranked communication skills as being the most crucial to managerial competency."[5]

Richard McCormick, president of Northwestern Bell, underlined the importance of specific communication skills as follows:

> We have to be better observers, better listeners. We have to be able to tell one another, clearly and concisely, what we're learning from our customers. We have to be able to sell our ideas to one another, on how to best serve those customers. We have to be able to sell our products and services. We have to be able to persuade legislators and regulators that federal rulings have changed the game and that state level changes must follow. On every front, we have to be good speakers . . . good writers . . . good listeners.[6]

Arthur Klein of the Mullican Company in Louisville, Kentucky, in a presentation entitled, "What Speech Communication Competencies Are Desirable for Prospective Employees in Public Relations," made a strong detailed analysis indicating the need for speech communication competencies in public relations.[7]

Alice Magill of the Southern Baptist Convention in Nashville, in a presentation, pointed out the need for communication skills in church work: "Communication skills are just as important to today's church vocations workers as they were to Jesus, if these workers are to be effective in persuading others to believe their message."[8]

- Carl Terzian, communication consultant, reported that because of the increased importance of public speaking to the executive "many corporations retain experts to concentrate on researching and cataloguing material, writing manuscripts, screening and soliciting invitations and coaching executives on speech discipline and techniques."[9]

- A booklet prepared by Albert L. Furbay, in cooperation with the National Employment Association, cited the following communication skills as valuable assets in employment: a positive approach, self-confidence and poise, intelligibility and good English, organized thinking, ability to get along with people, persuasive skill, and listening.[10]

- In a booklet prepared by the Speech Communication Association on "Speech Communication and Careers," several surveys indicated the importance of speech competency:

  > A recent study in Pennsylvania found that top management regarded communication in the organization as their most vital educational need. Management identified the following competencies as the most important for success: effective speaking, working efficiently with individuals and groups, effective communication in the organization, effective reading skills, and listening skills.

  > A project sponsored by the Committee for Economic Development studied over 5,000 people holding key posts in the federal service. They concluded that the professional's activities required that they be able to communicate their knowledge effectively and defend it persuasively both inside and outside the agency.[11]

- In a survey of 250 chief executive officers selected from the annual *Fortune* 500 listing of the country's most important companies, the following communication skills were indicated as being important in determining who got promoted: ability to argue logically, communicate clearly and concisely, and sell your ideas.[12]

- *Spectra*, a publication of the Speech Communication Association, reported that the American Management Association offers an introduction to public speaking course in various cities around the country. The association charges about $900 for a three-day course, which covers introductory talks, impromptu speeches, delivery, organization, audience analysis, answering questions, how to convince and persuade, and speaking on special occasions.[13]

Will public speaking and other communication skills be worth jobs, promotions, money, and satisfaction to you? You can count on it! By working on these skills now, you will be far ahead of many of those interviewing with you for jobs.

What Is Public Speaking?

Every communicative event, even those involving the same person, is unique, because people and situations change with time. In spite of this, there are common

Professionals use public speaking to give instruction and communicate important information.

elements in each communicative situation. Public speaking shares seven elements with other forms of human communication: sender, message, channel(s), receiver(s), feedback, barrier(s), and communication situation.

The *sender* is the person who sends the message. The *message* is developed by the sender and represents the meanings the sender chooses to share with the receiver. Messages consist of verbal and nonverbal symbols. Verbal symbols are words that represent the meanings intended; nonverbal symbols are means other than words, such as facial expressions, body movements, and vocal stress, that are used to represent meanings. The *channel* is the means by which the message is sent. Examples of channels for communicating messages are the telephone, a handwritten letter, or television.

The *receiver* is the person receiving the sender's message. The messages are received through the five human senses; for example, a television advertisement is received through the eyes (sight) and ears (sound). *Feedback* is the response message(s) sent by the receiver to the sender during and/or after the message has been received and understood. Feedback can consist of verbal and/or nonverbal symbols. *Barriers* include all of the factors, both internal and external, that interfere in accurate sending and receiving of messages. The *communication situation* includes both the physical aspects of the speech setting itself (place, time and layout of room and objects) and the relationship between the speaker and listener (roles and attitudes).

Figure 1-1 is a model of the seven elements. It parallels the picture on page 7.

These seven basic elements function on three levels of human communication—intrapersonal, interpersonal, and public communication. **Intrapersonal communication** refers to the communication you have with yourself. At this level, for example, you might be thinking about what topic you will use for your first speech assignment. **Interpersonal communication** refers to the communication you have with one person or a group of people in which the roles of the sender and receiver change often. At this level, you might ask a friend, "What kinds of questions will be on the midterm exam?" Your friend then answers your question (feedback) and asks you about your study plans. Thus, the process continues with you now being the receiver.

Public speaking is the process of one person using spoken language in a continuous message to call up an intended response within a specific group. The sender in public speaking is called the speaker, the message is called a speech, and the receivers are called the audience. At this level of communication, you (as speaker) might be giving a report (speech) to your classmates (audience) through speaking in public (channel). During your report, your classmates nod and look interested (feedback). You communicate in your classroom at the time your class meets (communication situation) and either hallroom noise or individual listener's contrary thoughts could interfere with accurate communication (barriers).

Our definition of public speaking focuses on two characteristics that distinguish it from intrapersonal or interpersonal communication—one, the use of a

Figure 1-1   Seven Elements of Communication

continuous oral message and, two, a situation for interaction that focuses the audience's attention on the speaker. While there may be interruptions in the form of comments, questions, or applause, the focus of attention usually stays on the speaker and his speech. Because of this attention, you usually think and plan more carefully before speaking publicly than you do for intrapersonal or interpersonal communication.

Before speaking, the speaker makes careful choices regarding the kinds of materials, organization, and style that are most likely to produce the desired response in the audience. Chapter 2 will help you assess your current levels of skills relating to public speaking. During the speech, the audience will make continuous choices regarding its reactions to the speaker and the speech. These choices will be reflected in nonverbal feedback during the speech. An experienced speaker will use this continuous feedback to adapt his or her choices during the speech. Finally, after the speech, the audience responds. Whether the *actual* audience response is the *desired* response will depend largely on the effectiveness of the speaker's initial choices and his or her adaptation of those choices during the speech. Your goal in this course will be to become increasingly skilled in both making effective choices *as a speaker* in order to maximize the occurrence of the desired audience response and in making choices *as a member of a speech audience* in order to make appropriate choices regarding the content of the speeches you listen to. Chapter 3 is designed specifically to help you develop ''audience'' skills; however, you will be working actively on both speaker and audience skills throughout the course.

What Are the Main Types of Audience Response?

Most public speaking teachers classify audience response in terms of the speaker's general purpose. The three basic classifications are to inform, to persuade, and to entertain. Most speakers work for all three basic responses at some time in each speech, but they have a single purpose to guide their overall speech choices.

An **informative speech** is one in which the speaker's general purpose is to have the audience understand something new or gain a new perspective on something audience members already know. Examples of informative speeches would be a teacher's lecture on DNA molecules or someone's explanation of the effects of a new IRS tax law on student tax breaks. The skills in developing and delivering an informative speech are basic to each of the other types. Therefore, Chapters 4–12 will assist you in developing skills basic to all understanding. A **persuasive speech** is one in which the speaker's general purpose is to have the audience believe and/or do something new. Examples of persuasive speeches would be a political candidate encouraging an audience to vote for her and a representative of the YMCA urging a group to start an exercise program. Your persuasive speaking skills will build on those developed in Chapters 4–12; specific skills in encouraging people to make a change will be developed in Chapter 13. An **entertaining speech** is one in which the speaker's general purpose is to have audience members enjoy themselves. Examples of entertaining speeches would be an after-dinner speech at a golf tournament and a humorous tribute delivered at a banquet. Entertaining speeches also build on the basic skills developed throughout the text.

Some speeches combine these general purposes. These special-occasion speeches are classified by the event itself, such as a graduation speech or a keynote speech. You will work on the specific skills for handling special-occasion speeches in Chapter 14.

LEARNING BY UNDERSTANDING

1. List two situations where you might use public speaking in your chosen profession.

2. List seven basic elements involved in public speaking.

3. For the picture on page 7 state one example for each of the seven elements of human communication.

4. In which level of communication is the man third from the end of the front row in the picture on page 7?

5. What are the two characteristics of public speaking that distinguish it from other levels of communication?

6. Identify the following as intrapersonal communication, interpersonal communication, or public speaking.
   a. A lawyer summarizing a case to a jury
   b. A person criticizing herself for sleeping through her public speaking class
   c. Two foremen talking about the problems of employee tardiness
   d. A committee meeting to decide arrangements for a graduation party
   e. A manager giving a monthly report to a board of directors

7. List the three main purposes for a speech.

8. Identify the type of speech each of the following speech titles most likely represents.
   a. "Baseball Umpires: Their Training and Licensing"
   b. "Take Up Swimming: Recreation for All Ages"
   c. "My Mother, the Pool Shark"
   d. "Recognizing Local Birds and Their Nests"

ANSWERS:

1. Giving reports and teaching others are typical examples. If you are unsure, the speaking experience described later in the chapter will be helpful.
2. Speaker, speech, channel, audience, feedback, barriers, and communication situation
3. SENDER: the man standing at the left
   MESSAGE: what the man standing is saying
   CHANNEL: speaking in public
   RECEIVER: the man sitting second from the left in the front row
   FEEDBACK: smiles from the men in the second row
   COMMUNICATION SITUATION: a lecture hall with chairs pointed toward the sender
   BARRIER: the man fourth from the left in the second row could be thinking about something else
4. A tough question! He might well be in the intrapersonal level, thinking about whispering something to the man on his left.
5. A continuous oral speech by the speaker and a situation that focuses attention on the speaker
6. a. public, b. intra, c. inter, d. inter, e. public
7. To inform, to persuade, and to entertain
8. a. informative, b. persuasive, c. entertaining, d. informative

What Can I Learn from Classical Sources to Improve My Public Speaking?

It was not until the Golden Age of the Greek city-states that public speaking training became an important part of a person's education. These skills gained importance because of the democratic form of government in Greece and the use of a court system in which people often pleaded their own cases. Public speaking was known as the art of *rhetoric* and was truly a ''survival'' skill for citizens. Aristotle, who made the most important and lasting contributions to the study of rhetoric, defined rhetoric as the art of finding the available means of persuasion.[14]

In 336 B.C., Aristotle described most of the five basic areas of speaker preparation—invention, organization, style, memory, and delivery. They remain the basis of speaker preparation today. *Invention* refers to the process of research and thinking that determines the content of a speech. *Organization* refers to the process of ordering the parts of a speech. *Style* refers to the process of selecting words to make the speech vivid, appropriate, and clear. *Memory* refers to the process of a speaker's memorizing the overall order of his or her speech and specific parts of the speech so that it can be delivered without notes. *Delivery* refers to the process, involving both vocal and bodily action, of presenting a speech.

Aristotle stressed that the speaker's choices must be made in terms of a specific audience. Aristotle focused on the emotions of the audience and their influence

Public speaking was a crucial and highly valued skill in the democracy of ancient Greece.

on audience response. This orientation is the basis of what we now call *audience analysis*, the careful study of a particular audience in order to achieve a desired response. This analysis is then used to guide the speaker's choices in preparing a speech.

Since Aristotle's time scholars have developed his ideas. Many of those refined ideas are still used today. About five hundred years ago, public speaking became part of a liberal arts education in universities and colleges.

Public speaking is considered a basic part of a liberal arts education because it can help individuals in so many ways.[15] The communicating skills which you develop in a public speaking course help you function at your greatest potential as a person. These important skills include clearly expressing an idea, thinking creatively and logically, synthesizing information, and adapting to a variety of other people. These skills not only will help you as you complete your college education, but also will be fundamental to your personal and professional lives.

What Can I Learn from Modern Sources to Improve My Public Speaking?

We have made great strides since Aristotle's time in understanding the human brain, human interaction, and effective communication. Studies by communication researchers and others have helped us understand the bases for audience attention, motivation, information processing, memory, and attitude change.[16] Other advances include greater understanding of communication apprehension, language usage, credibility, effective persuasive appeals, and the effects of the physical environment on the communication process. These developments from psychology and modern communication theory will help you make more effective choices. Your improved choice making will help you deliver speeches that are more likely to accomplish your desired purposes. It will also help you use the physical setting for speeches to your best advantage to accomplish your purpose.

From this research, we learn that audience members already know and believe many things that will influence how they react to you and your speech. This combination of audience attitudes, interest, and knowledge about a particular topic has been called a *frame of reference*. It includes information audience members already have about you and your topic, attitudes they have formed about you and your topic, their interests, their feelings about themselves, and their degree of openness. The audience's frame of reference serves as a filter system through which the audience deals with new information and ideas. Most people understand something new in terms of what they already know, and they process new information so that it fits into their current frame of reference.[17] Research indicates that people can reject, mishear, misunderstand, or forget information because of their attitudes before hearing it.[18]

Although an audience is a collection of individuals, there are usually similarities among its members that will help you understand its frame of reference. By analyzing your audience ahead of time and understanding as much as possible about its frame of reference, you, as a speaker, will be able to make choices that will lead to understanding and thoughtful choice making by the audience. This process of speaker and audience choice making is illustrated in Figure 1-2.

In this text, we will use the five basic areas described by Aristotle to help you develop your skills. We will also share with you modern research, theory, and, best of all, the experiences of other students and of veteran teachers within each of these areas to help you make the best choices. This combination of classical and modern sources will help you develop effective public speaking skills.

Might I Lead an Audience to Make Bad Choices?

An important question! As you develop strength as a public speaker, the likelihood that you will influence the choices of your audience will increase. There are many examples throughout history of the powerful negative (and positive) effects speakers can have through a public message. Therefore, the choices you make as a public speaker are very important and will reveal a great deal about your own personal ethics. This is especially important because some audiences are misinformed or biased about your topic and you could mislead them, intentionally or not.

This question is also a difficult one. In part, this question is asking to what extent you are responsible for the choices your audience makes. As you will see in Chapter 3, we believe that the role of the listener is an active and responsible one. Nevertheless, listeners have the right to assume that you have made your choices of organization, style, etc., carefully and are communicating them in a responsible way.

How Can I Make Ethical Choices as a Speaker?

Ethics can be thought of as the study of individual and social good and can be measured by the results of actions.[19] So, a basic question regarding the ethics of your speech becomes, What are you asking your audience to think and do? Many

Figure 1-2 Speaker and Audience Choice Making

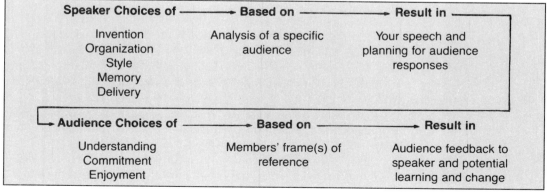

Speaker Choices of →	**Based on** →	**Result in** →
Invention Organization Style Memory Delivery	Analysis of a specific audience	Your speech and planning for audience responses

Audience Choices of →	**Based on** →	**Result in** →
Understanding Commitment Enjoyment	Members' frame(s) of reference	Audience feedback to speaker and potential learning and change

The knowledge and attitudes your audience already has will influence their understanding of your message.

speakers have found it helpful to ask themselves questions about the **ends**, or results, for the audience. These questions are usually best answered by considering how beneficial the ends are for a particular audience. For example, if you were to explain a new diet plan for losing weight to your class, you would first be concerned with whether trying this diet would be in the audience's best interest. To decide this you would need to know the effectiveness and safety of the diet as well as other concerns for a college audience, such as cost of the plan. The more the diet plan was safe, effective, and affordable, the more ethical would be the desired speech results.

In addition to considering the ethics of the end results, it is also important to consider the ethics of the **means** to get the desired results. The means relate to your choices in selecting (e.g., invention) and presenting (e.g., delivery) the speech's content. Most ethical speakers attempt to use both personally involving content and logical/factual content so that audiences can clearly understand and work to make their own careful choices. For your speech on diet, you would want to present accurate and full information and use language that was clear to *this* audience. While you would want to work for emotional involvement and commitment, you would also want your audience to know and understand the benefits of the diet plan.

The skills you develop in this course will help you to make effective *and* ethical choices for your speeches. This will have benefits not only for your audience, but also for you. One of the additional benefits of your making ethical choices is that your audience will respect you and you will respect yourself. This is one reason why public speaking is considered an important part of a liberal arts education.

LEARNING BY UNDERSTANDING

1. Match the five areas of speaker preparation and their descriptions.

    a. The process of mastering the overall order and specific parts of the speech so it can be delivered without notes

    b. The process of ordering the parts of a speech

    c. The process, involving both vocal and bodily action, of presenting a speech

    d. The process of research and thinking that determines the content of a speech

    e. The use of language symbols to make the speech vivid and clear

    1. invention
    2. organization
    3. style
    4. memory
    5. delivery

2. Which of the following accurately describe an audience's frame of reference?
    a. An audience's frame of reference includes what members already know about a particular topic.
    b. An audience's frame of reference can cause the audience to distort information.
    c. An audience's frame of reference does not influence responses to the speaker.
    d. An audience's frame of reference is understood through audience analysis.

3. Which of the following are *speaker choices* and which are *audience choices*?
    a. Organization of speech
    b. Acceptability of speaker's language
    c. Style of speech
    d. Behavior resulting from a speech

4. What two questions can help a speaker decide if a speech is ethical for a particular audience?

5. Which of the following are *ends* and which are *means*?
    a. Deciding that losing two pounds a week was a safe rate
    b. Deciding that using only one expert's comments is enough
    c. Deciding to minimize technical nutrition language
    d. Deciding that fats in a person's diet should be reduced

ANSWERS:

5. **a.** ends, **b.** means, **c.** means, **d.** ends
4. What are you asking the audience to think or do? What means are used to encourage the audience to make choices?
3. **a.** audience, **b.** speaker, **c.** speaker, **d.** audience
2. a., b., d.
1. **a.** memory, **b.** organization, **c.** delivery, **d.** invention, **e.** style

LEARNING BY INTERACTING

One way to better understand the process of communication during a public speech is to create a visual representation of it. This representation, called a model, shows the elements involved in the process and the relationship among the elements.

We suggest that you work with others to build your own model that visualizes the process of public speaking. As a starting point, each member of your small group could bring a personally developed model or an example of an already developed model. From these sources, you might want to add other elements to the seven common elements already described.

LEARNING BY SPEAKING

The following interviewing and speaking experience is an excellent way to learn more about the use of public speaking skills. It also reveals some of the choices speakers are making and the choices they ask their audiences to make.

If you have determined your professional goals, write down the specific job you hope to have in five years. If you have not yet determined specific professional goals, select one of the following areas that is closest to your personal interests:

Religion
Government
Education
Business
Law
Medicine
Military

Locate a practicing professional who holds the job or works in the area you have chosen. Make an appointment to interview that person to learn about the public communication skills he or she uses on the job. (If you are unable to arrange this, interview a college teacher in your major field.)

We suggest that you plan a list of questions before the interview. You might start with the following:

1. What kind of communication situations are you most often involved in?
2. When do you speak before a group of people in your job? In your personal life?
3. What topics do you give speeches on?
4. How do you prepare for your speeches?

Add at least three questions of your own.

Share your questions and the person's answers in a two- to four-minute talk to your class. Your purpose is to inform the class of what you learned from the interview.

REVIEW

Public speaking is a powerful communication tool that is linked to success in many professional fields. It differs from other levels of communication in that the speaker gives a continuous oral speech in a situation where the audience's attention is focused on the speaker. The process of public speaking is one of choice making by both speaker and audience.

Aristotle described most of the five basic areas in which public speakers make choices as invention, organization, style, memory, and delivery. These choices are made in terms of an analysis of the specific audience and result in the speech and the speaker's anticipation of audience response. As the audience members receive, understand, and assess the speech, they will make choices based on their frame of reference. The audience choices result in feedback to the speaker during the speech and potential learning and change. Research and experience since Aristotle's time have increased our understanding of audience choice making, which, in turn, has helped speakers make better choices.

A continuing concern of the public speaker is making ethical speaking choices. This is largely determined by keeping the best interests of the audience in mind.

NOTES

1. Robert E. Allen, "Effective Preparation for Career Opportunities within the Corporate World," *Vital Speeches of the Day* 49 (December 1, 1982):111.

2. Bradley Hitchings, ed., "When It's Your Turn to Book a Speaker," *Business Week* (Sept. 12, 1977):121.

3. Carl R. Terzian, "Going to Communicate: Try Speaking!" *Public Relations Journal* 32 (May 1976):16.

4. Pamela M. Birchoff, "Increasing Employability," *Change* 10 (June–July 1978):67.

5. Allen, "Effective Preparation," 110.

6. Richard D. McCormick, "Business Loves English," *Vital Speeches of the Day* 51 (November 1, 1984):52.

7. Presentation made by Arthur Klein at Career Opportunities Conference at Bowling Green, Kentucky, April 28, 1973.

8. Presentation made by Alice Magill at Career Opportunities Conference at Bowling Green, Kentucky, April 28, 1973.

9. Terzian, "Going to Communicate," 16.

10. Albert L. Furbay, "Career Opportunities for Liberal Arts Majors," National Employment Association, Washington, D.C.

11. "Speech Communication and Careers," Speech Communication Association, Washington, D.C.

12. W.J. Heislar, "Promotion: What Does It Take to Get Ahead?" *Business Horizons* (April 1978):57.

13. "Value of Public Speaking Course," *Spectra* 20 (November 1984):5.

14. Lester Thonssen and A. Craig Baird, *Speech Criticism* (New York: Ronald Press, 1948):57.

15. Frank H. T. Rhodes, "The Role of the Liberal Arts in a Decade of Increased Technology," *Vital Speeches of the Day* 50 (June 15, 1984):533.

16. Mark A. McDaniel, "The Role of Elaborative and Schema Processes in Story Memory," *Memory and Cognition* 12 (January 1984):46.

17. For example, International Communication Association's annual *Communication Yearbooks.*

18. For a summary of this research see the most recent "Attitudes and Opinions" in *Annual Review of Psychology.*

19. Thonssen and Baird, *Speech Criticism.*

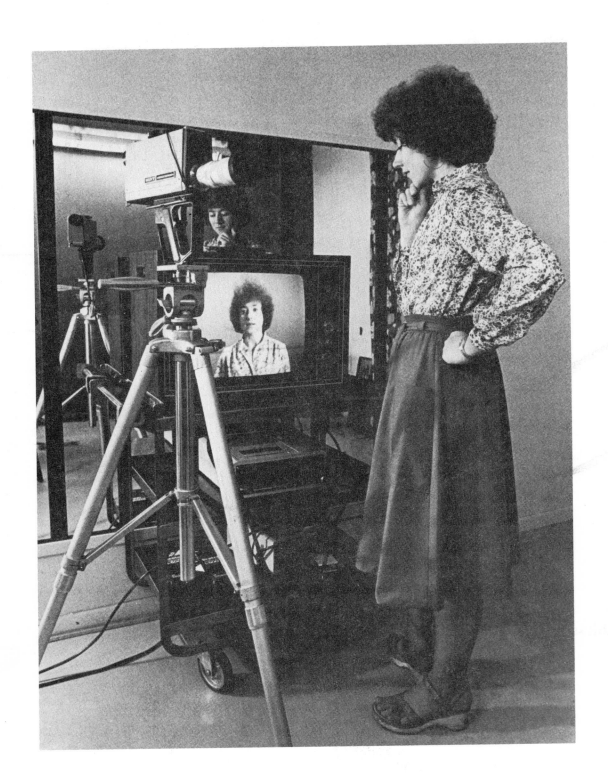

2

ASSESSING YOUR SKILLS AND GETTING STARTED

In this chapter, you'll be . . .

LEARNING BY UNDERSTANDING

- Why it is helpful to identify specific skills for improvement
- What skills may be important for success in your future job
- How to locate chapters for improving specific skills
- Seven basic steps for preparing a short speech
- Symptoms of communication apprehension
- Three characteristics of communication apprehension
- How much anxiety is desirable for a good performance
- Methods for managing nervousness before speaking

LEARNING BY INTERACTING

- How your feelings of communication anxiety compare with those of others in the class

CHAPTER OUTLINE

I. Everyone can assess and then develop speaking skills.
    A. Each person has a unique combination of already-developed, developing, and not-yet-developed speaking skills.
    B. It is helpful to assess your personal strengths and to identify specific skills for improvement.

II. One way to assess public speaking skills is by completing the Inventory of Public Speaking Skills in this chapter.
    A. The inventory helps you determine your relative skill development.
    B. Skills should be developed using two guidelines.
        1. Because speaking skills are interconnected, earlier skills will influence later skills.
        2. Attitudes and skills influence each other.
            a. Poor attitudes detract from effective speaking.
            b. Positive attitudes are essential to skill development.

III. Seven basic steps help a speaker prepare a short speech.
    A. Choose a topic of interest and value to the speaker and the audience.
    B. Determine the audience's level of knowledge of that topic.
    C. Research additional information.
    D. Decide what information can be given in the time limit.
    E. Decide the order in which to give the information.
    F. Develop notes for reference during the speech.
    G. Practice several times, keeping within the time limit.

IV. Nervousness before an audience concerns most beginning public speakers; it is called communication apprehension.
- **A.** Typical symptoms of this nervousness are sweaty palms, a fluttery stomach, a dry mouth, flushed skin, tense muscles, and irregular breathing.
- **B.** There are three characteristics of communication apprehension.
  - **1.** Communication apprehension is natural because people are uncomfortable in situations with unknown and/or potentially embarrassing consequences.
  - **2.** Communication apprehension is expected by your classmates and teacher.
  - **3.** Communication apprehension is desirable; a moderate amount of anxiety is necessary for a best performance.
- **C.** Certain behaviors can help you cope with communication apprehension.
  - **1.** Take several deep breaths before going up to speak.
  - **2.** Consciously relax your muscles.
  - **3.** Walk calmly to the front of the room, take time to organize your notes, and establish eye contact with your audience.
  - **4.** Use audience involvement procedures at the beginning of the speech.
  - **5.** Use a visual aid or demonstration and natural gestures to consume extra energy.
  - **6.** Remind yourself before you speak that you know more about your topic than your listeners do.

2

ASSESSING YOUR SKILLS AND GETTING STARTED

Know Thyself —*Oracle at Delphi*

PREVIEW

No one is a "born" speaker. All of us can develop our public speaking skills. The purpose of this chapter is to help you accurately assess your personal speaking-related skills and to identify areas for improvement. This accurate assessment will enable you to focus your learning on specific areas. We also want you to start developing your skills by knowing some basic steps in preparing a short speech.

A common self-assessment that beginning speakers make is that they are nervous about speaking in front of others. The symptoms and characteristics of speech anxiety are discussed in this chapter and suggestions are offered for coping with these feelings of nervousness.

How Should I Start Developing My Public Speaking Skills?

In ancient Greece, a famous temple was built to honor Apollo, considered the god of prophecy. A wise saying was carved into the temple—"Know Thyself." "Know Thyself" can be interpreted to mean that everyone has areas of highly developed skills, developing skills, and other skills that are not yet developed. Each person brings to the public speaking situation a unique bundle of abilities. You are unique. For example, you have a particular way of speaking. This way is so unique that a complex machine called a spectrograph can distinguish your particular "voice prints" from those of any other person. If you wanted to change the speed or volume of your speech, you could. Each of your skills can improve.

We have found that it is desirable to determine specific areas for improvement so that you can direct and concentrate your learning efforts. Some people, instead of describing their areas for improvement, criticize themselves for not being perfect.

We suggest that those people take off their black-and-white referee shirts and give up their whistles. Description leads to a more accurate and positive self-understanding. For example, a professional golfer who is attempting to improve her game would identify those areas in which she is losing strokes. She might discover that she is using more than thirty-six strokes for putting or that she is hitting too few greens "in regulation." Specifically describing areas that need improvement is more valuable than saying, "I'm not hitting well, so I'll try harder next time."

Without concentrating on specific skills, trying harder or making excuses is not likely to lead to improvement. The same applies to public speaking. Being able to "know thyself" by describing your strengths and specific areas for improvement enables you to direct your learning toward total speaking effectiveness.

How Can I Describe My Skills?

Because it is desirable to describe the current levels of your public speaking skills, we recommend that you complete the Inventory of Public Speaking Skills (IPSS) on page 24. We developed this inventory on the basis of the component skills involved in listening to, preparing, and delivering speeches. Many other students have found this a helpful way to describe their current skills.

How Did I Do on the Inventory?

Using the Inventory of Public Speaking Skills, you will be able to identify less-developed skills and specific areas for improvement. To assist you in identifying skills to be improved, we have included the average scores of 503 beginning public speaking students (page 25). The number in the first column is the average score for that particular skill. The next seven columns of numbers are the percentages of students who marked that level of skill development for each skill. In those areas where the number you have chosen to describe your current skill development is higher than the average of typical beginning students, your skill is probably quite well developed already. In those areas where the number is lower than the average, you can identify skills for special work.

How Do I Decide What Skills to Work On?

The first way is by comparison with other people—with the averages and percentages of the 503 students. A second way is by comparing the skills with your personal goals for using speaking skills. Your interview with a practicing professional from Chapter 1 could have helped identify many of your likely future uses. If, for example, you will be using public speaking skills for public relations purposes, then analyzing the audience, developing your credibility, choosing words, and delivery will be especially important. If, as a manager, you will be using public speaking skills for communicating information and procedures to your employees,

INVENTORY OF PUBLIC SPEAKING SKILLS

For each of the skills identified in the Inventory of Public Speaking Skills, circle the number which best describes our current level of skill development.

Skill	Current Skill Development						
	Little Skill Development				High Skill Development		
Understand meanings while listening	1	2	3	4	5	6	7
Analyze while listening	1	2	3	4	5	6	7
Give feedback	1	2	3	4	5	6	7
Ask questions	1	2	3	4	5	6	7
Choose a specific speech topic	1	2	3	4	5	6	7
Choose a specific speech purpose	1	2	3	4	5	6	7
Develop main points	1	2	3	4	5	6	7
Organize main points	1	2	3	4	5	6	7
Analyze an audience	1	2	3	4	5	6	7
Research a speech topic	1	2	3	4	5	6	7
Support main points	1	2	3	4	5	6	7
Develop logical arguments	1	2	3	4	5	6	7
Develop emotional appeals	1	2	3	4	5	6	7
Develop my credibility	1	2	3	4	5	6	7
Develop an introduction	1	2	3	4	5	6	7
Develop a conclusion	1	2	3	4	5	6	7
Develop an outline	1	2	3	4	5	6	7
Choose words	1	2	3	4	5	6	7
Use visual aids	1	2	3	4	5	6	7
Handle nervousness	1	2	3	4	5	6	7
Be assertive	1	2	3	4	5	6	7
Articulate and pronounce words correctly	1	2	3	4	5	6	7
Practice a speech	1	2	3	4	5	6	7
Remember a speech	1	2	3	4	5	6	7
Deliver a speech	1	2	3	4	5	6	7
Think on my feet	1	2	3	4	5	6	7
Plan for audience response	1	2	3	4	5	6	7
Adapt to feedback	1	2	3	4	5	6	7
Adapt to the setting	1	2	3	4	5	6	7
Handle questions	1	2	3	4	5	6	7
Handle criticism	1	2	3	4	5	6	7
Determine if I accomplished my goal	1	2	3	4	5	6	7
Identify areas for further improvement	1	2	3	4	5	6	7
Change audience's attitudes	1	2	3	4	5	6	7
Change audience's actions	1	2	3	4	5	6	7
Talk on short notice	1	2	3	4	5	6	7
Handle special occasions	1	2	3	4	5	6	7

RESULTS OF INVENTORY OF PUBLIC SPEAKING SKILLS

		Little Skill Development				High Skill Development			
		Percentages							Location
	Averages	1	2	3	4	5	6	7	in Text
Understand meanings while listening	5.17	1	1	8	15	34	27	14	Chapter 3
Analyze while listening	4.26	2	2	12	19	28	27	10	Chapter 3
Give feedback	4.40	2	7	14	28	22	19	8	Chapter 3
Ask questions	4.45	1	6	19	27	26	16	5	Chapter 3
Choose a specific speech topic	4.24	1	11	18	27	24	14	5	Chapter 4
Choose a specific purpose	4.20	2	8	19	30	23	12	6	Chapter 5
Develop main points	4.57	1	3	12	31	31	19	3	Chapter 5
Organize main points	4.37	2	5	14	26	28	21	4	Chapter 7
Analyze an audience	4.07	4	11	19	30	17	12	7	Chapter 4
Research a speech topic	4.57	1	4	16	24	31	19	5	Chapter 5
Support main points	4.72	1	3	11	25	33	21	6	Chapter 5
Develop logical arguments	4.69	1	4	12	25	31	20	7	Chapter 9
Develop emotional appeals	4.10	9	4	18	26	25	13	5	Chapter 8
Develop credibility	4.53	3	2	15	26	30	19	5	Chapter 8
Develop an introduction	4.67	1	6	10	26	29	19	9	Chapter 7
Develop a conclusion	4.71	0	4	13	31	23	21	8	Chapter 7
Develop an outline	4.41	2	6	18	25	26	16	7	Chapter 7
Choose words	4.39	1	4	14	29	28	18	6	Chapter 10
Use visual aids	4.11	3	11	24	21	23	11	7	Chapter 6
Handle nervousness	4.37	3	12	13	22	25	16	9	Chapter 2
Be assertive	4.23	4	7	15	30	27	14	3	Chapter 11
Articulate and pronounce words correctly	4.66	1	4	14	27	25	20	9	Chapter 11
Practice a speech	4.52	2	8	11	27	24	20	8	Chapter 11
Remember a speech	4.42	4	6	11	28	27	18	6	Chapter 11
Deliver a speech	4.16	4	9	13	28	29	14	3	Chapter 11
Think on my feet	4.28	3	5	21	26	27	13	5	Chapter 11
Plan for audience response	3.74	14	6	15	30	21	13	1	Chapter 11
Adapt to feedback	4.42	3	6	12	29	29	15	6	Chapter 11
Adapt to the setting	4.42	3	6	9	30	32	18	2	Chapter 11
Handle questions	4.55	3	5	11	28	26	21	6	Chapter 14
Handle criticism	4.49	4	6	14	24	26	18	8	Chapter 14
Determine if I accomplished my speech goal	4.59	3	4	14	23	28	21	7	Chapter 12
Identify areas for further improvement	4.54	4	2	11	28	28	19	8	Chapter 2
Change audience's attitudes	4.24	2	8	19	38	20	14	4	Chapter 13
Change audience's actions	3.90	5	8	20	36	20	9	2	Chapter 13
Talk on short notice	3.79	9	16	16	26	17	12	4	Chapter 14
Handle special occasions	4.03	7	7	17	33	21	11	4	Chapter 14

then organizing main points, using visual aids, and handling questions will be extremely important.

There are two things to keep in mind here. First, the less-developed and more personally important skills may need your direct attention. But you should not exclude work on other skills; since skills are interconnected and built on each other, it will be helpful to develop all of them. Second, feedback from your teacher and classmates will provide other viewpoints of your relative development of each skill. For some skills, you may not see yourself as accurately as others do. For example, beginning public speaking students almost always see themselves as more nervous than their classmates and teacher do.

How Can I Develop My Skills?

The preceding inventory summary sheet identifies chapters in this book for developing each skill. As you develop your skills, remember that public communication skills are interconnected. Some earlier skills will influence later skills. For example, how well you develop and support main points, choose words, and practice your

Discussing the results of your IPSS with a classmate provides another viewpoint of your speaking skills.

speech will influence how well you deliver your speech. Thus, it is important to learn and apply each skill.

Remember, too, that attitudes and skills influence each other. If, for example, you lack confidence in your speaking abilities, you are probably going to use your skills less effectively. Positive attitudes will greatly help your skill development and use.

By identifying, learning, and practicing the skills and attitudes that are most important to you, your overall skill development in public speaking will increase rapidly. Also, by carefully watching the other people in the class and observing how they use their skills, you will be learning even when you are not directly practicing your skills.

How Do I Get Started?

A good question! Many beginning speakers feel they should fully develop all of the skills listed on the inventory before they speak in class for the first time. Actually this is not possible. Practice is an important part of developing each skill. Start sharing your ideas right away. You will begin to develop the basic skills of public speaking, and you will begin to experience the art of adapting ideas to specific audiences. While later chapters will describe speech preparation more fully, we have listed seven basic steps in preparing for a short speech to get you started.

BASIC STEPS IN PREPARING A SHORT SPEECH

1. Choose a topic of interest and value to you and your audience.

2. Determine your audience's level of knowledge of that topic.

3. Research additional information (if you do not know enough about the topic to talk to this particular audience).

4. Decide what information you can share within your time limit.

5. Decide the order in which to give the information.

6. Develop notes (not a script) to which you can refer during the speech.

7. Practice several times, staying within the time limit.

LEARNING BY UNDERSTANDING

1. Give one reason why it is helpful to identify specific areas for improvement.

2. What are five IPSS skills that will help you succeed in your future job?

3. What chapter in this book will help you develop your skills in developing an outline?

4. Give an example of how public communication skills are interconnected.

5. How can knowing the relationship between attitudes and skills help improve your public speaking skills?

6. What should you do before starting research for a short speech?

ANSWERS:

1. It will help you concentrate on important areas for development.
2. If you have difficulty answering this, you might check your notes from your interview (Chapter 1).
3. Chapter 7.
4. For example, if you had not fully understood the meanings intended by a public speaker, you would be less effective in your assessment of the speech. You might check your example with someone else in the class.
5. By maintaining positive attitudes, you will develop skills more effectively.
6. Choose a topic of interest and value to you and your audience. Determine your audience's level of knowledge of that topic.

What If My Big Problem is Nervousness?

Most beginning public speakers identify their lack of confidence about speaking in front of others as an important area that needs improvement. This feeling—which usually has some of the following symptoms: sweaty palms, fluttery stomach, dry mouth, flushed skin, tense muscles, and irregular breathing—is called *stage fright*. The actual source of the nervousness is the idea of communicating to a large group. Today, stage fright is often called *communication apprehension*. This term focuses on the source of the apprehension—communication itself—rather than on the location of the communication.[1]

Communication apprehension can be defined as a lack of confidence in speaking with people. It is almost universal among people. A recent study indicated that fear of speaking to groups and fear of heights are the two most widely held fears in our society.[2] These two fears have several characteristics in common. They both involve being in unusual situations with unknown dimensions. On a rooftop or a mountain, we do not know when the wind will blow or if the footing is solid. In a speech, we do not know how the audience will react (or how we will). Both situations have potentially negative consequences. We could fall and hurt ourselves. The audience could laugh and embarrass us.

Other factors may contribute to nervousness besides the unusual situation. Some people have difficulty choosing an idea; others have good ideas but difficulty organizing them; some people have difficulty doing research for a speech because they have trouble using a library effectively. Not being as well prepared as you want to be can cause nervousness.

What Does All This Mean?

In perspective, this means that many people are nervous about giving public speeches. If you feel this way, too, you will be interested in what experience and research have shown about communication apprehension.

First, nervousness is *natural*. We tend to be uncomfortable when we are in unusual situations with unknown dimensions and potentially embarrassing consequences. As you recall your first date or the first time you water-skied, you probably will remember similar feelings.

Even outstanding speakers have communication apprehension. Cicero said, "I turn pale at the outset of each speech and quake in every limb and in all my soul." William Jennings Bryan, described as the "most effective political convention speaker of all time," indicated that "he felt nervous before his famous 'Cross of Gold' speech, but the knowledge that he had a good conclusion kept him going."

This natural reaction is probably an example of what has been described as the **general adaptation syndrome**, or the tendency to "fight or flight."[3] This reaction dates back to prehistoric times, when our ancestors faced snarling saber-toothed tigers and fight or flight were their two available choices. Luckily, you have more choices in a speaking situation, as we will point out later.

Secondly, communication apprehension is *expected* because it is natural. Your teacher, who has had considerable experience speaking and working with other students, expects some nervousness. Even your teacher, who knows how to handle nervousness, probably feels it on the first day of each new class or before giving a public speech to an unfamiliar group.

Your classmates also expect you to feel nervous. As they prepare for their speeches, they are likely to feel nervous, too. In fact, you are probably the only one in your class who expects you should be free of communication apprehension.

Finally, besides being natural and expected, communication apprehension is *desirable*.

You're Putting Me On!

No, a moderate amount of anxiety is necessary for your best effort. Each of us has an optimal level that differs from that of other people. Football players, for example, work hard to get "psyched up" before a game; and the halftime talk by the coach helps get the team "up" again for the second half. After you get to know your class and teacher, you may have to raise your anxiety level in order to do your best. If you think back to your last semester of high school, you may remember how your lack of anxiety reduced your motivation to study for final exams. So, while too much anxiety is undesirable for a best performance, too little is also undesirable.

In summary, a moderate degree of anxiety is natural and expected, and leads to your best effort.

How Can I Handle My Nervousness?

As your skills in public speaking develop and you have more opportunities to practice, you naturally will develop more confident communication.[4] However, at this early stage you can practice being confident even though you might not feel it yet. As indicated earlier, attitudes and skills influence each other. Considerable research suggests that your attitudes and feelings about yourself can be changed by first changing behaviors related to those attitudes.

Specific behaviors to increase confidence include (1) taking several slow, deep breaths before going up to speak; (2) consciously relaxing your muscles, first by tensing them and then quickly releasing all tension; (3) walking calmly and slowly to the front of the room, taking a minute to get your notes organized, and looking for a moment at the audience to establish contact; (4) using an audience involvement procedure at the beginning of the speech, such as a question asking for a show of hands, to remind yourself that the audience is on your side; and (5) using a visual aid, such as a chart, or demonstration at the beginning and natural gestures to consume your extra energy. These procedures will help you feel better physically and orient you to the new perspective of being in front of others. We also assume that you will be well prepared and motivated; so a sixth behavior is to remind yourself that you know more about your topic than the audience does and that you really want to share this information with your listeners.

What If I Say, ''I'm Really Scared''?

If you are one of the small percentage of people with strong anxieties about speaking in public, we appreciate your feelings. Because of their concern, speech communication professionals have developed ways of measuring communication apprehension and programs for reducing it.[5] One that has worked well with our students is "Building Speech Confidence."[6] It is an individualized program based on visualization and muscle relaxation. If your communication apprehension is strong, we recommend that you talk with your teacher about such programs.

LEARNING BY UNDERSTANDING

1. Which of the following are typical symptoms of communication apprehension?
   a. Direct eye contact
   b. Flushed skin
   c. Dryness in your mouth
   d. Tense muscles

2. Communication apprehension is _____ , _____ , and _____ .

3. A _____ amount of anxiety is desirable for a good performance.

4. List six behaviors you could use to cope with feelings of nervousness before giving a public speech.

ANSWERS:

1. b., c., d.
2. Natural, expected, desirable
3. Moderate
4. (1) Taking slow deep breaths before speaking; (2) consciously relaxing your muscles; (3) walking calmly, organizing your notes, and looking at the audience before speaking; (4) using audience involvement early in your speech; (5) using visuals, demonstrations, and natural gestures to consume your energy; and (6) reminding yourself of your preparation and motivation. You might have added others from your own reading and experience. If you have something that really works for you, share it with others in your class. They will appreciate it.

LEARNING BY INTERACTING

Get together with several other people in your class and share your feelings about your communication apprehension. Try to discover which types of public speaking situations are most uncomfortable for you.

Discuss the similarities and differences among the levels of anxiety in your group and the means of coping with these feelings you believe would be most helpful.

REVIEW

Self-assessment is an important beginning to the development of public speaking skills. By recognizing the skills you already have and those that need to be developed, you will be able to start right away and use this course of study to your best advantage.

Many beginning public speakers are self-conscious about their nervousness in speaking before a group. However, a moderate amount of what is called communication apprehension is natural, expected, and desirable for doing your best job. There are several practical ways to cope with such nervousness.

NOTES

1. Lynne Kelly, "A Rose by Any Other Name Is Still a Rose: A Comparative Analysis of Reticence, Communication Apprehension, Unwillingness to Communication, and Shyness," *Human Communication Research* 8(Winter 1982):99.

2. "Fear," *Spectra* (New York: Speech Communication Association, 1973), 4.

3. Hans Selye, *The Stress of Life* (New York: Knopf, 1953).

4. Anthony Mulac and A. Robert Sherman, "Behavioral Assessment of Speech Anxiety," *Quarterly Journal of Speech* 60(April 1974):134; and W. Clifton Adams et al., "Effects of Radio Announcing Experience on Self-Perceived Anxiety," *Western Speech Communication* 39(Spring 1975):120.

5. Kelly, "A Rose by Any Other Name," 109.

6. James W. Lohr, *Building Speech Confidence, A Program for Coping with Speech Anxiety* (Skokie, Ill.: National Textbook Company, 1976).

3

LISTENING TO PUBLIC SPEECHES

In this chapter, you'll be . . .

LEARNING BY UNDERSTANDING

- How listening to public speeches differs from interpersonal listening
- Four skill areas and component skills needed for effective listening
- How to understand a speaker's meanings
- Criteria for assessing messages
- Two reasons why audience feedback is vital to public speakers
- Nonverbal behaviors that can communicate feedback to a speaker
- How to ask effective questions
- How to give constructive feedback

LEARNING BY INTERACTING

- Developing criteria to assess a speech

LEARNING BY LISTENING

- Receive, understand, assess, and respond to a live or videotaped model speech

CHAPTER OUTLINE

I. Listening in public speaking situations differs from interpersonal listening.
   A. As a part of an audience, you are not the only one with whom the speaker wants to communicate.
   B. Generally, you do not give verbal feedback during the speech.

II. Four sets of skills are involved in effective listening.
   A. Actively receive the message in order to remember important parts of the speech.
   B. Understand the message as the speaker intended it so that you can explain the speaker's message.
   C. Assess and then judge the speech.
   D. Send feedback—of your reactions—to the speaker.

III. Actively receiving messages is the first set of skills involved in effective listening.
   A. Set listening goals.
      1. You may decide how you will benefit from the content of the speech.
      2. You may decide the overall quality of the speech.
   B. Concentrate on the important words and ideas.
      1. Your listening goal will direct your concentration.
      2. A speaker's transitions will direct your concentration.
   C. Refocus your attention.
      1. Keep your listening goal in mind; it will help you refocus and remember.
      2. Be physically and mentally prepared to listen and to provide connections with your own experience.

IV. Understanding the message as the speaker intended is the second set of skills involved in effective listening.
   A. Attach appropriate denotative meanings to the words chosen by the speaker.
      1. You can understand the overall denotative meanings—the actual things or ideas to which the words refer—by identifying the purpose, main points, and support of the speech.
      2. These will be verbally highlighted in the introduction and in transitions and non-verbally highlighted when the speaker pauses, speaks more slowly, and stresses individual words.
   B. Attach appropriate connotative meanings to the speaker's words.
      1. Connotative meanings are the feelings and attitudes which a speaker reflects.
      2. Connotative meanings are also directly reflected in the speaker's nonverbal behavior and style of the speech.

V. Assessing the speech is the third set of skills involved in effective listening.
   A. Determine appropriate criteria or standards on which to base a decision for content or quality assessment.
   B. Apply the criteria to the speech by concentrating on those parts directly related to particular criteria.
   C. Make a judgment about the speech based on the chosen criteria.

VI. Sending feedback is the final set of skills involved in effective listening.
  A. Determine the appropriate channel for sending the feedback message.
    1. Audience members typically send nonverbal feedback during the message through facial expressions and body movements.
    2. Audience members typically send oral feedback during question-and-answer periods following the speech.
  B. Actually communicate clear verbal and nonverbal messages.
    1. Audience members can send nonverbal messages during the speech by means of eye contact or lack of it, posture, gestures, and facial expressions.
    2. Audience members can send oral messages after the speech in the form of questions and comments.
  C. Use constructive criticism to help a speaker improve.
    1. Constructive feedback should begin with "strokes" that indicate what a speaker did well.
    2. Constructive feedback should include specific suggestions for speaker improvement.

3

LISTENING TO PUBLIC SPEECHES

It takes two to speak the truth—one to speak and another to hear.   —*Henry David Thoreau*

PREVIEW

Do you know that you probably spend over 40 percent of each day listening?[1] You listen to many messages and make choices about the information, ideas, and recommendations they contain. The choices you make might include deciding what toothpaste to buy, when the world's oil supply will run out, or whom to vote for in a political race. By becoming a more effective consumer of public speeches, you will be able to make better choices.

Effective listening in this class is important for another reason. Developing speaking skills is a team effort. Your classmates will need your careful receiving, understanding, assessing, and responding to help them develop their speaking skills. Your feedback will help them assess the effectiveness of their speaking. And their effective listening will help you, too. Listening to others' speeches will be an important learning experience. Even though this is a speaking course, you actually will be spending more time listening.

The component skills for effective listening in both situations are similar. The difference is that, in your daily experiences, you will assess the value of the content of the speech, while in class you will also assess the speaker's effectiveness.

How Is Listening to Public Speeches Different from My Normal Listening?

Listening is defined as the process of receiving, attending to, and assigning meaning to aural stimuli.[2] There are at least two differences between public listening and interpersonal listening. First, when you are part of an audience, you are not the only one with whom the speaker wants to communicate. The speaker will not always be focusing directly on you, and the speaker's content may not always be directly of interest to you.

A second difference is that you are usually not able to give verbal feedback during the message. Even though the speaker is interested in your responses, it would be distracting for each person in the audience to question and comment throughout the speech.

What Skills Do I Need to be an Effective Listener to Public Speeches?

You need four basic skills to listen effectively in a public situation: actively receiving the speech; understanding the speech as the speaker intended; assessing the speech; and sending feedback that indicates your reactions to the speech. These four skill areas and their component skills are listed in Figure 3-1.

When you have successfully received the speech, you will be able to remember its important parts, such as the specific purpose and the main ideas. After successfully understanding the speech, you will be able to explain the speaker's ideas. After successfully assessing the speech, you will be able to state your judgments about the speaker's choices and/or your use of the speech's content. After successfully sending your feedback, the speaker will understand your reactions.

Figure 3-1 Component Skills for Effective Listening

Actively Receiving the Speech
   Setting listening goals
   Concentrating on the important words and ideas
   Refocusing your attention

Understanding the Speech as the Speaker Intended It
   Attaching appropriate denotative meanings to the speaker's words
   Attaching appropriate connotative meanings to the speaker's words

Assessing the Speech
   Selecting appropriate criteria
   Applying the criteria to the speech
   Making a judgment about the speech

Sending Feedback That Indicates Your Reactions
   Determining appropriate channels to use
   Sending clear verbal and nonverbal feedback

ACTIVELY RECEIVING SPEECHES

The component skills in actively receiving speeches are *setting listening goals, concentrating on the important words and ideas,* and *refocusing your attention.* The tendency in public listening is to be passive and let the speaker do all the work. In fact, effective listening is hard work! It is easy to be distracted by other people in the audience and by your own thoughts. These create a barrier to accurate understanding. To overcome passiveness and distractions, you should set a listening goal prior to or early in the speech.

What Is a Listening Goal?

A *listening goal* is a statement of what you want to accomplish by listening to a particular speech. This goal represents your motivation for being in the audience. And motivation can make the difference between good and poor listening.[3] A friend of ours, doing research on effective listening, was trying to discover what preparation helped people listen better. He worked out many preparations and tested each carefully. One day he told one of his test groups that he would give ten dollars to the top person on the listening test. You guessed it! The people in the group trying for the money reward got the highest listening scores that day.[4] Find some positive reason to listen, and you will be way ahead.

Becoming distracted is natural therefore listeners need to continually refocus their attention on the speaker's message.

You can set a listening goal by deciding how you can benefit from the speech. Your goal may be to learn new information, discover the qualifications of someone for public office, or remember jokes. Or it may be to help someone improve his or her speaking skills. For example, if you are listening to a local politician give a campaign speech, your listening goal may be to understand a suggested remedy for a local problem. By setting a specific goal before the speech, you can preview those areas on which you specifically want to concentrate during the speech.

A listening goal may also be chosen early in the speech. The speaker's stated purpose may help you set your own listening goal. A speaker's goal, often stated in the introduction, gives you a preview of what the speech will be about and what organizational pattern will be used to present the information. For example, turn to page 323 and read the first paragraph of G. J. Tankersley's speech. Imagine that you have just listened to this paragraph and decided to set a listening goal. If you set one like *to remember at least five of the character traits and thinking habits recommended which make success possible*, then this listening goal will mentally prepare you for what is to come and give you a motivation for listening. Having the speaker's purpose in mind will help you review what you already know about the topic, predict the main points, or remember any unanswered questions you have about the topic. And these would provide extra motivation.

Your listening goal may also be to assess the overall quality of the speech you hear. This assessment, the result of such a listening goal, is called **rhetorical criticism**. The analysis television commentators make of an important presidential address is an example of rhetorical criticism. The assessments you will make of your classmates to aid their skill development will also be examples of rhetorical criticism.

The second component skill in actively receiving speeches is to concentrate on important words or ideas. A clearly specified listening goal will guide the focus for your listening. For example, for the listening goal *to remember at least five of the character traits and thinking habits which make success possible*, you would listen for the stated traits and habits. A speaker will often guide your listening with transitions like, "The first trait I wanted to mention is empathy," to focus your attention on the parts of the speech that will help you attain your listening goal.

The third component skill in actively receiving speeches is to continually refocus your attention. Research indicates that most people do not continually focus on one stimulus for longer than about eight seconds.[5] However, because you can listen and understand at a much faster rate than people usually speak, you can keep your listening goal in mind, review important information you have already heard and refocus your attention on the information needed to accomplish that goal. Therefore, effective listening is a process of continually refocusing your attention on the important parts of the speech which will enable you to remember the speaker's key ideas.

How Should I Remember What I Hear?

Psychologists tell us that there are two types of memory—**short-term memory** and **long-term memory**.[6] Short-term memory refers to how many items can be perceived at once. It is easily disrupted, has a limited capacity, and involves automatic retrieval. Long-term memory refers to what is relatively permanently stored in our memory. It has an unlimited capacity and involves retrieval procedures. If information is not carefully transferred from short-term memory into long-term memory, it is usually forgotten in less than thirty seconds.[7] This may have happened to you with another person's name or phone number.

There are techniques for remembering things—some tend to work better for certain individuals and in specific situations.[8] Some people visualize the thing or idea; some repeat it to themselves; some write notes. One helpful technique for remembering key ideas in a speech is to summarize them in your own words. This additional mental step provides words that you can remember more easily and forces you to repeat the information.[9]

Being physically and mentally ready to listen will help you remember and refocus your attention. Listening is more difficult if you are tired or if you have had a large meal right before a speech and then settle back in the potentially passive role of an audience member. You can be mentally ready to listen by being open and positive toward the speaking situation. If you keep your listening goal in mind, you can remind yourself of the personal benefits you are working toward.

A final behavior that is helpful in remembering and refocusing your attention is to make a transition from the previous speech or experience to the speech itself. This will be especially important in this class, where you often will be listening to speeches on a wide variety of topics, one right after the other. For example, if you have just heard a speech on three quick checks to make before buying clothing and the next speaker is going to tell you about two ways farmers are suffering from inflation, you might note that everybody wants to come out ahead in financial matters. This will provide a mental connection or bridge between the two speeches and help you move your attention to the new concern.

LEARNING BY UNDERSTANDING

1. How is listening in public different from listening interpersonally?

2. Match the four listening skill areas and their results:

   receiving   **a.** Speaker understanding your reactions
   understanding   **b.** Important speech parts remembered
   assessing   **c.** State your judgments
   feedback   **d.** Explain speaker's ideas

3. What are the three component skills in actively receiving the speech?

4. What are three ways you can transfer information from short-term memory to long-term memory?

ANSWERS:

1. You are not the only one with whom the speaker is communicating. You generally do not give verbal feedback during the speech.
2. **a.** feedback, **b.** receiving, **c.** assessing, **d.** understanding
3. Setting listening goals, concentrating on the important words and ideas, and refocusing your attention
4. Repeat it, write it down, or visualize it.

UNDERSTANDING THE SPEECH
AS INTENDED BY THE SPEAKER

After actively receiving and remembering the message, you must attach appropriate *meanings* to the **verbal and nonverbal symbols** you receive from the speaker. Understanding the message is challenging because meanings are not contained in the words or actions themselves but are attached in the minds of the listeners. Therefore, it is possible that you will attach somewhat different meanings to words than those the speaker intended. Perhaps you have attended a sermon or a speech with a friend and later discovered that you each attached different meanings to the speaker's message. That is because we each listen from our own frame of reference.

Because of our past experiences, we all know different things and feel different things about subjects. When a speaker says, "We all know what it's like to get angry when something doesn't work," each member of the audience will recall somewhat different experiences and feelings. While the general response may be similar, each audience member will react somewhat differently.[10] Attaching different meanings becomes even more likely when the speaker is very different in background from the audience. The more people are different, the more different will be the meanings they attach to symbols.

An effective speaker is careful to select verbal and nonverbal symbols that accurately communicate his or her intended meanings. The term *meaning* here refers to the idea or object that people call to their minds when they hear (or see) a symbol. This type of meaning is called *denotative meaning* and is the agreed-on definition we usually find in dictionaries.

But we also know that symbols have a personal meaning—feelings and attitudes beyond the agreed-on meaning. For example, we all know the definition of the symbol "money," but it has a quite different personal meaning to each of us. We call this more personal meaning *connotative meaning*.

As a listener remember that the words represent not only the speaker's overall meaning but also his or her feelings and attitudes for those ideas. Your goal in effective listening is to understand the *full* meanings of the speaker. Therefore, you need to work to attach appropriate denotative *and* connotative meanings to the symbols chosen by the speaker.

How Do I Figure Out
the Overall Meaning the Speaker Intends?

To determine the overall denotative meaning the speaker is trying to communicate, you should identify the speaker's purpose, his or her main points, and the support used to illustrate or prove those points. The effective speaker usually will state the specific purpose early in the message and highlight it nonverbally by pausing, speaking more slowly, and stressing particular words. In the introduction, a speaker may also indicate the organizational pattern to be used. Listening aids may be used throughout the speech to help you follow the main ideas and identify the supporting points and data for illustration or proof. You might actually visualize in your mind the outline the speaker is using. In most public speaking situations, you can take notes. Notetaking is an excellent procedure for identifying the purpose, main points, and support, as well as providing a fine memory aid.

After previewing the organizational pattern to be used, an effective speaker will usually refer to an upcoming main idea by using connections called ***transitions***. Thus, a speaker may say, "I'd like to share with you three promising approaches that emerged from my research on how to find a job after graduation. First, let's look at . . . Now, let's look at a second approach . . . Finally, a third approach. . . ." It would be quite easy to take notes from this speaker, wouldn't it? Typically, speakers will support or illustrate the main ideas immediately after presenting them. You might mentally note or write down the main clarifying or supporting data if one of your criteria is whether the speaker provided adequate support.

How About the Speaker's Feelings?

Understanding the appropriate connotative meanings is more difficult. Connotative meanings are most often reflected in the speaker's nonverbal behavior and in the style of the speech. For example, a calm, direct tone of voice combined with direct eye contact and natural body movements would indicate the speaker's feelings of confidence. An intense stare and a loud tone of voice might indicate the speaker's strong feelings about the topic and a more personal involvement.

Connotative meanings are also reflected in the words a speaker chooses. There are different ways of expressing the same idea. For example, the speaker could refer to a particular woman as a "female," "honey bunny," "chick," "babe," or "person," and each choice would reveal something different about the feelings and attitudes in her or his connotative meanings. Therefore, an effective listener considers not only what literal meanings a speaker's words have but also what personal meanings they reveal.

How Do I Put the Speaker's Words and Actions Together?

Verbal and nonverbal symbols that communicate how the speaker meant the main message to be received are called metacommunication. ***Metacommunication*** means "communication about communication." These additional symbols give you a better idea of the connotative or personal meanings the speaker attaches to the speech. Verbal metacommunication often begins with such phrases as, "The reason I share this with you is . . ." or "I feel this is important because. . . ." Such messages disclose something about the speaker's personal feelings regarding the topic. Nonverbal communication might be an intense look; a strong gesture; a change to a firmer, faster, or louder voice tone—any of which could accompany or directly follow the point being made.

In summary, translating the denotative meanings will help you to understand the main ideas the speaker is trying to communicate. Translating the connotative meanings will help you to understand the speaker's feelings and attitudes. Meta-communication will help you check the consistency between the denotative and connotative meanings.

LEARNING BY UNDERSTANDING

1. What guides can a speaker give in a speech to help audiences understand the overall denotative meanings?

2. List three nonverbal behaviors that would suggest a speaker's strong personal involvement in the speech.

3. Which of the following represent denotative meanings (D) and which represent connotative meanings (C)?

   a. A speaker says, "An athlete begins to decondition after seventy-two hours without exercise."
   b. A speaker shakes a fist while speaking.
   c. A speaker uses a visual aid containing recent statistics.
   d. A speaker looks you right in the eye while concluding a speech.

ANSWERS:

1. Stating the goal and main points in the introduction, using transitions
2. A speaker could speak loudly, use strong gestures, or maintain eye contact.
3. a. D, b. C, c. D, d. C

ASSESSING THE SPEECH

The third skill area in effective listening is assessing the speech on the basis of appropriate criteria. There are two basic situations for using effective listening skills to make an assessment. The first is listening where your goal is to make a personal choice about the speaker's ideas and recommendations for you. In this type of situation, you, as an audience member, are deciding what to do as a result of the speech. Examples might be listening to an army recruiter urging you and others to enlist or to a politician asking for your vote. In these examples, your major choice is not whether it was a good speech but whether the ideas have value for you.

In the second kind of listening situation your goal is to assess the effectiveness of the speaker's choices of means in accomplishing a particular speaking outcome. This is the type of listening you will mainly do in this class. While you may be personally concerned about the content, your assessment of whether it was an effective speech will be more important in helping your classmates develop their speaking skills.

The three component skills involved in assessing both listening situations are determining appropriate criteria, applying those criteria to a speech, and making a judgment about the speech. In Appendix A we have included sample critique forms for each of the three main types of audience response.

What Are Criteria?

Criteria are the standards or reasons on which you base a judgment. Criteria for assessing public speaking indicate the parts of the speech you will observe as you listen. There are two advantages to setting criteria for your listening choices. The first is that criteria will improve your listening choices. Developing your skills in assessing will help you become a more thoughtful consumer of things and ideas. For example, if your goal in listening to a political campaign speech is to determine a candidate's qualifications for office, it would be important to determine if the candidate had logical arguments, not if he or she dressed well. The second advantage in setting criteria is that you will be able to explain to others the judgments you make.

For your daily out-of-class listening choices, your primary decision will be whether or not to accept the ideas and recommendations of the speaker. Your criteria would indicate which things would be important to you in making the decision. In the example of listening to a political campaign speech, you would decide ahead of time what qualities the candidate would have to reflect in a speech to earn your vote. You might decide to vote for a candidate who (1) is trustworthy, (2) has arguments that are logically sound, and (3) has basic values similar to yours.

How About In-Class Criteria?

For your listening choices in class, your criteria will also include the kinds of behaviors effective speakers use to accomplish their purposes. These criteria will include behavior that research and experience have shown are the skills an effective informative, persuasive, or entertaining speaker would use, such as developing rapport with the audience in the introduction.

We suggest that you build on your own experiences as a listener to public speeches to develop a list of criteria for assessing the quality of a speech. A good place to start might be to consider the teachers, clergy, politicians, and other public speakers you have heard who were effective in accomplishing their goal. Ask yourself, What made them effective? Or you might start by considering ineffective speakers, and ask the opposite question. You could then translate the negative behaviors into positive ones. As you develop your own public speaking skills, you will learn more about the kinds of speaker choices that lead to effective speeches. This will enable you to make your criteria more specific and practical for your assessment.

How Can I Apply Criteria to a
Specific Speech and Make a Judgment?

To apply your determined criteria to a particular speech, direct your attention to the necessary parts of the speech and observe those parts directly related to the criteria. Because it is challenging to direct your attention to many different aspects of a speech at one time, your teacher may ask you to observe only a few criteria for the first speeches in class and to add criteria for the speeches that follow.

To make an overall judgment, you could add together your relative judgments on each of the criteria. Sometimes numbers can be assigned to your judgments to make the overall judgment easier to express. We have found that is a helpful way to reflect someone's developing speaking skills.

SENDING FEEDBACK

Your feedback influences the speaker. A summary of research on the effect of audience feedback on the speaker concludes: "Positive feedback improves attitudes, feelings, and efficiency, while negative feedback produces a deteriorating effect."[11] Communicating your reactions is important to the speaker both during the speech (so adjustments can be made) and after the speech (so the speaker can determine how well his or her purpose was attained).

Does My Individual Feedback Really Make a Difference?

Speakers make many choices based on their analysis of how much the audience knows about the topic and what the attitudes, interests, and expectations of the listeners are. But each speech remains flexible. An effective speaker is continually sensitive to the feedback from the audience and makes necessary adaptations to audience reactions during the speech. The speaker will adapt to those audience members who most clearly indicate their response.[12] For example, a speaker may be using biased words that make you feel uncomfortable. But if some members of the audience are smiling and others are not giving any clear feedback, the speaker probably will continue to use that type of language. To communicate your reactions, send nonverbal feedback. If others in the audience are responding in a similar way, the speaker may change her or his words based on the feedback.[13]

The two main skills involved in sending feedback are determining the appropriate channel to use and sending clear verbal and nonverbal feedback.

How Do I Choose the Appropriate Channels?

Your facial expressions and body movements can communicate messages to the speaker. Typically, you can only give oral feedback during an organized question-and-answer period after the speech. Some speakers may invite you to interrupt them with questions during the speech; but this is unlikely if the audience is large, the speech is timed, the setting is formal, or the speaker is giving specific information. Thus, during the speech, you will communicate your feedback nonverbally.

Audiences nonverbally communicate their feedback to the speaker as they listen.

What Nonverbal Behaviors Will Communicate My Meaning to the Speaker?

Several nonverbal behaviors you can use as an audience member are suggested in Figure 3-2.

What Kind of Verbal Feedback Is Appropriate after a Speech?

It is helpful to differentiate between feedback in situations where your goal is to focus on the content of the speech and situations where your goal is to focus on the quality of the speaker's choices. In the first type of situation, the speaker will not expect you to make an overall assessment of the speech or to comment on the quality of the introduction. The speaker will expect questions about specific points or requests for additional support for a main idea. By reassessing your listening goal and reviewing your notes on how well the speaker met your criteria, you can determine what questions you should ask before deciding what, if any, action you will take because of the speech. For example, let's imagine you were listening to a speaker explain the benefits of composting, and your listening goal was to determine the appropriateness of the speaker's suggestions for your small backyard garden. One of your criteria was, Did the speaker provide enough detail so that I can actually do it? You noted that the speaker's second suggestion was to throw the ashes from your fireplace on the garden; but he did not say how much is good for the garden or what time of year to put them on. Thus, you have two specific questions to ask.

Figure 3-2 Nonverbal Behaviors Used By Audience Members*

Audience Nonverbal Behavior	Meaning
Maintaining eye contact Leaning forward Taking notes	*Interest*
No eye contact Frequent shifting of body position Slouching	*Disinterest*
Nodding head	*Understanding*
Looking quizzical	*Uncertainty*
Nodding head	*Agreement*
Shaking head	*Disagreement*

*These behaviors were adapted from the list of positive and negative audience behaviors determined by Blubaugh (Jon Blubaugh, "The Effects of Positive and Negative Audience Feedback on Selected Variables of Speech Behavior of Normal College Students," Ph.D. diss., University of Kansas, 1966).

The following guidelines for audience questions will help you encourage answers that will lead to your listening goal:

GUIDELINES FOR AUDIENCE QUESTIONS

1. Make sure your question is of interest to the total audience. If it is purely personal, talk to the speaker later.

2. Adapt to the speaker's knowledge and experience when phrasing your question.

3. If you really want the speaker's views, do not imply the answer to your question by saying, "Don't you think it would have been better to . . .?"

4. Be as brief as possible. Do not make a speech yourself.

5. Avoid attacking or offending the speaker.

What Kind of Feedback Is Helpful for In-Class Speeches?

If you are listening in a situation where you will be asked to assess and/or to comment on the quality of the speaker's choices, the question-and-answer period probably will focus on the speaker's goals and the means the speaker used to accomplish them. The following formula will help you give such feedback.

Strokes for what went well and Specific suggestions for improvement = Helpful feedback

We suggest this formula for several reasons. First, on completing a classroom speech, speakers desire some positive feedback. These strokes reduce the tension they feel as they wonder how the speech went and also enable them to concentrate more fully on your suggestions. Secondly, the word *and* is important in this formula. When trying to give constructive feedback to others, we often forget the good things, or we cancel them by saying, "I really liked . . . *but.* . . ." The word *but* psychologically cancels the positive statement. Third, the formula also indicates that, as good as a speech might have been, there are usually areas for improvement. Specific suggestions are more helpful and more easily used by a speaker. For example, saying, "Tell three or four specific ways that SQ3R will raise our grades" is more helpful to a speaker than, "Be more interesting."

LEARNING BY UNDERSTANDING

1. What three component skills are involved in assessing a speech?

2. Give an example of a criterion for assessing an in-class speech.

3. When judging a speech that will result in action, it is helpful to _____ your criteria before listening to the speech.

4. What are the two component skills in sending feedback?

5. Tell two reasons why an audience's feedback is helpful to the speaker.

6. Two types of nonverbal behavior an audience member can use to communicate to the speaker are

_____.

7. What nonverbal behaviors could communicate the following reactions during a speech?

   a. Disagreement
   b. Agreement
   c. Misunderstanding

8. Which of the following are effective questions? Improve those that are ineffective according to the guidelines given.

   a. "Why did you present your main points in that order?"
   b. "Don't you think that more statistics were needed to prove your second main point?"
   c. "How many times did you think we had to hear that information on traffic deaths before we'd remember it? I think you told us four times."

9. Give an example of constructive feedback, which follows the formula in the text, to another student in this class.

ANSWERS:

9. Your example should fit the "strokes *and* suggestions" formula. For example, "I thought you really caught our attention by your personal experience of failing your final exam last semester AND I believe that the speech would be more valuable to us if you would tell three or four specific ways that SQ3R will raise our grades."

8. Item "a." is effective; "b." is weak because it implies the answer; and "c." probably would put the speaker on the defensive because the question is stated as an evaluation or attack.

7. **a.** shaking your head; **b.** smiling, nodding; **c.** looking quizzical

6. Facial expressions and body movement

5. It helps adaptation during the speech and assessment of success afterwards.

4. Choosing the appropriate channel, sending clear feedback

3. Determine

2. An example might be Did she give clear examples?

1. Determining appropriate criteria, applying the criteria to the speech, making a judgment

LEARNING BY INTERACTING

Work in small groups of three or four. (It will be helpful if you do some thinking ahead of time so that the group will have some ideas to start with.) Each group should select one of the following types of speeches: informative, persuasive, or entertaining.

Each group should develop a list of the criteria (standards) that an effective speech of that type should meet. Some of your criteria will concern how well the speaker accomplishes particular goals, and some will concern the means for accomplishing these goals. Make your criteria as specific as possible. When your group has completed its list, review it to make sure each criterion is stated clearly. Try to organize your criteria under several broad categories.

After the groups are finished, share the criteria. Compare what the groups have developed. Work together until, as a class, you can agree on a list of standards for each type of speech. There will be some standards common to all lists and some specific for each type of speech. Compare your lists with the speaker critique sheets in Appendix A and any your teacher may share with you. Adjust your lists so that they will assist your listening outside the class and be most helpful for giving feedback in class.

LEARNING BY LISTENING

This experience will enable you to practice the four skill areas of effective listening. We suggest that you and your classmates listen to the same speech and use your understanding of the materials in this chapter to help you do the following:

1. Write down your personal listening goal for this speech soon after the speaker begins.

2. Write the speaker's specific purpose.

3. Write the speaker's main points and one support or illustration of each point.

4. Write how the speaker seemed to feel about the topic and the verbal and nonverbal behaviors that indicated this to you.

5. Use the list of criteria for an informative speech that you developed earlier. It will be challenging to observe all aspects to which your criteria refer, but give it a try.

   a. Write down at least one sentence, phrase, or idea the speaker said for each criterion.
   b. To help you assess how well each criterion was met, you might use a continuum from 1 (lowest) to 7 (or 9) (highest). This will help you compare your assessment with others and communicate your assessment to the speaker.

6. Develop two questions you could ask the speaker to help you accomplish your listening goal. Also, prepare a "strokes and suggestions" statement to help the speaker improve her or his speaking skills.

Share your responses with others and discuss the similarities and differences.

REVIEW

Effective listening to public communication is an important part of being a thoughtful consumer of information and ideas. Listening as a member of an audience, however, is challenging because you are in a potentially more passive role. The basic skill areas involved in effective listening are actively receiving the speech, understanding the speech as the speaker intended, assessing the speech, and sending feedback to the speaker. An important factor in effectively using these skill areas is finding some personal motivation to listen.

This chapter focused on the component skills involved in each of the basic skill areas and offered recommendations for their application to your daily listening.

NOTES

1. Larry Samovar, Robert D. Brooks, and Richard E. Porter, "A Survey of Adult Communication Activities," *The Journal of Communication* 19(December 1969)301; and E. T. Klemmer and P. W. Snyder, "Measurement of Time Speech Communicating," *The Journal of Communication* 20(June 1972):142.

2. Andrew D. Wolvin and Carolyn Gwynn Coakley, *Listening* (Dubuque, Iowa: Wm. C. Brown, 1982), 48.

3. Charles R. Petrie, Jr. and Susan D. Carrel, "The Relationship of Motivation, Listening Capability, Initial Information and Verbal Organizational Ability to Lecture Comprehension," *Communication Monographs* 32(August 1976):194.

4. Conversation with Jon Blubaugh, Professor, Dept. of Communication, University of Kansas, February 24, 1975.

5. Jon Eisenson, J. Jeffery Auer, and John V. Irwin, *The Psychology of Communication* (New York: Appleton-Century-Crofts, 1963), 251.

6. Robert N. Bostrom and Enid S. Waldhart, "Components in Listening Behavior: The Role of Short-Term Memory," *Human Communication Research* 6(Spring 1980):221.

7. Kenneth L. Higbee, *Your Memory: How It Works and How to Improve It* (Englewood Cliffs, N.J.: Prentice-Hall, 1977), 14.

8. Mark A. McDaniel and Edmund M. Kearney, "Optimal Learning Strategies and Their Spontaneous Use: The Importance of Task-appropriate Processing," *Memory and Cognition* 12(July 1984):361.

9. Richard Heun, Linda Heun, and Vi Martin, "Computer Modeling of Comprehension in Listening and Reading," paper presented at the annual meeting of the International Communication Association, Minneapolis, Minn., 1981.

10. Andrew D. Wolvin and Carolyn Gwynn Coakley, *Listening* (Dubuque, Iowa: Wm. C. Brown, 1982), 48.

11. James C. Gardiner, "A Synthesis of Experimental Studies of Speech Communication Feedback," *Journal of Communication* 21(March 1971):28.

12. Ross Buck, "Nonverbal Receiving Ability," in *Nonverbal Interaction*, ed. J. M. Wiemann and R. P. Harrison (Beverly Hills, Calif.: Sage Publications, 1983), 217–22.

13. Maureen O'Sullivan, "Measuring Individual Differences," in *Nonverbal Interaction*, 243–70.

4

CHOOSING SPEECH TOPICS AND ANALYZING AUDIENCES

In this chapter, you'll be . . .

LEARNING BY UNDERSTANDING

- How to get a general and specific topic for your speech
- Three characteristics of an effective specific topic
- Why audience analysis is important
- How to analyze your audience

LEARNING BY INTERACTING

- Analyzing an audience on a chosen speech topic

LEARNING BY SPEAKING

- One-minute introduction of a classmate

CHAPTER OUTLINE

I. The first step in speech preparation is choosing a specific topic.
   A. It is helpful to begin with a general topic.
      1. Concentrate on an area of personal expertise or concern.
      2. Or choose something from a general topic list.
   B. Brainstorm specific topics within the general topic area.
      1. Brainstorming is the process of generating as many ideas as possible without evaluating them.
      2. Group brainstorming can lead to more and varied ideas.
   C. It may be helpful to determine the component parts of a topic and then to converge on a specific topic.
      1. Your specific topic should be within your range of interests and expertise.
      2. Your specific topic should be of interest to your audience.
      3. Your specific topic should fit the occasion for the speech.

II. The second step in speech preparation is analyzing your audience.
  A. Collect descriptive information about your audience.
    1. Descriptive information helps you to infer the audience's frame of reference.
    2. Descriptive information helps you to select appropriate materials for the speech.
  B. Describe your audience's frame of reference for your specific topic.
    1. The audience's frame of reference is the combination of the audience's knowledge, attitudes, and interests, as well as its expectations of how you will handle the speaking situation.
    2. The audience's frame of reference is determined by using the descriptive information and information related to the specific topic.
  C. There are two types of sources of information for audience analysis—direct and indirect.
    1. To get information from direct sources, you might ask questions, either directly or by questionnaire.
      a. Start with general questions and then ask specific questions.
      b. Ask about the audience's knowledge, attitudes, and experiences and about its expectations of the speech.
    2. Indirect sources, which are used if no direct source is available, would be printed materials and groups somehow related to your audience, such as "parent" organizations.
      a. Indirect sources can provide descriptive information about your audience.
      b. Information from indirect sources can help you establish credibility and rapport.

4

CHOOSING SPEECH TOPICS AND ANALYZING AUDIENCES

For of the three elements in speech making—speaker, subject, and person addressed—it is the last one, the hearer, that determines the speech's end and object.   —Aristotle

PREVIEW

Many students think that selecting a topic is the hardest part of speech preparation. Often the topic-choosing situation is described as an "all or nothing" problem. Some students say, "I can't think of anything to talk about!" Others say, "There are so many topics to choose from." If your problem is choosing one topic from many, the solution is converging. If your problem is finding a topic in the first place, the solution is brainstorming. You will work on both of these skills in this chapter. Also, many students start with a very general idea and spend a great deal of time looking for information on that broad topic. It is very important to focus on a specific topic early in your preparation so that you can use your time effectively and efficiently.

Choosing an effective topic for a speech is more complex than choosing one for an English theme or a term paper. Instead of communicating with one teacher, you will be communicating with a whole class. Not only do your classmates want to learn something from your speech, but also they expect you to adapt to their knowledge and interests. It will certainly help your grade when your teacher sees that your classmates are interested, leaning forward, and listening closely to you. Consider the effect on your teacher if class members are bored, talking among themselves, andd yawning! To effectively adapt to your audience you will need to know them well. Audience analysis and adaptation are essential to good speeches and will be the focus later in this chapter.

How Do I Discover a General Topic?

For all your speaking experiences your choice of a general topic will be guided by the general purpose for the speech. As you remember from Chapter 1, the general purpose is determined by the basic type of audience response you wish to occur. This general purpose will almost always be determined for you by the communication situation itself (such as the expectation that you will inform your listeners as a keynote speaker at a professional conference), or by a request from the person asking you to speak (such as your teacher telling you the general purpose as part of your speech assignment).

Also, for most of your public speeches outside this class, your general or specific topic will be selected for you. For example, as a student, you may be asked to give an oral report of your major findings from a term paper. As a business leader, you might be asked to explain the plans for a civic project or to present a quarterly report on a department's productivity. A police officer might be asked to talk about specific security precautions. School board members might be asked to explain their reasons for supporting a school bond issue. Parents might communicate their questions about the school bond issue or their concerns about new regulations in their school district.

To find something to talk about for your in-class speeches when you do not have any general topic in mind, consider areas in which you are personally concerned and/or knowledgeable. We believe that "everyone is 'an expert' on some subject. . . . The speaker who does not have anything worthwhile to talk about probably does not exist."[1] Direct experiencing and thinking are usually the basis for expertise. As the British philosopher and activist Alfred North Whitehead said, "Firsthand knowledge is the ultimate basis of intellectual life." As a starting point, you might make a list of things you know quite a bit about or can do quite well. Examples for speech topics might include your experiences at funerals, your ability to budget your money or time, or the benefits of general education. Another area of concern might be your personal gripes. What bothers you? Bicycle theft or the insensitivity of restaurant employees might serve as the basis for initial general topic selection. Representative examples of your personal interests might be in the areas of personal relations (talking with children), job-related activities (needed leadership characteristics in business), recreation (the safe use of recreational vehicles), current issues (the impact of inflation on the cost of schoolbooks), or specific personal experiences (your indecision about getting married).

If none of these probes in areas of personal expertise or concern give you a general topic, then you might wish to choose a topic area from a general list. The list of general topic areas in Figure 4-1 probably includes several items of particular interest to you. Pick one of these general topic areas if you do not have one based on expertise or concern.

Brainstorming, a process of generating as many ideas as possible without evaluating them, is helpful with either of the two general ways of generating topic areas. In addition to using brainstorming to generate topic areas, it is also used to generate a number of specific topics within a general topic area. The focus is on quantity, not quality. Because the purpose of brainstorming is to generate as many choices as possible, evaluation, which means criticizing or approving a topic or an idea, is not used. When several people brainstorm together, more ideas are developed. For this reason it is used by many organizations to develop creative ideas.

Here is a list of specific topics, within the general area of "the library," that was generated by a group of students brainstorming:

- How to use the library
- How to check out books
- How to check out magazines
- Can I take newspapers out?
- How to find an article I'm looking for
- How to find articles on a particular topic
- How to find articles in newspapers
- How to ask the librarian for specific information
- How to find good articles
- How to find pictures
- How to check out pictures
- Where's the quietest place?
- When is the library open?
- How to use the library on weekends
- What kinds of things will librarians do for you?
- What if the library closes before you've finished your work?
- How to use the vertical file
- What's in the library besides books and magazines?
- What if you want copies of something on microfilm?

Figure 4-1   General Topics for Speeches

Spare-time Activities	Personal Experiences	Personal Awareness	Group Memberships
crafts	success	safety	political
sports	failure	health	religious
games	pride	hopes	social
reading	fear	fears	professional
music	challenge	skills	service
pets	exhaustion	aging	activist
arts	love	physical appearance	environmental

Lifework	Society	Human Relationships	
fields	government	friendship	
professions	politics	parents	
part-time jobs	laws	aging	
superiors	current events	marriage	
interviews	crime	conflict	
salaries	energy	foreigners	
training	technology	neighbors	

How does the new copyright law affect making copies?

What if I want to type notes in the library?

How to get books that aren't currently in the library

What if the library doesn't have something I need?

How Can I Focus on Something to Cover in a Short Speech?

Essentially, the problem here is *converging* on a specific speech topic from your list of possible topics. Converging is the process of dividing a topic into its components or parts and then selecting one specific topic. This is the "many topics" side of the "all or nothing" dilemma of specific topic selection. Most of us begin preparing a speech by selecting a general topic, such as "leadership skills," "gripes," "recreational vehicles," or "health foods." Some general topics are so large that they cannot be covered meaningfully in a brief speech. In fact, these topics contain hundreds of specific topics, any of which could be used for a speech.

If your selected topic is still too big, the next step is to converge or divide a topic into its components or parts and then select one specific topic. As you can see in Figure 4-2 each entry is divided into smaller parts as the topics move from the top of the diagram to the bottom. For this example of converging, we used the first brainstormed topic from the list about "the library." We selected a general topic we thought would be of interest to you and divided it into its parts. Thus, the parts of "using the library" would be knowing when it was open, what contents it had, where the contents were, and so on. Then we narrowed the "contents" part even further. Knowing that you are about to do research on a speech topic, we thought that "locating articles" would be of particular interest to you.

LEARNING BY UNDERSTANDING

1. If your problem is "nothing to talk about," the skill you would use is _____ ; if your problem is "too many topics to talk about," the skill you would use is _____ .
2. Two areas from which to get general topics before brainstorming include _____ .
3. Describe the processes of brainstorming and converging.
4. Take one of the general topics or areas of personal interest and brainstorm until you have at least twenty-five topics within that area. Try using a tape recorder to save time and keep the ideas flowing.

ANSWERS:

1. Brainstorming; converging
2. Personal expertise or concern; general topic list
3. Brainstorming is a process of generating as many ideas as possible without evaluating them. The process of converging involves dividing a topic into its components or parts and selecting one of these to work with.

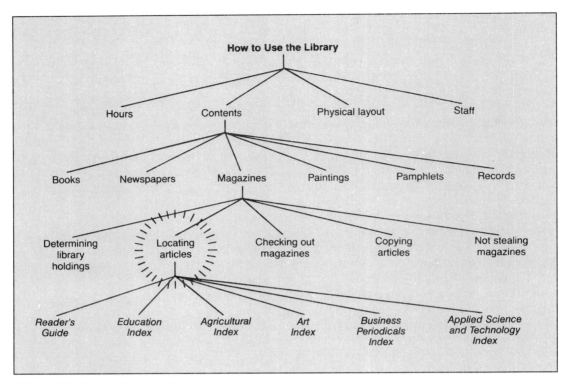

Figure 4-2 Converging on a Specific Topic

▓ *Which One Should I Choose for My Specific Topic?*

As Figure 4-3 shows, the specific topic you select should have two primary characteristics: first, it should be a part of your audience's interests; second, it should be within your own interests and expertise. The shaded area in Figure 4-3 shows the overlap between the audience's interests and your own.

If you are not sure about your topic, ask several members of your prospective audience how interested they would be in learning more about it. If they answer very, you are on the right track. If they say not very, consider choosing another topic.

Of course, it is best to ask all of your audience members. Our students have developed a way to do this efficiently. Several students write questions on a ditto master. When the ditto master is filled, copies are run for all members of the audience. After audience members have answered all of the questions, the questions are cut apart and returned to the appropriate speakers. In this way the speakers can confidently go on with their preparation knowing how interested the audience is. They also learn if there are a few who are not very interested, and they can plan how to interest those specific people. Figure 4-4 contains sample questions. The first one checks interest in the general topic, and the second checks interest in the specific topic.

General references indicate the availability of needed information on a specific topic.

Your selected topic may interest you enormously and you may even have some basic information about it, but, if you do not have enough information to add to the audience's current understanding, then you should develop your expertise. If

Figure 4-3 Finding a Specific Speech Topic

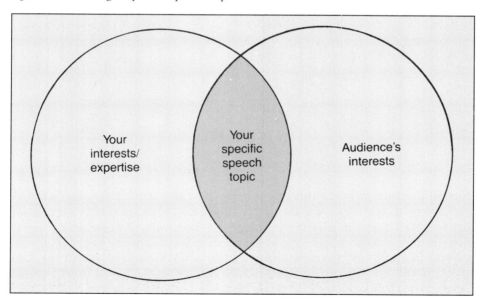

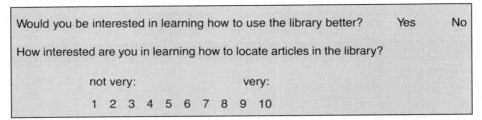

Figure 4-4   Sample Audience Survey Questions

this is the case, make sure there is sufficient time and research material to allow you to become well informed.

In addition to being in an area of your interest and expertise and in an area of audience interest, your topic choice should also fit the occasion for your speech. The occasion will imply certain audience expectations, as well as a time limit for your speech. For example, if you were asked to give an after-dinner speech at an awards banquet, the audience would probably expect a twenty-minute speech, more inspirational than technical. For your classroom speeches your audience will expect to learn about a wide variety of topics, and the major goal will be focusing on a topic that will have value for the class. Taking time to choose such a topic communicates to your classmates that you respect the value of their time. As you prepare to speak on occasions outside of class, you will find that busy people appreciate the work you do to make their listening time valuable to them.

LEARNING BY UNDERSTANDING

1.   What are the three characteristics of an effective specific topic?

2.   For G. J. Tankersley's speech, "Success Is Not A Trivial Pursuit" in Appendix B (page 322), assess how well his choice of a specific topic met the three characteristics.

ANSWERS:

2. Well done, especially on the second characteristic

1. Within the speaker's interest and expertise, within the audience's interest, and adapted to the expectations of the occasion

Why Is It So Important to Adapt to My Specific Audience?

A good question to ask at this point. If you look ahead to Figure 5-1, you will notice that considering your audience is part of every phase of speech preparation. As we talked about in Chapter 1 (the basic process of communication) and in Chapter 3 (the challenges of effective listening), audience members tend to process information based on their own points of view. To accomplish public speaking goals, as well as interpersonal goals, it is vital to understand the people with whom you are talking. The reasons for this will become even clearer as we work with the process of audience analysis.

Audience analysis is the process of describing your audience's frame of reference relevant to this specific topic and occasion. The audience's frame of reference, composed of knowledge, attitudes, interests, and expectations, acts like a filter for new information and ideas.[2] The audience members' relevant frame of reference could include too little information, strong attitudes against you or your topic, or so little interest that they become bored with your topic. Or it could be that the members are not open to new information and ideas.

The audience will also have certain expectations about you and your speech. For example, members may expect you to speak for a specified length of time, to be organized, to use informal language, and to answer questions after the speech. If you do not meet their expectations, any of these factors could cause them to filter your speech so that they incorrectly heat, understand, assess, or remember your message. In audience analysis you will identify the similarities in the audience's knowledge, attitudes, and interests and discover expectations about your speech.

Your attempt to identify similarities in your audience is important for two reasons. The most obvious is that you will be developing *one* message for many people. And while you know that all people are unique, there are similarities which will enable you to accomplish your speech purpose with the entire audience. Secondly, we know that people influence each other when they are in a group situation. Audience members in public speaking settings do this even though they may not actually talk to each other.[3] Therefore, by focusing on similarities, you can use shared, positive responses to lead the audience to understand and accept you and your message.

The first goal in audience analysis is to *collect basic descriptive information about your audience.* This information will allow you (1) to choose the general topic which is within the needs and interests of your audience, (2) to focus on a specific part of that topic which will be especially valuable for that audience, and (3) to make specific content and delivery choices that will lead to desired audience responses. The second goal in audience analysis is to use the basic descriptive information and other sources to *describe the audience's frame of reference for your specific topic.*

What Information Do I Need about My Audience to Accomplish Audience Analysis Goals?

First, research descriptive information about your audience. Following are some helpful categories of information:

Age	Political Preference
Social Class	Religious Preference
Economic Status	Physical Fitness Level
Group Memberships	Personal Needs
Marital Status	Professional Goals
Geographic Origin	Issues of Concern

This information could be fed into a computer (and often is in advertising and political research) to get a general audience description. After you have chosen your specific topic, there will be other pieces of information to gather. For example, if you were going to compare on-campus and off-campus living, you would want to know the current living arrangements of audience members.

This information will be valuable throughout your speech preparation and delivery, both in making basic decisions and in fine-tuning the supporting materials. You could avoid criticizing someone's home state, for example, or unify audience members by referring to their common experiences, such as doing research for their next speech. You will further develop your skills in appealing to a specific audience in Chapter 8.

Once you have chosen your specific topic, you will use the basic descriptive information and additional information to answer four questions about your audience. The answers will determine the members' frame of reference for the specific topic and will help you select and successfully accomplish a specific speech purpose. The four questions are What do they already know? How interested are they? What are their attitudes? What are their expectations? (See Figure 4-5.)

How Can I Discover the Necessary Information about My Audience?

There are various sources for finding descriptive information and for answering the four questions. Some of these are *direct sources* and some are *indirect sources*. Direct sources are people knowledgeable about an audience; they can give specific answers to questions. Indirect sources are written materials or inferences; they cannot

Identifying the similarities among individual listeners in an audience allows a speaker to effectively deliver his or her message.

give specific answers to questions. Direct sources are best and will be especially helpful for your in-class speeches.

You already have some basic descriptive information about your classmates. In fact, in this class you may know more of the people and know them better than in any of your other classes. Thus, your own observations are one source of information. A second source is interviews with typical members of the audience. You can question typical audience members directly or by means of a questionnaire. You will want to know what they already know about your topic, their attitudes toward you and your topic, their interests as they relate to your topic, and their expectations about how you will handle the speech situation. In other words, you want to know about their frame of reference.

If you are speaking to, say, a social or service group that has weekly or monthly meetings, you might interview the person who asked you to speak. That person, who may be the vice president or program chairperson of the group, will be aware of the audience's level of understanding and know how members have reacted to previous speakers. Someone who had previously spoken to the group also could be an excellent source of information.

The best way to interview these sources is to ask general questions first and then more specific ones. The first general question usually concerns the audience's interests. Thus, you might begin by asking, "How interested is this audience in gardening?" This could be followed with more specific questions—"What does the audience know about the effects of mulching?" or "What are members' attitudes toward chemical fertilizers?" or "How many members of the audience have gardens?" If you discover that your audience has little interest in your general topic or specific topic, perhaps you should change your topic.

But if you decide to keep your topic, connect it with the audience's interests. For example, if your audience is interested in saving money or in maintaining good health, you could connect your topic of mulching with the money saved by growing vegetables or with the health benefits of eating better food. Sometimes you will find that your audience is interested in your general topic, but you may need to change your specific topic to better relate to members' interests. For instance, they might be interested in sports in general but not in lacrosse in particular.

Finally, ask about audience members' expectations. Why are they there? What kind of a talk do they expect? How long should it be? Should you leave time for questions? These will all be helpful things to know.

In summary, the more direct the source of your information is to your audience, the better you can answer the four questions to understand its frame of reference. If you have a direct source, ask specifically for descriptive information and about the audience's knowledge, attitudes, interests, and expectations.

What If I Don't Have a Direct Source?

If you do not have a direct source to answer the four questions, you will have to depend on indirect sources. Even if you have a direct source, the information you can gather from indirect sources may help you develop credibility with your audience.

Figure 4-5 Audience Analysis Form with Sample Answers

I. Speech Situation
  A. Speaker: *Linda Heun*
  B. Audience: *public speaking class*
  C. General Purpose: *to inform*
  D. General Topic: *alcoholism*
  E. Specific Topic: *alcoholism on college campuses*

II. Audience Description
  A. *Twenty-four audience members*
  B. *Ages from eighteen to twenty (except for five people between twenty-five and forty)*
  C. *Half women and half men*
  D. *Majority freshmen and sophomores*
  E. *Most have taken basic psychology or sociology*
  F. *Twelve are in religious and/or service groups (less likely to drink); eight are in social groups (morre likely to drink)*
  G. *Most have tried drinking (inferred from USA Today survey, 1985)*
  H. *Most are aware of the six students from our campus killed last spring break from drunken driving*

III. Questions to Determine Frame of Reference toward Specific Topic
  A. *What do you know about college alcoholism?* — Open-ended question on audience knowledge
    1. *What percent of our class drinks?*
    2. *What percent of college students are alcoholics?* — Specific questions about the tentative main points
    3. *What are the symptoms of alcoholism?*
    4. *What do you think are the cures for alcoholism?*
  B. *How interested do you think the class is in learning more about alcoholism?* — Question on audience interest
  C. *What are your attitudes about drinking?* — Open-ended question on audience attitudes
  D. *What do you think my speech will be like?* — Question on audience expectations
  E. *What similarities will there be among audience members?* — Question on information for class description
  F. *What else should I know about the class to help me with my speech?* — Catchall question to probe for information not asked directly

IV. Audience Inferred Frame of Reference Toward Specific Topic
  A. Interest
    1. *Not high*
    2. *Not seen as a problem*
  B. Knowledge
    1. *Most drink socially*
    2. *Most have seen someone drink too much*
    3. *Do not know much about alcoholism as a disease*
    4. *Know about Alcoholics Anonymous*
  C. Attitudes
    1. *Most favor drinking*
    2. *Believe drinking expected of college students*
    3. *Believe it takes years to become an alcoholic*
    4. *Believe they could quit if it were harmful*
  D. Expectations
    1. *Five-minute speech*
    2. *Preachy talk rehashing old information*

Printed information about your audience can be a helpful indirect source. Perhaps the group has a newsletter or has been written up in the press. You can often infer the group's interests from the kinds of projects they are involved in. Another source of indirect information is a group's "parent" group. If, for example, you were asked to talk to a local chapter of the National Organization for Women, you could read information from the national NOW office. If you were talking to the local Blue Key Chapter, you could read information about the Kiwanis. If you were talking to a local fraternal or professional group, you could read its national publication.

In addition to materials written by the group itself, there are materials written *about* groups or types of people. For example, there are periodicals devoted to the elderly, farmers, teachers, students, parents, and businesspeople. Check the periodicals in your library. Also, general sources often have articles about groups or types of people. A source which could be especially valuable is *USA Today*. This newspaper has up-to-date summary articles about groups, as well as articles indicating how certain issues affect specific groups. *USA Today* recently published the following statistic about the changing political orientation of college students:

> College freshmen who consider their political views "middle-of-the-road" declined 2.9% this year as more students shifted to liberal and conservative positions.[4]

This would be a helpful general piece of information for speeches to your class audience.

An indirect source can provide information about an audience to help you develop a general description of its members. You can also draw inferences about an audience's frame of reference from this information. Often you can determine how much audience members know about a subject from their age and education. Attitudes sometimes can be inferred from knowing the audience's group memberships—social, religious, or political. For example, members of the Sierra Club no doubt have favorable attitudes toward conservation of natural resources and unfavorable attitudes toward industrial pollution. An audience's interests also can be inferred from members' sex, age, and education. Obviously, some of the data available from indirect sources may not be very helpful for your particular speech topic. For example, it may not matter at all what religious, occupational, social, service, or political groups your audience is connected with if you are talking about mulching the garden. It would, however, be important to know about members' gardening knowledge and experience.

The audience analysis in Figure 4-5 includes a basic audience description, questions asked of two typical audience members, marginal notes to indicate the information sought, and the inferred audience frame of reference for the specific topic. As one result of the audience analysis in Figure 4-5, the speaker decided to keep the specific topic and to raise audience interest early in the speech.

After analyzing your audience, you will know a great deal about its frame of reference and will be able to prepare an effective speech. This information will help you choose and refine your speech topic, specific purpose, and main points. From your analysis of the audience's interests, you will have information to use in preparing your introduction and developing rapport. From your analysis of its attitudes, you will be able to choose supporting materials and develop arguments. You also will know what the audience expects in terms of the length of your talk, how formal it will be, whether you should prepare for questions, and if you should use demonstrations or visual aids.

LEARNING BY UNDERSTANDING

1. List the four things you want to learn about an audience from an audience analysis.
2. What two kinds of sources help you determine the audience's frame of reference?
3. What are two expectations an audience might have about your speech?
4. What are two indirect sources of information about an audience?
5. Your in-class speech on the need for a national energy policy went well. You told your mother, who mentioned it to her neighbor, a teacher at the junior high. The neighbor decided that the topic would coincide with her next unit and asked your mother to ask you to come to the class to talk on that subject. How could you refuse? What would you do? What information would you want to know in order to adapt to junior high students? How would you get that information?

ANSWERS:

1. Knowledge, attitudes, interests, expectations
2. Direct sources, indirect sources
3. Your answers might include the length of the speech, the formality of the speech, or the quality of the speech.
4. Indirect sources could include written information about the audience or information about the parent group.
5. Assuming you agreed to talk, you would want to learn about the junior high students' knowledge, attitudes, interests, and expectations. Their teacher would be one direct source of information, the students themselves would be another.

LEARNING BY INTERACTING

With several other people in your speech class, do an audience analysis for your class similar to the sample audience analysis in this chapter.

Choose a general and specific topic of interest to you and within your expertise.

Decide what descriptive data you want to have about your audience. Collect this data, based on the group members and your knowledge of others in the class.

Develop at least five questions and formulate "average" answers for the class.

Based on the answers, describe the class's frame of reference for your chosen topic.

LEARNING BY SPEAKING

Share basic descriptive information with one other person in your class. Use the suggested list on page 63 for ideas. Add new categories that you think would be helpful in getting to know this person.

From your interview, select appropriate information for helping the rest of the class know this person. Plan a one- to two-minute introduction. Your partner will also introduce you.

This experience will provide information which will help you adapt to the class audience in your later speeches.

REVIEW

In this chapter, you worked on the basic skills involved in selecting and developing an appropriate speech topic based on audience analysis. All later steps of speech development are also influenced by an analysis of your audience. Your audience analysis provides the basis for these choices by helping you understand the frame of reference through which the audience will filter your message.

The most effective audience analysis uses direct sources to answer the following questions: What do the audience members know about my topic? How do they feel about my topic? How interested are they in my topic? What are their expectations for the speaking situation?

NOTES

1. Robert C. Jeffrey and Owen Peterson, *Speech*, 2d ed. (New York: Harper and Row, 1985), 122.

2. Timothy G. Plax and Lawrence B. Rosenfeld, "Dogmatism and Decisions Involving Risk," *Southern Speech Communication Journal* 41(Spring 1976):266.

3. John Hocking, Duane Margreiter, and Cal Hylton, "Intra-Audience Effects: A Field Test," *Human Communication Research* 3(Spring 1977):243.

4. " 'Middle-of-the-Road' Politics," *USA Today*, March 13, 1985, p. 1A.

5

DEVELOPING SPEECH TOPICS

In this chapter, you'll be . . .

LEARNING BY UNDERSTANDING

- Guidelines for writing an effective specific purpose
- Benefits of developing a central idea
- How to develop main points and subpoints
- How additional materials can develop, clarify, or support your main points
- Twelve communication procedures to develop, clarify, and support your speech
- When to use developing, clarifying, or supporting materials
- Five ways to research a speech
- How to use your library for researching your speech

LEARNING BY INTERACTING

- Using a variety of methods to research a speech topic

LEARNING BY SPEAKING

- A three- to four-minute informative speech that describes an important experience in your life

CHAPTER OUTLINE

I. The first step in developing your topic is stating a specific purpose.
  A. The general purpose of a speech—to inform, to persuade, or to entertain—is defined in terms of audience response.
  B. A specific speech purpose will combine the assigned general purpose and the specific topic you have selected.
    1. A specific purpose should be within the audience's current knowledge and beliefs.
    2. A specific purpose should have certain basic characteristics.
      a. It is stated in a sentence.
      b. It states the general purpose.
      c. It focuses on the specific topic to be covered.
      d. It states the intended results in terms of outcomes for the audience: new knowledge, change, or enjoyment.

II. The next step in developing your topic is stating a central idea.
  A. A central idea indicates what you want the audience to remember from your speech and is based on the results of your audience analysis.
  B. A central idea leads directly to your main points, focuses your research, and can be used in the introduction to preview your speech.

III. The next step in developing your topic is determining main points.
  A. The main points should be based on your central idea.
  B. The main points should be carefully worded.
    1. They should not overlap each other.
    2. They should cover all parts of the central idea.
    3. They should contain only one main idea.
    4. They should be stated in simple and complete sentences.

IV. The next step in developing your topic is determining the number of main points and subpoints.
  A. The number of points and subpoints depends on the audience's frame of reference.
  B. The number of points and subpoints is also based on the time available.

V. The next step in developing your topic is determining subpoints.
  A. Determine the necessary subpoints to allow audience understanding.
  B. Consider how many subpoints can be fully developed within the time limit.

VI. An important step in developing your speech is discovering additional material about your main points.
  A. Additional material can serve three basic functions in your speech.
    1. Additional material can develop a main point.
      a. Developing material is used if the audience does not already know or fully understand the main point.
      b. Developing materials are especially important in informative speeches.
    2. Additional material can clarify a main point.
      a. Clarifying material is used if a main point is not clearly understood.
      b. Clarifying materials are especially important in informative speeches.

   3. Additional materials can support a main point.
      a. Supporting materials are used when an audience does not fully accept a main point.
      b. Supporting materials are especially important in persuasive speeches.
   B. There are twelve kinds of communication procedures that can serve as additional material to develop, clarify, or support your points.
      1. Definitions explain what concepts mean denotatively.
      2. Examples are specific instances of a concept.
      3. Illustrations are detailed actual or hypothetical examples of a concept.
      4. Narrations describe personal experiences.
      5. Details are specific characteristics of a concept.
      6. Descriptions are verbal pictures of a concept or an example of a concept.
      7. Statistics are numerical descriptions of the size or frequency of a concept.
      8. Comparisons show how one concept is like another concept.
      9. Analogies are comparisons of a concept with a known, simpler visual concept.
      10. Contrasts show how one concept is different from another concept.
      11. Testimony or quotations are a direct statement of another's opinion about a concept.
      12. Repetitions restate a concept in the same or similar words.

VII. There are five main ways to research material to add to the main points.
   A. One way to research for your speech is reading.
      1. You can find recent materials in the library.
         a. The *Reader's Guide to Periodical Literature* will help you find magazine articles.
         b. The *New York Times Index* and *Facts on File* will help you find newspaper articles.
      2. You can find books on your subject in the library.
         a. Books in the library are indexed in the card catalog.
         b. Books are a less current source of information.
      3. You can find brief overviews of your topic in the library.
         a. Encyclopedias offer brief overviews of topics.
         b. *Who's Who in America* gives facts about people.
      4. You can find specific information in almanacs.
   B. A second way to research is to listen.
      1. Use the skills you have developed in listening to find materials.
      2. The interview is a research tool.
         a. Have a specific listening goal when you interview someone.
         b. Start with a general question and move to more specific questions.
   C. A third way to research is to observe.
      1. Have a specific observational goal when researching.
      2. Observation provides first-hand information about your topic.
   D. A fourth way to research is to experience.
      1. Experiencing provides personal data.
      2. Experiencing provides understanding so you can communicate connotative meanings.
   E. A fifth way to research is to think.
      1. Thinking helps make your speech unique.
      2. There are guidelines for your creative thinking.
         a. Understand all aspects of the problem or situation.
         b. Do not be boxed in by artificial procedures or available limits.
         c. Consider alternative formats for your answers.
         d. Brainstorm for many different kinds of possible solutions.

5

DEVELOPING SPEECH TOPICS

The mind of the orator grows and expands with his subject. Without ample materials, no splendid oration was ever yet produced. —*Tacitus*

PREVIEW

How do I get from my topic to an actual speech? is a question all public speaking students must answer. This chapter and Chapter 7 will help you develop the skills for preparing a speech on your chosen topic. The skills include choosing main points and subpoints to develop your specific topic, selecting additional materials to develop each point, and organizing this material into a unified whole. All of these skills will involve using your audience analysis results and doing topic-related research. Figure 5-1 shows these sequential skills and Figure 5-2 provides an example.

In this chapter, we will work on selecting a specific approach which leads to your main points and subpoints, as well as the skills involved in finding appropriate materials to develop fully your topic.

▧ *Where Do I Start?*

We have found that many beginning speakers want to start writing as soon as they have decided on a specific topic. While it feels good to start writing immediately, this method of topic development almost always takes more total time—the speaker writes too much, writes beyond the borders of the specific topic, or discovers a lack of supporting information on the topic. Instead, after choosing your specific topic and analyzing your audience's frame of reference for that topic, you need to decide on your *approach* to selecting main points for this topic. An essential consideration in choosing your approach is the audience's current interests, knowledge, attitudes, and expectations. For example, relating to the audience in an informative speech means adding to what members already know. You are attempting to add two to five new "bricks" (main points) to their current "wall of learning," as visualized in Wall A of Figure 5-3. In this way you can avoid

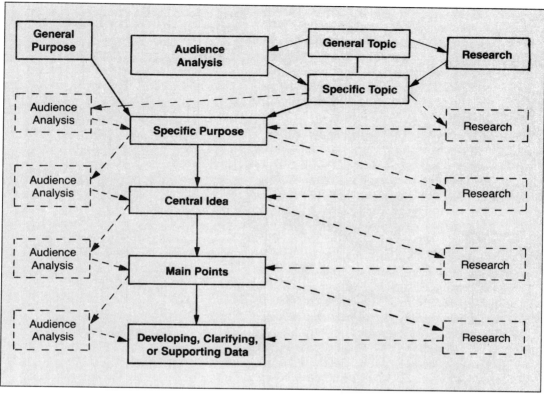

Figure 5-1 Developing a Speech

losing audience members by communicating above their level of knowledge, as visualized in Wall B of Figure 5-3, or boring them by communicating information they already know, as visualized in Wall C of Figure 5-3.

Here are some possible approaches to selecting main points for a specific topic. Each represents a way of developing a specific topic. What others would you add to the list?

APPROACHES TO TOPIC MAIN POINTS

1. Reasons for or against
2. Main types
3. Advantages or personal benefits
4. Means or procedures
5. Behaviors related to topic
6. Solutions

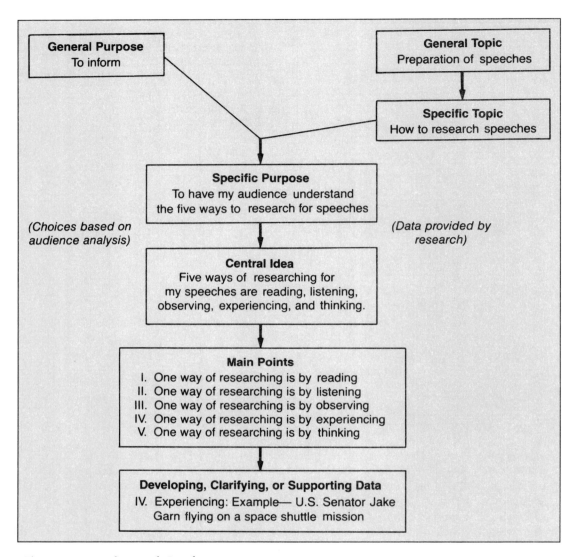

Figure 5-2 Sample Speech Development

7. Steps

8. Criteria

9. Characteristics

10. Historical background

Based on your audience analysis and your time limit, you will decide the most valuable approach to the main point for a specific audience. For example, given the topic of alcoholism on campus, possible main points include (1) reasons for campus alcoholism, (2) characteristics of a campus alcoholic, (3) procedures for

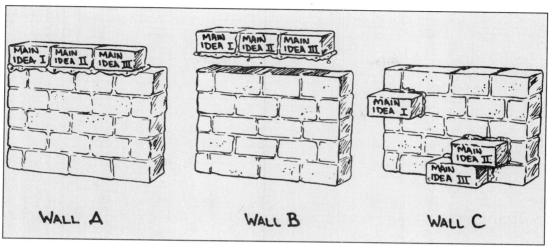

Figure 5-3   Communicating Useful Information to an Audience

avoiding alcoholism, or (4) procedures for overcoming alcoholism. Effective questioning and inference making during your audience analysis will help you to choose the most valuable approach for your audience. Each of these approaches would provide ample material for a four- to seven-minute speech. Instead of choosing one approach to the main points, however, many beginning speakers include several approaches in one short speech. You would not have time to say very much about any of the possible approaches if you tried to cover all of them in four to seven minutes.

If you do not already know a great deal about your specific topic, you may need to do some research before choosing an approach to your main points. Then make sure there is adequate information available to develop the approach you choose. The suggestions at the end of this chapter will help you to do effective research on your specific topic. At this stage of your choice making, look for brief overviews of your topic to give you an idea of the approaches available.

My Teacher Says I Should Have a Specific Purpose!

There is a reason why teachers are concerned with **specific purposes**. A clear purpose specifies the desired audience response. With this in mind you can direct your preparation efficiently and effectively toward attaining that speech purpose. This is the same reasoning that leads individuals and organizations to go through a careful process of goal setting. A major form of goal setting used by organizations is called Management by Objectives (MBO). In processes like this, specific objectives are developed which coordinate the behaviors of the people working toward a goal. The objectives are carefully worded in sentences so that everyone understands the desired outcomes.

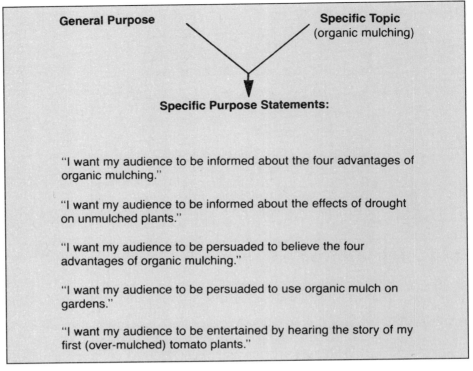

Figure 5-4   Sample Specific Purpose Statements

As described in Chapter 1, the general purposes of speeches are defined in terms of audience responses. A speech to inform should help the audience to understand new information. A speech to persuade should encourage the audience to hold a new belief or to take a new action. The purpose of an entertaining speech is to have audience members enjoy themselves. Therefore, the first step in developing a specific purpose for your speech is to connect your topic with a general purpose. Since the goal of public speaking is attaining the desired audience response, your specific purpose statement must also include the specific new knowledge, commitment, or enjoyment which will result.

Your specific purpose, therefore, combines in a sentence your general purpose, your specific topic, and the desired audience response. Figure 5-4 visualizes these connections with examples of specific purpose statements. Stating the specific purpose in terms of *audience response* instead of *speaker behavior* is important. To determine the accomplishment of the specific purpose statements in Figure 5-4, you would have to check the audience response. However, if you state your purpose in terms of your behavior (for example, "I want to tell my audience about the four advantages of organic mulching."), it would be easy to feel successful after you have finished telling the audience—regardless of the response.

In summary, the important characteristics of a specific purpose statement are listed below.

CHARACTERISTICS OF A SPECIFIC PURPOSE STATEMENT

1. It is stated in a sentence.

2. It states the general purpose.

3. It focuses on the specific topic to be covered.

4. It states the intended results in terms of audience outcomes: new knowledge, attitude or behavior change, or enjoyment.

How Do I Get to My Main Points from a Specific Purpose?

Many people find it helpful to use a middle step—writing out a central idea—to move from the specific purpose to the development of main points. The **central idea** is the concept the audience will remember, believe, and/or act on if the message is successful. The central idea is the main idea, the component parts of which are your **main points**. The central idea also might be called your thesis statement, proposition, theme, or thesis. In any case, it describes the key thing your audience will remember after your speech. Two examples are shown in Figure 5-5.

Write your central idea in *one* sentence. Determine if the main parts of that sentence work together to form a coherent idea. If the parts of your sentence do not go smoothly together, you should reconsider your choice of the main divisions

Figure 5-5   Formulating a Central Idea

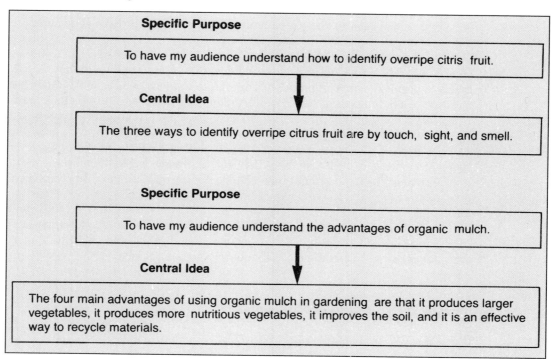

Specific Purpose

To have my audience understand how to identify overripe citris fruit.

Central Idea

The three ways to identify overripe citrus fruit are by touch, sight, and smell.

Specific Purpose

To have my audience understand the advantages of organic mulch.

Central Idea

The four main advantages of using organic mulch in gardening are that it produces larger vegetables, it produces more nutritious vegetables, it improves the soil, and it is an effective way to recycle materials.

for your speech. For example, consider the following central idea for a speech to persuade audience members to quit smoking:

Central Idea: The important things to know about the dangers of smoking are my brother's attempts to quit smoking, the dangers to your health, the negative effects on your finances, and the 1985 statistics of the number of deaths from smoking-related diseases.

While the sentence does mention ideas that are all related to quitting smoking, the first and fourth parts are examples of specific supporting material. You might mention them to help your audience understand a main point, but they are not main divisions of the topic. The second and third parts of the sentence, however, *are* main divisions of the topic. The central idea, which you prepare early in your speech development, helps you determine the parts of the topic you think would be most effective for this audience. For example, you might decide to limit your speech to the two main areas mentioned in parts two and three. Your central idea would then be

Central Idea: Two important things to know about smoking are the dangers to your health and the negative effects on your finances.

Why Do the Extra Step of a Central Idea?

A central idea leads you directly to your main points. The central idea also helps you focus your research on those areas you will use in your speech. And you can use your central idea in the introduction to your speech to help your audience understand and remember the speech as a whole.

Like your specific topic choice and your choice of approach, your choices regarding your central idea should be audience-based. Your audience analysis will help you decide the most appropriate central idea to focus on. The most important question to ask yourself is, Based on the audience's knowledge of this topic area, what are the most important points to focus on to accomplish my speech purpose?

For example, if you were speaking about identifying overripe fruit in the grocery store, you would want to know if your audience members had ever shopped for fresh fruit. If they had, they might already know the basic ways to test for overripe fruit. You might then change your central idea to ''the three ways grocery stores try to camouflage overripe fruit.'' If you were speaking about the advantages of mulching, and you were talking to a group that recently had participated in ecology-related projects, you could focus on the two advantages of improving soil and recycling. Again, effective questioning and inferring during your audience analysis will help you choose your central idea.

How Do I Choose My Main Points?

If you follow our suggestion, your main points will be explicitly stated in your central idea. All the central ideas given earlier directly state the main points. If, for example, your purpose is *I want my audience to understand an improved way of studying chapters for taking tests* and your central idea is *The five steps in the SQ3R method of studying are survey through skimming, ask yourself questions, read the chapter, recite orally what you remember, and review your notes*, then your main points would be

    I. Survey through skimming.
   II. Ask yourself questions.
 III. Read the chapter.
 IV. Recite orally what you remember.
   V. Review your notes.

Let's take the central idea regarding mulching developed earlier and state the main points that would cover all parts of that idea.

Central Idea: The four main advantages of using organic mulch in gardening are that it produces larger vegetables, it produces more nutritious vegetables, it improves the soil, and it is an effective way to recycle materials.

Main Points:
    I. Using organic mulch in gardening will produce larger vegetables.
   II. Using organic mulch in gardening will produce more nutritious vegetables.
 III. Using organic mulch in gardening will improve the soil.
 IV. Using organic mulch in gardening is an effective way to recycle materials.

How Many Main Points Should I Have?

This is an important question for a public speaker to answer. If you were to write a paper on your speech topic, the answer would likely be as many as it takes to deal fully with your topic. Once you have chosen the topic, such as the causes for campus alcoholism, it is your responsibility to research and communicate the best available information regarding that topic. You assume you are writing to cover the topic adequately and you typically do not have a specific reader in mind (other than your teacher if the paper is for a class). Also, if your paper turned out to be quite lengthy, a reader could read it in several shorter sessions or skim over parts he or she was already quite familiar with. But when you are talking to a specific audience, who must listen and comprehend at your chosen rate of delivery, you must limit the number of points you will talk about.

For your classroom speeches, your time limit will most likely be from three to five minutes for earlier speeches and from ten to fifteen minutes for later speeches. In speaking situations outside your class, you will rarely have more than forty-five minutes to cover your topic. Your speech will contain an introduction and a conclusion, as well as the main body. The introductory and concluding materials orient the audience and provide closure, and they are shorter in proportion to the body of the speech. Assuming the introduction and conclusion would be about one minute long, you could estimate the length of your main points by dividing the remaining minutes by the number of main points. For a four-minute speech, if the introduction and conclusion are one-half minute each, you could include three main points, each being about one minute, or two main points, each being one and one-half minutes. Even a longer speech should not cover more than five main points.

LEARNING BY UNDERSTANDING

1. State three benefits of developing a central idea.

2. For the general speech topic, "Getting a College Degree," choose three different approaches to main points for the topic. For each approach, write a central idea.

3. Write the main points for each of the central ideas developed for #2.

4. Examine Randy Larsen's speech on lasers in Appendix B and write his specific purpose, central idea, and main points.

5. The following is a description of a card game.[1] After you have read the description, would you be able to play the game? If not, indicate the missing concepts or terms that the description assumes you know.

Dom Pedro (or Snoozer)

Dom Pedro (or Snoozer) is the same as Pedro Sancho with the joker (called Dom Pedro or Snoozer) added to the pack. The joker ranks below the deuce of trump in play and counts 15 points for the taker of the trick in which it is played. It does not score low, but is a trump and wins over any card in plain suits. The game is 50 or 100 points.

ANSWERS:

1. It leads directly to your main points, it focuses your research, and it is useful for the introduction of your speech.

2,3. Use the list of approaches to topic main points in this chapter. You might check with someone else in the class to see if your central ideas were well adapted to your class.

4. Specific Purpose: "I want my audience to understand the medical applications of lasers."
   Central Idea: To understand the medical applications of lasers, you should know their history, the variety of current medical uses, and the future uses of lasers.
   Main Points: I. The laser has a long history.
   II. There are many medical uses of the laser.
   III. Lasers are light waves of the future in medicine.

5. When we read the description, we did not know what Pedro Sancho was. We also did not know what "the pack" referred to. Was this the entire deck? What other terms or concepts were new to you? Check with someone else to compare your understanding.

How Do I Develop Each Main Point?

In developing your main points, determine what parts need to be covered in order for your audience to understand fully the main point. The necessary parts, or subdivisions, of your main points are called **subpoints**. For example, consider the following main points for an informative speech on substance abuse:

    I. There are psychological dangers to substance abuse.
   II. There are physical dangers to substance abuse.
 III. There are social dangers to drug abuse.

Under each main point you would list specific dangers. You would discover these specific dangers, such as the psychological dangers of dependency and paranoia, through research. If you found many dangers, you would then select the most relevant for your speaking situation.

How Do I Determine How Many Subpoints to Include?

Your decision on the number of subpoints should be tentative at this point in your planning. You might change your mind after completing your research. You might find more information on one main point than another. The tentative decision should be based on your time limit and how much information you feel you should add to the audience's understanding. As you consider the number of subpoints, keep in mind that you want to do more than just list them. As we will be talking about in the next section, you want to add materials that will make your main and subpoints not only understandable, but also interesting and memorable to your audience. Leave enough time so that you can develop each main and subpoint with additional materials.

Sometimes in doing your research you find information that causes you to shift subpoints. Using the substance abuse example, you might find a great deal of material about Main Point II.—the physical dangers of substance abuse—that would be new and valuable for your audience. You could change your specific topic to focus only on the physical dangers. The main physical dangers would then become your main points, and you would look for the divisions of each physical danger for your subpoints.

What Added Material Would Help My Audience Understand My Main Points and Subpoints?

Although people think and learn differently, almost everyone learns new ideas from some form of example and an understanding of how the example relates to the main idea. Thus, you should look for various communication procedures that help people understand new ideas. If, for example, you wanted to support your main idea that many professional athletes are involved in humanitarian causes, you might mention that baseball player Rod Carew is actively involved in the fight against multiple sclerosis. This example adds to your audience's understanding and belief of your main ideas.

Specifically, the additional material in your speech serves three purposes: to develop, to clarify, or to support your main ideas. Material used to **develop** a main point implies that the main point is not already known or fully understood by the audience. Material used to **clarify** implies that the main point is known or partially known but is not clearly understood or even misunderstood. Development and clarification are most often used in informative speeches. The **support** function implies that the main point is known but not fully accepted by your audience.

Supporting material, which is used primarily in speeches to persuade, should lead to new belief or action on the part of your audience. Some additional material can do more than one function. For this reason, and for ease of reference, we call it ***DCS material***.

Besides being appropriate to your audience's informational needs, there is another essential characteristic for DCS material. It should be directly relevant to the concept. If your specific purpose is to have your classmates understand and be able to recognize how speakers can lie with statistics, then your examples, illustrations, quotations, etc., would all be intentionally misused statistics. Reasons why speakers lie or examples of speakers' unintentional misuse of statistics would not be relevant.

In addition to relevancy, two other characteristics are desirable for almost all DCS material: typical and recent. Imagine that your friends ask you what they should study for their final exam from a teacher you had previously. If you can tell them the main types of questions the teacher used last semester in the class, that would likely be of real value. On the other hand, if you had the class ten years ago (not recent) and told about the one 5-percent-bonus essay question (not typical), you would be much less helpful. The more typical and the more recent your material is, the more valuable it will be for developing, clarifying, and supporting your points. The best DCS material is summarized below.

CHARACTERISTICS OF EFFECTIVE DCS MATERIAL

1. appropriate to your audience's informational needs
2. directly relevant to your point
3. typical
4. recent

Table 5-1 summarizes twelve specific communication procedures that can help develop, clarify, or support your main points. Check marks indicate the most likely purposes for these communication procedures, the kinds of speeches in which they usually occur, and the most likely source or sources of each. You will notice that the word *concept* appears frequently in the definitions. Learning psychologists use this word to refer to words, groups of objects, experiences, and conditions, as well as to ideas, beliefs, and processes. For our purposes, the word generally will refer to ideas, beliefs, or processes.

DEFINITION

A ***definition*** is an explanation of what a concept stands for. It is the denotative meaning of the concept. If, for example, you use the word *ecosphere*, which is unfamiliar to your audience, you can develop the audience's understanding by defining the word. Or if you use a word with many or abstract meanings—for example, *socialism*—you can clarify your use of the term by defining it.

In the following example, Jeanne Greenberg, chairman of Personality Dynam-

TABLE 5-1 DCS Materials

Term	Definition	Purpose			Kind of Speech			Source				
		Develop	Clarify	Support	Informative	Persuasive	Entertaining	Reading	Listening	Experiencing	Observing	Thinking
Definition	Explanation of what a concept means	✓	✓		✓		✓	✓				✓
Example	Specific instance of a concept	✓	✓	✓	✓	✓	✓	✓	✓	✓	✓	
Illustration	Detailed actual or hypothetical example of a concept	✓	✓	✓	✓	✓	✓	✓	✓	✓	✓	✓
Narration	Description of a personal experience	✓		✓	✓	✓	✓			✓	✓	
Detail	Specific characteristics of a concept	✓	✓	✓	✓	✓	✓	✓			✓	
Description	Verbal picture of a concept or an example of a concept	✓	✓		✓		✓	✓		✓	✓	
Statistics	Numerical description of the size or frequency of a concept	✓	✓	✓	✓	✓	✓	✓			✓	
Comparison	Shows how one concept is like another concept	✓	✓		✓		✓	✓			✓	✓
Analogy	A comparison of a concept with a known, simpler visual concept	✓	✓		✓		✓	✓				✓
Contrast	Shows how one concept is different from another concept		✓		✓		✓	✓			✓	✓
Testimony or Quotation	Direct statement of another's opinion about a concept	✓	✓	✓	✓	✓	✓	✓	✓			
Repetition	Restatement of a concept in the same or similar words		✓	✓	✓	✓	✓	✓				✓

ics, Inc., used definition to clarify the meaning of 'high-tech' to provide the basis for her profile of the successful high-tech salesperson:

> Before describing our findings, let me take a minute to define high-technology. . . .
> In point of fact, high-tech has become a buzzword, which some have used to describe everything from the space shuttle to the electronic typewriter.
> Let me try to be more specific.
> We consider something to be high-tech when it offers a significant departure from the past.[2]

James Watkins, chief of naval operations for the U.S. Navy, also applied definition to clarify how United States and Russian leaders use the word *peace* to mean different things:

> For us [the United States], peace is the absence of war and relaxation of tensions. For the Soviets, in contrast, peace implies a movement to the condition when world-wide victory of socialism has made war obsolete. It is, thus for them a term for a process of struggle and challenge.[3]

The most helpful definitions are brief and are stated in words the audience will understand.

EXAMPLE

An *example*—a brief, specific instance of a concept—is the most common procedure for development, clarification, and support. It helps an audience mentally picture your idea. An effective example is chosen with the specific audience in mind and refers to situations with which the audience is familiar and comfortable.

In a speech regarding the advocacy of people's interest in Washington, D.C., Dorothy Ridings, president of the League of Women Voters of the United States, used example as follows:

> I want to raise one more example of an effective grassroots lobbying effort: the Voting Rights Act amendments of 1982. . . .
> . . . Working in coalition with other civil rights organizations, we activated our grassroots network, bringing pressure to bear on members of Congress from their home districts. We targeted members of the Senate whose votes were crucial and our Leagues responded with newspaper ads calling on Senators to support extension, and a flood of letters and phone calls to their offices, as well as with a variety of other pressure techniques.[4]

James Zumberge, president of the University of Southern California, used the following example in a speech. He was trying to communicate the importance of understanding other cultures when we are trying to market our products abroad. It is also an excellent example of audience analysis.

> Let me give you another example. Peter Ueberroth was successful in negotiating an Olympic contract with Japan's TV broadcasting company, Nippon Hosokyoku, because as an experienced international negotiator, he and his team did their homework. They studied and thoroughly familiarized themselves with the Japanese style of bargaining and were thus equipped to anticipate the various strategies of the NHK team. These efforts resulted in a very favorable Japanese contract for the 1984 Olympic Games.[5]

Because Zumberge's example was recent and the Olympics were especially important to his southern California audience, this example had a considerable impact.

ILLUSTRATION

Illustrations are detailed examples. Illustrations are often used to visualize a problem (as in a case study) or to show a step-by-step solution to a problem.

Calvin Gross, president of the National College of Education, used illustration to develop his point about the advantages of teaching for mastery of a subject.

> At TWA, a pilot-in-training has to learn everything and then do it perfectly—100 percent, no sampling—before going on to the next step. Graduates can do everything they are supposed to do. They can prove it and so can their school.
>
> To me, that's a mighty reassuring piece of knowledge when Flight No. 355 from La Guardia settles down at 8:13 p.m. on a foggy runway at O'Hare. I'm glad to know that the fellow or gal up front didn't pass the unit on blind approaches with a mark of 95 percent. I'd hate to take repeatedly a chance of one in twenty that the pilot would overlook something or wouldn't know what to do.[6]

NARRATION

Narration is a description of a personal experience. It adds human interest to your speech and often a degree of suspense as the audience waits to hear the end of the narration or how it relates to your main point. Because narration usually develops and maintains attention, it is often used in the introduction of a speech.

Ted Tedesco, at that time city manager of San Jose, introduced his speech on European cities with this colorful lead-in to his idea of new approaches to conventional ways of doing things:

> I was driving back to San Jose from the beach a few weeks ago, and just before the freeway entrance the traffic began backing up. Looking ahead, we saw that every car had stopped briefly to talk to a hitchhiker. It was hot; I was annoyed, but curious. Why in the world would everyone pull over for the hitchhiker? What made him so unusual?
>
> Finally reaching him I discovered why. On a piece of cardboard with a thick crayon, he had printed "home" and everyone was stopping to find out where "home" was.[7]

It is often effective to refer back to an introductory narration later in your speech or in your conclusion.

DETAIL

Providing *detail* helps an audience understand your point more fully by showing its specific characteristics. This procedure helps if you are introducing a new idea, talking about an unfamiliar situation, or suggesting a new solution to a problem.

Randy Larsen of Humboldt State University used detail in his first-place informative speech at the 1985 American Forensic Association's National Individual Events Tournament. In the following excerpt he added detail to communicate the simplicity of the laser process:

> The word "laser" is an acronym formed from the first letters of the words *L*ight *A*mplification by *S*timulated *E*mission of *R*adiation. Of these five com-

ponents, ''Stimulated Emission,'' a concept theorized by Albert Einstein way back in 1917, is the cornerstone of the laser's production. Stimulated emission is the actual process by which a cylinder filled with a pure substance, for example, neon or argon, has its contents funneled into a coherent, nondefracting beam of light. The resulting beam is of pure color and according to Alan Mauer's 1982 book *Lasers*, may be three times hotter than the surface of the sun.[8]

DESCRIPTION

Description is a detailed verbal picture of a concept or an example of a concept. Description usually depends on the vividness of words for total understanding. Edward Eddy, president of Chatham College, used description to develop the idea of the Niger River in West Africa as the serene, yet deadly, life support of that country:

> We saw below us the men washing themselves and their clothes in the river and we watched the women drawing water and carrying it on their backs for miles inland. We observed the cattle and goats drinking . . . And the children laughing as they swam . . . And the fishermen hoping for one last catch. It was a magnificent painting with the broad strokes of activity muted only by a certain serenity. Nothing could be more perfect—and nothing more deadly. Because beneath the surface of the Niger, schistosomiasis thrives. Small parasitic flatworms, carried by snails, enter the blood vessels of man and mammal and attack the liver.[9]

STATISTICS

Statistics numerically describe the size or frequency of a concept. Statistics are powerful means of developing, clarifying, or supporting because they give the audience concrete information. But numbers, especially large ones, out of context can be meaningless to an audience. They are far more effective if they are used in a comparison. For example, if you told your audience there are 370,000 deaths each year in the United States due to cancer, the audience might attach a connotative meaning to the number but would lack a precise denotative meaning for it. It would be more helpful to say there are 1000 deaths each day due to cancer. Numbers that are rounded off also are easier to understand.

If you use statistics in your speech, be sure that you understand their meanings and that you use them so your audience will understand them, too. Misleading an audience by using statistics carelessly will confuse your listeners' reasoned choice making.

John McCabe, president and chief executive officer of Blue Cross and Blue Shield of Michigan, used the following statistics to impress on his audience the high cost of medical care:

> Americans are now spending $360 billion a year, or 10.6 percent of our gross national product, for health care. That's more than $1,500 for every man,

woman, and child in the country. And some experts say we may be spending 14 percent of the G.N.P. by the end of the century.[10]

Willard C. Butcher, chairman of the Chase Manhattan Bank, used statistics to visualize the extent of the federal deficit:

> In fiscal 1984 the United States overspent its income by $175 billion. Our national debt last year soared to more than $1.5 trillion. That debt required an interest expenditure of more than $150 billion.
> To put these numbers in perspective, compare them with the experience during the Kennedy Administration some 20 years ago, just before the huge buildup of the Vietnam War. In 1964, President Kennedy's *entire budget* was $115. That's $35 billion less than our interest cost to service the national debt last year.[11]

And, finally, Richard Capen, senior vice president, Copley Newspapers, stressed the small amount of time young people spend in church by using statistics to make his point:

> By age sixteen, our children have spent 15,000 hours watching television. If they went to Sunday School every other week from the time they were born until age fifteen, they would have only 400 hours of formal Christian education.[12]

Notice how all three speakers compared the basic statistic they wanted the audience to know with something which would help make the number more meaningful.

COMPARISON

Comparison is a means of developing, clarifying, or supporting your point by saying one concept is like something your audience already knows. Using the information you gathered during your audience analysis, you will be able to choose a concept with which the audience is already familiar. You can then show how the idea you are developing is similar to that concept. The effectiveness of your comparison depends on choosing a concept for comparison that is already clear to your audience.

For example, if you are talking to a group of business executives about maintaining high standards of achievement in education, you could compare this with the quality control of manufactured products. We have heard students make effective comparisons between taking care of your body and taking care of your car, between developing a relationship with another person and developing a productive garden plot, and between the weather on Mars and the Arizona desert.

John McCabe used comparison to stress the dangers of making a national decision which would limit needed health care for those who cannot pay. He compared data regarding health care in Britain and the United States as follows:

> I think it never seriously occurs to Americans that there might be something the country wants, but cannot afford. The concept of economic limitations has

not traditionally been part of our mental landscape. But here we are wanting to help people, but forced to think how the *cost* of our medical miracles will be borne.

The British have made that decision. They ration expensive health care. Kidney failure occurs at the same rate among Britains and Americans. Yet only one-third as many British patients get expensive kidney dialysis. Patients over the age of 55 are excluded altogether. Chemotherapy for cancer is limited to those who are young and likely to be cured. Only one-tenth as much coronary bypass surgery is performed per capita in England.[13]

ANALOGY

An *analogy* is a comparison of an abstract idea you want your audience to understand with a simple, concrete idea which your audience already knows. Jesse Jackson used analogy to communicate his concept of America's ethnic tradition:

> We're more like a bowl of vegetable soup than a melting pot. First of all, vegetable soup is more digestible than steel . . . The second point is that in the vegetable soup, you may have a tomato base and that is the homogeneous dimension of American culture. . . . But beyond that base . . . there is corn and beans, peas and chunks of meat floating up on the top of that soup . . . And when it gets hot, those elements do not lose their identity, but each one of them has extracted from it some of its vital juices. And that's what makes the soup tasty.[14]

Beverly Beltaire, president of PR Associates, Inc., also used analogy to stress information as "America's Biggest Business" as follows:

> It is information—knowledge reproducing itself like rabbits on fertility drugs— that has made it all possible. Whatever miracles may come next—whether cheap, clean energy or a cure for cancer—they will flow from the same source: the wellspring of knowledge.[15]

CONTRAST

Contrast shows how your idea differs from another idea, preferably one that the audience already understands. John Silber, president of Boston University, used contrast to clarify the difference between the tuition advance fund he was proposing for funding higher education with an existing student loan program. This was especially effective because his audience was familiar with the loan program and its problems. By contrasting his suggestion to the major deficiencies of the loan program, he vividly highlighted the advantages of his own ideas.

> Before discussing such a plan in detail, I want to point out that it would differ fundamentally from our present loan program. First, repayment would be contingent upon income . . . Second, repayment could be carried out over a very long period of time—the approximately forty-five years comprised by the

contemporary working lifetime. Third, although the amount to be repaid would include a one-time service charge for administrative and other costs, there would be no interest charged on the advance . . . Finally, there would be no question of default. Anyone who received an advance from the trust fund would make annual payments through withholding until the advance was paid back.[16]

TESTIMONY OR QUOTATION

While we encourage you to make a unique contribution to the understanding of your speech topic, there will be times when it is effective to use the words of others. You may use the words of someone who is a respected source for your audience. In either case, make your quotations brief. Select *testimony* or *quotations* that do not need additional explanation. If you have to say, "What she meant was . . .," you may not have chosen your quotation carefully.

Win Borden, president of the Minnesota Association of Commerce and Industry, used this humorous quotation to begin a graduation address:

> The political satirist Art Buchwald gave another short speech at a graduation ceremony at Georgetown University. Let me repeat his entire speech.
> "I'm here today to congratulate 987 men and 856 graduating persons. I have examined your grades. Your collective entry into the world of business marks the end of the free enterprise system as we know it.
> "Thank you."[17]

Carole Howard, a division manager for AT & T Information Systems, used quotation to support her suggestions for women moving into senior management.

> Seventh, we shouldn't be so quick to share our weaknesses with others. Men have always known that to move up in the corporate ladder they must move into jobs for which, on the surface, they had few qualifications—for example, a marketeer transferring to a factory manager's job for production experience. We must do the same—with confidence, not foreboding. . . . Take some chances. As Flip Wilson observed, "You can't expect to hit the jackpot if you don't put a few nickles in the machine."[18]

REPETITION

Repetition restates a concept in the same or similar words. Repetition helps an audience remember your ideas. To develop, clarify, or support your ideas with intelligent audiences, it is usually more helpful to use similar words or phrases as repetition rather than repeating exactly those you used originally to express your ideas. This has the double impact of allowing the audience to hear the idea several times and aiding its understanding when it hears it in slightly different ways. In the following speech excerpts Jesse Jackson used repetition to develop his idea of ethnic identity:

I'm concerned about the ethnic development of black people and other peoples. But being black ain't enough. Being Arab ain't enough. Being female, being male ain't enough.[19]

Lastly, be ethnic, be ethical, be economic, be excellent, excellent, excellent. The only protection against genocide is to remain necessary. Be necessary. Do your thing so well that even your enemies have to say, "I don't like him, but we need him."[20]

▓ *Which Developing, Clarifying, and Supporting Materials Should I Use?*

Because it is unlikely that you would use all twelve in any one speech, you will have to make some choices. If you go back to your audience analysis for each main point, you will be able to determine if the audience does not know your main point, knows it only slightly, or does not fully accept it. If the audience members do not know the main point, you would use developing materials; if they know it slightly, you would use clarifying materials; and if they are uncertain or disagree, you would use supporting materials. By keeping your general purpose and the results of your audience analysis in mind, you will be able to select appropriate materials and find one or more sources for those materials.

▓ *Where Do I Find These Materials for My Speech?*

There are basically five ways you can research: reading, listening, observing, experiencing, and thinking. Many students only read to research for a speech, often using only one article or one book. While this may be a good way to discover your topic and main points, it is preferable to do research in several sources and types of sources. By using many sources, you can bring new insights, understanding, and awareness to your audience and greatly increase its interest and attention.

Let's start with research by ***reading***, not because it is always best or always first but because it is often an excellent way to get background material that will make the other ways of researching more meaningful. You may also find yourself returning to reading material to confirm information you learn from the other types of research. While your main source for reading material will be the library, you could also ask someone who knows a great deal about your topic to recommend reading material. Materials will differ in their timeliness, scope of coverage, depth, and point of view. By knowing the kind of material you are looking for, you will be more likely to use an appropriate source. Table 5-2 gives you a brief overview of the kinds of things you might look for and the library sources that contain them.

LEARNING BY UNDERSTANDING

1. What three functions does additional material for the main points of your speech accomplish?

2. Below are the twelve communication procedures and examples of each one. Match the letter of the example with the number of the procedure that goes with it. Then rank each of these procedures for effectiveness in communicating an informative speech to your classmates. For example, if you think that statistics would be most effective for your classmates, put (1) in front of statistics.

Examples

a. Vitamin A deficiency leads to poor night vision. Poor night vision results from vitamin A deficiency.

b. Vitamin A deficiency is different from deficiency in the B vitamins. Vitamin A deficiency only affects the eyes, whereas B deficiencies affect all the body's organs.

c. People who are deficient in vitamin A are characterized by poor night vision, eye strain, acne, and dandruff.

d. Of animals deficient in vitamin A 98 percent had infections.

e. Vitamin A is like the film in a camera: it photographs what you see and can be used up.

f. Adelle Davis said, "Perhaps no glare is so destructive to vitamin A in the eyes as sunlight on clean snow."

g. Vitamins are chemicals essential for the normal functions of cells.

h. You can test your vitamin A adequacy when you drive at night. The lights of oncoming cars destroy vitamin A in your eyes. If you can see almost immediately after a car passes, you have enough vitamin A. If you are blinded for fifteen seconds or more, you are deficient.

i. Vitamin A is a colorless substance found in animal foods.

j. My development of eyestrain resulting from vitamin A deficiency began about four months after I started writing this book. I spent long hours writing on white paper with light reflecting off the paper.

k. Vitamin A deficiency is similar to vitamin C deficiency in that supplying large amounts almost immediately reduces the symptoms.

l. My brother had severe vitamin A deficiency.

Procedures

1. DEFINITION
2. EXAMPLE
3. ILLUSTRATION
4. NARRATION
5. DETAIL
6. DESCRIPTION
7. STATISTICS
8. COMPARISON
9. ANALOGY
10. CONTRAST
11. TESTIMONY or QUOTATION
12. REPETITION

ANSWERS:

1. Developing, clarifying, and supporting
2. a. 12, b. 10, c. 5, d. 7, e. 9, f. 11, g. 1, h. 3, i. 6, j. 4, k. 8, l. 2.
Check your ranking of most effective procedures with several other people in your class. Discuss differences in your rankings.

TABLE 5-2 LIBRARY RESEARCH SOURCES

If You Want:	Type of Sources:	Specific Examples:
Overview of topic	Encyclopedias	*Encyclopaedia Britannica*
Current events (*brief*)	Newspapers	*Facts on File*
Current events (*commentary*)	Magazines	*Atlantic Monthly* *Saturday Review* *New Republic*
Background/Depth	Books	See Card Catalog
Quotations	Magazine articles	*Hoyt's New Cyclopedia of Practical Quotations*
Human interest stories	Newspapers Magazines	*Current Biography*
Varied points of view	Articles from opposing magazines	*Reader's Guide to Periodical Literature*
Statistics	Almanacs	*World Almanac,* *Information Please Almanac*
Pictures	Vertical file Some magazines	*Index to Illustrations*
Historical perspective	Books Bound issues of magazines	See Card Catalog, *Reader's Guide to Periodical Literature*

Where Can I Find Recent Information on My Topic?

There are several sources of recent information in your library. The *Reader's Guide to Periodical Literature,* an index for many types of magazines, is published twice a month and is a good place to begin your search for recent information. The entries in the *Reader's Guide* are alphabetized by subject, author, and, sometimes, title. Unless you have an author or title to look under, it will be helpful to think of several subjects under which you might find material for your topic. For example, if you have decided to talk about alcoholism on campus, you might look under the words *drinking, student, habit,* and *alcoholism.*

Each author and subject entry in the *Reader's Guide* contains the following information: (1) title of the article; (2) author's name, if known; (3) special features of the article, such as illustrations or maps; (4) name of the magazine (abbreviated but written out in the "List of Periodicals Indexed" at the front of the issue); (5) volume number (appears before the colon); (6) page numbers (after the colon); and (7) date of the magazine. Here is how a sample entry looks:

ALCOHOL—COLLEGE STUDENTS

Busting the beer bust (drinking on campus); C. Leerhsen. il <u>Newsweek</u>.
104:96–7 O 29 '84.

Some fields have special indexes to related articles. Some examples are the *Agricultural Index, Business Periodicals Index, Education Index, Applied Science and Technology Index, Art Index,* and the *Index to Religious Periodical Literature.*

Book selections can be made in a library card catalog through an author's name, a book title, or a subject heading.

Newspapers are also a helpful source for recent information. One of the best sources for news articles is the *New York Times Index. Facts on File* is a weekly digest of articles from a number of large newspapers. Newspapers are also helpful for learning attitudes toward your topic at a particular period of time. For example, in a speech on current attitudes toward cocaine, you could quote newspaper articles about attitudes toward cocaine in the 1920s for a comparison.

The United States government is another source of up-to-date information. Many libraries receive government publications regularly. These pamphlets and books are the result of research conducted by governmental agencies. To discover what publications are available on your topic, check the *Monthly Catalog of United States Government Publications*.

How Do I Find Books on My Topic in the Card Catalog?

In a card catalog, books are alphabetized according to title, author, and subject. Early in your research, you could check under general subjects related to your topic to find helpful books. Later, when you have discovered particular books, you can check to see if your library has the book and where you can find it. The index card for each book contains helpful information. Figure 5-6 shows a sample title card from a card catalog like the one in your library.

If you need up-to-date information for your speech, be sure to check the

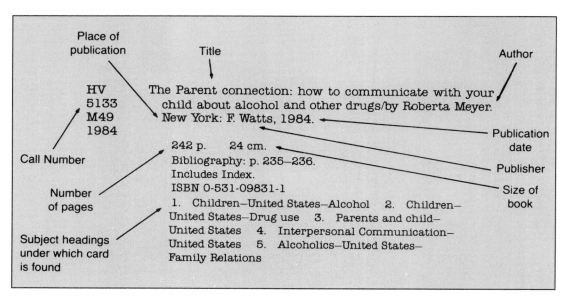

Figure 5-6   Sample Title Card

publication date of the book. And remember that, because it takes time to publish a book, the information will be about a year or so older than the date of publication. Another important bit of data is the number in the upper left-hand corner of the card. This will either be the Library of Congress or Dewey Decimal classification number, depending on the filing system used by your library. This number will direct you to the place in the library where you can find your book. Most libraries have pamphlets and posted directories that indicate how the numbers on the card relate to the location of the book in the library. It is helpful to become familiar with the location system your library uses.

What If I Want a Brief Overview of My Topic?

There are numerous general and specialized encyclopedias in which you can find a brief overview of many topics. The *Encyclopaedia Britannica* or *The World Book* might be good places to start.

If you are looking for information about a particular well-known person, you could check *Who's Who in America* (published every other year) or *Current Biography* (published monthly). Examples of specialized encyclopedias include *Yearbook of the United Nations*, *An Encyclopedia of World History*, *McGraw-Hill Encyclopedia of Science and Technology*, and the *Encyclopedia of Jazz*.

What If I Need Specific Information about My Topic?

The *World Almanac* and *Information Please Almanac* are published annually and contain a variety of useful information and statistics. For example, if you want to find out the number of automobile accidents or births, the amount of rain, or the average income of Americans for any year, these would be excellent sources. The *World Almanac* is especially helpful for its chronology of important events of the preceding year and the *Information Please Almanac* for its descriptive articles on the year's developments in certain fields. The *Economic Almanac* has specific economic and business statistical data.

How About Listening?

There are lots of things you can learn through **listening** that you cannot learn through reading—for example, information that is too recent to have appeared in print or information from a source who has not written it down. Speakers on campus offer this kind of information. You may listen to the news or talk shows on National Public Radio, or you might interview someone who knows about your topic. For example, if you are preparing a speech on alcoholism on campus, talking to a guidance counselor on your campus about the problems at your school in the last five years would provide information you could not get otherwise.

You have already developed listening skills that will be valuable to you as a research tool. It will be especially important in an interview to have a specific goal in mind so that you can make the best use of your time with your subject. We suggest that you develop several questions ahead of time that will help you accomplish your listening goal. Additionally, we suggest that you begin with a general question and then move to more specific ones. You might begin by asking, "I'm preparing a speech on alcoholism. What can you tell me that will help me better understand the situation on this campus?" You could then have several specific questions ready, such as "How many students have come to you with this problem?" "What approach do you take with these students?" and "How do students overcome this problem?"

What Are Other Ways of Researching?

A third way of researchig is by **observation**. As with listening, you will learn a great deal because you spend much of your day observing things about the people around you. When you use this means as a research tool for your speeches, many of the skills you have already developed for effective listening will be helpful. If you have decided that observing is an effective way to research, then set a specific goal to be accomplished by your observation. Observation provides first-hand information about your topic. For example, you might want to research nonverbal communication by observing the local traffic court; your specific observational goal might be learning the nonverbal behaviors people show when they receive fines. You could learn about the aggressive tendencies of preschool children by observing several playground periods at a nursery school; here, your specific observational goal might be comparing male and female physical contact during anger.

A fourth way of researching is by **experiencing**. Research by experience can

Direct experience within a specific topic provides valuable information unobtainable through other means.

be a direct and personally meaningful way to gain information. Experiencing something provides the kind of understanding that helps you communicate connotative, as well as denotative, meaning to your listeners. You might need to spend a day with an elderly person or try to get to classes in a wheelchair to understand these experiences well enough to communicate them to an audience. Author George Plimpton frequently researches by experiencing. When he wanted to understand what it was like to be a professional football player, he actually went through the training camp of the Detroit Lions. The results? A successful book and a movie, both called *The Paper Lion*.

What's Left?

A last means of researching is ***thinking***, which helps you use each of the other methods. The process of thinking enables you to make an original contribution through your speaking. It helps you give your audience something unique that you have developed by thinking about the information you have researched.

Disciplined thinking is not easy. George Bernard Shaw, British writer and activist, said that he became famous and wealthy by thinking only once a month. Probably Shaw was talking about creative thinking or difficult problem solving, because we all spend quite a bit of our time thinking in some way. If you include assessing things we hear, daydreaming, reasoning, dreaming, free associating, and problem solving as examples, we all think every day. But, disciplined thinking is not easy.

How Can I Practice Disciplined Thinking to Prepare for My Speech?

That's a fair question and a difficult one to answer because there are many approaches to thinking, and everyone develops his or her own approach to this skill. While there is considerable research being done on various approaches to effective thinking, there is no one best procedure for all situations.[21]

Much of what we typically call thinking is done after you have completed your research and are analyzing the materials and developing arguments to support or develop your ideas. Here, we are referring to a more creative form of thinking in which you consider alternative possibilities and provide new perspectives on topics. This is especially important in finding new solutions to problems or new explanations for complex behavior. The following guidelines should help you improve this type of thinking.

GUIDELINES FOR EXPLORATORY THINKING

1. Understand all aspects of the problem or situation.
2. Do not be boxed in by artificial procedures or available limits.
3. Consider alternative formats for your answers.
4. Brainstorm for many different kinds of possible solutions.[22]

First, it is important to clearly identify the situation you are trying to understand or the problem you are trying to solve. Information and understanding gathered from the other four means of researching will be valuable here. Consider any aspect of the situation or problem that you do not have information about, and use the other four means of research to get the needed information.

Second, consciously avoid typical or traditional answers. The problem here is that we are so accustomed to using typical answers that we do not recognize we are doing it. Recognizing the limits we usually place upon ourselves is the biggest part of overcoming this restrictive factor, as the following problem will illustrate:

In this diagram are nine dots. You will have to avoid typical approaches in order to draw four straight lines that go through all the dots without letting your pencil leave the paper.

Third, it is important to consider alternative formats to view the situation or problem. This directly builds on the second suggestion. Here, it will be helpful to record the information that you gathered by using the other four research methods. We suggest you record your information on separate cards so you can change the order of the cards, spread them out to reveal all the information at once, and consider various sequences.

Fourth, you will want to brainstorm for many different kinds of possible solutions. As you know, this involves quickly suggesting many possibilities without evaluating them—no matter how farfetched they may seem. We have found that using a tape recorder is especially helpful for this; because you do not stop to write down your ideas, you can sustain the flow of creative energy. Imagine that it is the first snowfall of the year, and you and a friend want to go sledding but do not have a sled. Now quickly think of all the possible objects you could use as sleds.

Another approach to brainstorming is to ask *What if?* questions. What if the Rocky Mountains were where the Appalachian Mountains are? How would this have changed the course of American history? What if you were going on a month-long hike along the Appalachian Trail or a month-long wilderness canoe trip in northern Minnesota, and you could only take fifteen things? What fifteen things would you take? Thinking assisted by future-oriented *What if?* questions can produce interesting speech topics. For example, What if cars were outlawed because they use too much of our dwindling gas and oil supplies and pollute the air too much?

Creative thinking and problem solving are two characteristics that set humans apart from other animals. Thinking will help you make unique contributions through your speeches. Thinking is so important and exciting that we should try to avoid saying, ''Oh, I was *just* thinking.''

Here is a final, difficult problem for which you can use all of the suggested guidelines for exploratory thinking:

Many years ago, when a person who owed money could be imprisoned, a merchant in London had the misfortune to owe a huge sum to a moneylender. The moneylender, who was old and ugly, fancied the merchant's beautiful young daughter. He proposed a bargain. He said he would cancel the merchant's debt if he could have the girl instead.

Both the merchant and his daughter were horrified at the proposal. So the cunning moneylender proposed that they let Providence decide the matter. He told them that he would put a black pebble and a white pebble into an empty moneybag, and the girl would have to pick out one of the pebbles. If she chose the black pebble, she would become his wife, and her father's debt would be canceled. If she chose the white pebble, she would stay with her father, and the debt would still be canceled. But if she refused to pick out the pebble that was to decide her fate, her father would be thrown into jail and she would starve.

Reluctantly, the merchant agreed. They were standing on a pebble-strewn path in the merchant's garden as they talked, and the moneylender stooped down to pick up the two pebbles. As he did, the girl, sharp-eyed with fright, noticed that he picked up two black pebbles and put them into the moneybag.

He then asked the girl to pick out the pebble that was to decide her fate and that of her father.

Imagine that you're standing on that path in the merchant's garden. What would you have done if you had been the girl?[23]

How Do I Record the Information I've Learned from My Research?

It is helpful to take notes while you are doing each type of research. This will be especially important for the very specific information you will get while researching by reading. Figure 5-7 illustrates an effective procedure for taking notes on note cards. Figure 5-8 shows a sample note card for research by reading.

Baird, Knower, and Becker offer the following suggestions for clear notetaking.[24]

SUGGESTIONS FOR CLEAR NOTETAKING

1. Use small cards of a uniform size.

2. Aim to get the gist of an idea or an article.

3. Place one fact on each card.

4. Tag each card at the top with the topic or division under which the statement or fact falls.

5. Cite the exact source at the bottom of the card.

6. Quote accurately and avoid long quotations.

7. Try to note facts rather than general opinions.

8. Establish a general scheme for reading and classifying notes.

9. Write legibly.

Figure 5-7 Note Card Procedure

Write Specific Topic

Write brief quotation, statistics, summary of listening, observation, experiencing, or thinking

Accurately quote the source of your information. Write all data you would use in a bibliographic reference.

> Employees Paid to Lose
> Weight
>
>
> Overweight American Continental Corporation employees can earn
> $750 bonuses if they go on a health kick. Part of first program of its
> kind in country.
>
> "Medical and Nutritional News."
> Runner's World 20(May 1985):29.

Figure 5-8   Sample Note Card for Research by Reading

Should I Tell My Audience Where I Found the Materials?

Yes. The source for your materials is usually described for definitions, statistics, testimonies or quotations, and for such visual aids as graphs or charts. In communicating ideas and information that are not the result of your own thinking, observing, or experiencing, you should state the source of your materials in your speech. There are several advantages to this. First, your audience will know that you carefully researched your topic, and this will increase your credibility as a speaker on this topic. Second, you will be giving credit to the actual source of the material. When you write an English theme, you footnote information and ideas that are not your own; you also should verbally footnote your material in speeches. In listening to your data, your audience might wonder if your material is up-to-date or biased in some way. By communicating the source and date of your information, you will help answer these questions.

Here is an example of how you might include the source and date in your speech:

> In the medical and nutritional news section of the May 1985 issue of *Runner's World* a report on American Continental Corporation's first-of-its-kind health program indicated that overweight employees can earn bonuses of $750 if they go on a health kick.

How Can I Use the Developing, Clarifying, and Supporting Data in My Speech?

Remember, the purpose of the data is to clarify, develop, or support the appropriate main points. You might either state your main point and then include the clarifying, developing, or supportive data, or you might first state the data and then draw the conclusion of your main point. When you state your main idea first and then support it by your evidence, you are using deductive organization. When you present your data before your main idea, you are using inductive organization. For your next few speeches, you probably will use deductive organization. We will describe both kinds in more detail in Chapter 7.

LEARNING BY UNDERSTANDING

1. List the five means of researching a speech topic.

2. Decide the type of research represented by each of the following examples.

   _____ **a.** Going for an interview in an employment office to see what it is like to look for a job

   _____ **b.** Using the latest issue of *People* for information on what has happened to Linda Ronstadt

   _____ **c.** Watching people waiting for a delayed flight to see how they use time

   _____ **d.** Deciding which of the research conclusions regarding campus alcoholism are most applicable at your school

   _____ **e.** Hearing your father tell you his perspective on the defeat of the school bond issue

3. How does this note card differ from the recommended form?

JOBS WITHOUT A DEGREE

The vast majority of the 46,000,000 openings expected between 1986 and 1995 will require workers with less than four years of college, according to the U.S. Dept. of Labor.

"Good Jobs You Can Get without a Degree," Changing Times

ANSWERS:

1. Reading, listening, observing, experiencing, thinking
2. **a.** experiencing, **b.** reading, **c.** observing, **d.** thinking, **e.** listening
3. The card lacks the date of the magazine. That information would be important because it proves your facts are up-to-date.

LEARNING BY INTERACTING

Choose a speech topic that your speech classmates agree they would like to learn more about. In small groups, discuss the best methods for researching and developing the topic.

First, develop a central idea and three main points that your group would cover in such a speech. Then decide what clarifying, developing, and supporting materials would be most appropriate for each point. Write down your reasons for your choices. Plan to use at least two types of materials for each point.

Finally, beside each type of material, write which of the five ways to research you think would be the most appropriate means of getting the information. Use several ways of researching.

Compare your results with the other groups. Do you agree with each other's choices? Discuss any differences.

LEARNING BY SPEAKING

Prepare a three- to four-minute informative speech that describes an important experience in your life. Your topic should meet the three guidelines specified in Chapter 4. Use the steps for preparation suggested in Chapter 5. Use at least five of the means of developing, clarifying, or supporting procedures in your speech. Use at least three of the ways of researching to provide materials which help the class to understand your experience. Summarize your preparation by writing your:

General Purpose
General Topic
Audience Analysis (as in the sample Audience Analysis form in Chapter 4)
Specific Topic
Specific Purpose
Central Idea
Main Points

Include your additional speech materials under the main points they are developing, clarifying, or supporting. Include a bibliography in which you state the specific source you used for your three ways of researching.

REVIEW

In this chapter you have worked on skills in developing your specific speech topic. You have developed a specific purpose and a central idea and formulated main and subpoints which communicate the main meaning of your speech. Further, you are able to make your points more understandable and acceptable to your audience by adding developing, clarifying, and supporting materials. Finally, you have learned research skills in reading, listening, observing, experiencing, and thinking that will enable you to find the materials to make a unique contribution to the audience's understanding of your speech topic. You are now ready to move on to developing skills in organizing these materials.

NOTES

1. Paul H. Seymour, *The New Hoyle Standard Games*, rev. ed. (Chicago: Albert Whitman, 1934), 90.

2. Jeanne Greenberg, "A Profile of the Successful High-Tech Salesperson," *Vital Speeches of the Day* 51(May 15, 1985):478.

3. James Watkins, "Roads Diverging—Despair or Hope: Your Choice," *Vital Speeches of the Day* 51(February 15, 1985):283.

4. Dorothy Ridings, "Advocating the People's Interest in Washington," *Vital Speeches of the Day* 51(June 1, 1985):488.

5. James Zumberge, "Finding Our Way in the New Pacific Frontier: A New Trade Culture," *Vital Speeches of the Day* 51(April 1, 1985):368.

6. Calvin Gross, "Drumbeats and Dissonance: Variations on a Theme for Teachers," address delivered at the Sixteenth Annual Charles W. Hunt Lecture at the 1975 meeting of the American Association of Colleges for Teacher Education, as published in the *Proceedings of the Twenty-Seventh AACTE Annual Meeting*, 1975.

7. Ted Tedesco, "We Can Learn from Europe's Cities," *Vital Speeches of the Day* 43(January 15, 1977):209.

8. Randy Larsen, "Lasers" (Unpublished speech delivered at the 1985 American Forensic Association's National Individual Events Tournament, Towson, Maryland, April 15, 1985).

9. Edward Eddy, "The Quality of Life," *Vital Speeches of the Day* 44(January 15, 1978):173.

10. John McCabe, "Human Values: The Evolution of the Health Care System," *Vital Speeches of the Day* 51(March 1, 1985):305.

11. Willard C. Butcher, "The Federal Deficit: The Need for Bipartisanship," *Vital Speeches of the Day* 51(March 1, 1985):301.

12. Richard Capen, "Sex on Television, More or Less," *Vital Speeches of the Day* 44(January 15, 1978):173.

13. McCabe, "Human Values," 304.

14. Jesse Jackson, "The Good Signs of Life," *Vital Speeches of the Day* 44(January 1, 1978):189.

15. Beverly Beltaire, "Information: Gateway to Success," *Vital Speeches of the Day* 51(July 1, 1985):552.

16. John Silber, "The Tuition Advance Fund," *Vital Speeches of the Day* 44(January 15, 1978):216.

17. Win Borden, "Recommendations for Graduates: How You Play the Game of Life," *Vital Speeches of the Day* 51(April 15, 1985):400.

18. Carole Howard, ''Moving into Senior Management,'' *Vital Speeches of the Day* 51 (December 15, 1984):149.

19. Jackson, ''The Good Signs of Life,'' 189.

20. Address delivered by Jesse Jackson before the National Convention of the Speech Communication Association, Chicago, 1974, copies by Speech Communication Association, 8.

21. James R. Erickson and Mari Riess Jones, ''Thinking,'' *Annual Review of Psychology* 29(1978):61–90.

22. Adapted from Dennis Coon, *Introduction to Psychology* (St. Paul: West, 1977), 252.

23. Edward deBono, *New Think* (New York: Basic Books, 1968), 11–12.

24. A. Craig Baird, Franklin E. Knower, and Samuel Becker, *General Speech Communication* (New York: McGraw-Hill, 1971), 113.

6

USING VISUAL AIDS

In this chapter, you'll be . . .

LEARNING BY UNDERSTANDING

- Reasons why visual aids are important in speech development
- How visual aids can reduce nervousness
- Five main types of visual aids
- How to choose an appropriate visual aid
- How to find visual aids
- How to make your own visual aids
- How to use equipment for presenting visual aids
- How to overcome basic problems in using visual aids

LEARNING BY INTERACTING

- Choosing and preparing visual aids for a speech

LEARNING BY SPEAKING

- A three- to four-minute speech in which you introduce a new object to your class

CHAPTER OUTLINE

I. Visual aids are an important means of developing your speech topic.
   A. People pay more attention to a varied and interesting stimulus.
   B. People understand something better when they see it as well as hear it.
   C. People remember something longer if they see it as well as hear it.

II. Visual aids can reduce nervousness if handled properly.
   A. Provide any instructions so others can understand your aid.
   B. Talk with your audience, not the aid.
   C. Do not stand between your audience and the aid.
   D. Place your aid out of sight after you have finished using it.

III. There are five main types of visual aids.
   A. The first type of visual aid is an object or a model of an object.
   B. The second type of visual aid is a picture, drawing, or photograph of what you are talking about.
   C. The third type of visual aid is a chart, diagram, or graph used to present data in a concise way.
   D. The fourth type of visual aid is bodily movement that you do as a demonstration of something.
   E. The fifth type of visual aid is the listing of key words or statements for emphasis.

IV. It is important to choose the appropriate aid for a specific speech.
   A. A primary consideration in choosing a visual aid is the specific purpose of the speech.
   B. A second consideration in choosing a visual aid is the nature of your audience.
   C. A third consideration in choosing a visual aid is the physical setting in which you will speak.
   D. A final consideration in choosing a visual aid is the level of your skill in using aids.

V. There are many sources for ready-made visual aids.
   A. One source for visual aids is professionals who use models or objects related to your speech topic.
   B. Libraries are sources for visual aids.

VI. There are several types of visual aids which speakers typically make.
   A. Some of the most effective aids are speaker developed.
      1. Speaker-made charts and graphs allow you to make new combinations of information.
      2. Speaker-made charts and graphs allow you to simplify visuals from reading material so they are clear and easy for an audience to understand.
   B. Following basic guidelines will help you make effective visual aids.
      1. Decide what is the key relationship or concept to be shown.
      2. Decide what data should be included to show the relationship or concept.
      3. Decide what sizes the letters, numbers, and other parts of the visual aid should be.
      4. Decide how to emphasize the parts of the visual aid by colors and shapes.

VII. There is helpful equipment available for presenting visual aids.
    A. A flip chart and stand are basic visual-aid equipment.
    B. Posters are valuable for visual aids and are usually rested on a flip chart stand.
    C. An overhead projector uses transparencies and allows you to enlarge materials.
    D. An opaque projector enlarges and projects printed material directly from the source.
    E. Slide and film projectors are useful for longer speeches.

VIII. Beginning speakers face several problems in using visual aids.
    A. Speakers face problems in choosing the appropriate aid.
    B. Speakers face problems in practicing with the visual aid.
        1. Practice in the same (or similar) setting in which you will talk.
        2. Make sure everyone in the audience will be able to see the aid.
    C. Speakers need to follow the basic four guidelines (see II.) when presenting the aid during the speech.

6

USING VISUAL AIDS

A good picture is worth 2000 words!   —*Heun*

PREVIEW

In the last chapter you worked on developing your speech topic by the words you say. As you learned, developing, supporting, and clarifyng materials are important because they help your audience fully understand and remember your message.

In this chapter you will work on another method of developing your speech topic. Besides the words you say, you can aid your audience's understanding by appealing to the five senses: sight, sound, smell, taste, or touch. Stimulating the senses supplements spoken words and often explains or describes concepts, objects, or procedures more clearly and in more detail.

We are highlighting visual aids because they are the most common supplement. A chart showing the increasing size of the federal budget deficit or a photo showing how to do the Heimlich Maneuver are examples of visual aids. But our comments also apply to aids which appeal to other human senses. Sound or audio aids, such as cassette tapes of music selections, might be effective for a speech on music trends. Smell aids would be helpful in a speech on recognizing food spoilage. Touch aids might be valuable in a speech on identifying the quality of clothing before buying. And what would a speech (or sales presentation) on the high quality of American wines be without taste samples?

Why Are Visual Aids Given a Special Focus?

Visual aids are considered more important than audio, touch, and the other supplements. Visual aids are supplements to your speech which use the channel of sight to communicate information. They are likely to be beneficial in almost any speech while the others are used only in special situations. Because you are more likely to use visual aids, we will focus on them in this chapter. But please keep in mind that most of the recommendations for their use, such as pretesting to see if the aid can be sensed by all of your audience members, apply to the other supplements. In addition to greater use, there are three important reasons why visual aids are especially effective.

First, people **pay more attention** to a varied and interesting stimulus.[1] For example, consider how much easier it is to pay attention to a classroom lecture when the teacher uses the chalkboard or other visual aid. Visual aids can make your speech more stimulating. And this is even more important for the television-experienced audiences of today who are used to a great deal of visual stimulation.[2]

Second, people **understand something better** when they see it as well as hear it.[3] Most visual aids provide a true-to-life image, which shows the parts of something all at once. The speaker avoids possible misunderstandings which could occur if listeners missed several words, did not understand the words, or did not see their relationship to other words. Since audience concentration comes and goes, such difficulties occur often. By showing audience members a concrete image of what you are talking about, you can greatly aid their understanding and fill in any gaps which occurred as they processed the information. This is especially important for informative speeches where you are helping the audience learn something new. Consider how difficult it would be to understand how to complete an income tax form, how to prune a tree, or what the Kremlin looks like without a visual aid.

Third, people **remember something longer** if they see it as well as hear it.[4] You are applying the principle of repetition when you use a visual aid, and the reinforcement is stronger because you are sending the message through two different channels. In other words, if you are describing the Heimlich Maneuver at the same time a friend is demonstrating it on a classmate, the demonstration repeats and reinforces your verbal description.

Because of these three values of using visual aids, we suggest that you consider their use as a specific step in the preparation of every speech.

If I'm Nervous, Won't It Be Hard to Use a Visual Aid Effectively?

Planning ahead and practicing will help you avoid most problems. And most speakers actually find that using a visual aid helps them relax. First of all, the audience will turn its attention from you to the aid, taking you out of the spotlight for a moment. And, second, the physical activity of using the aid gives you a way to expend excess energy and relax your muscle tension. Here are several suggestions that will help you use your visual aid effectively and comfortably.

GUIDELINES FOR USING VISUAL AIDS

1. Provide any instructions your audience will need to understand the aid.
2. Talk to your audience, not the aid.
3. Do not stand between your audience and the aid.
4. Place your aid out of sight or turn it over after you have finished using it.

Later in the chapter we will work on some of the problems speakers face when using visual aids. First, however, you must carefully choose the visual aid(s) that will help you accomplish your speech purpose.

What Types of Visual Aids Are Available?

Many different kinds of visual aids are appropriate and useful in public speeches. We have found it helpful to group your options into five main types. As we talk about each type, we will consider the circumstances which would make it the appropriate choice for a specific speech. You will also learn how to prepare and practice with the aid so you can use it effectively as you deliver your speech.

The first type of visual aid is *an object or a model of an object*. Using a human skeleton while describing the main areas of physical stress from various sports or using an actual soccer ball while explaining the proper technique used to kick one are good examples. Objects and models are especially useful for informative speeches which call for a demonstration. Models are most valuable when they are true to scale, that is, proportional to the real object.

A second type of visual aid is *a picture, drawing, or photograph* of what you are talking about. Pictures can serve the same purposes as models and objects do, but they are often easier to handle during a speech. Some objects could be too large, too small, too smelly, or too wiggly to control before an audience. It is best *not* to pass photos or pictures while you talk as they divert much of the audience's attention from you. Also, as the audience would experience the aid at different times, you could not effectively coordinate it with your verbal message.

Possible disadvantages of pictures, drawings, or photos could include their small size and two-dimensionality. Because audience members cannot see all sides of an object at one time, they may develop inaccurate ideas of the object's other characteristics, such as its weight.

A third type of visual aid is *a chart, diagram, or graph* used to present information in a concise way. This type is especially valuable if you are dealing with numerical data. Most people have great difficulty imagining, understanding, and remembering numbers, especially large ones like city or state budgets. Also, the point you are making will often be more clear by showing the relationships between data rather than by presenting the specific data by themselves. Pie diagrams and bar graphs are especially valuable for showing these relationships as Figure 6-1 shows. We have found *USA Today* to be a valuable source for clear and interesting bar graphs and charts. The visual impact of seeing the great differences in the slices of the pie (e.g., Federal Budget Squeeze, Agricultural Work Force) or the lengths of the lines of a bar graph (e.g., the other three charts) adds strength to your idea because it clarifies the relationships among data.

A fourth type of visual aid is *bodily movement that you do*, as a speaker, to demonstrate something while you talk. These movements go beyond the natural gestures you use as you talk—they actually demonstrate a process or procedure. There are many procedures which you can best explain by doing them, such as showing the audience a muscle relaxation technique. You probably have used body

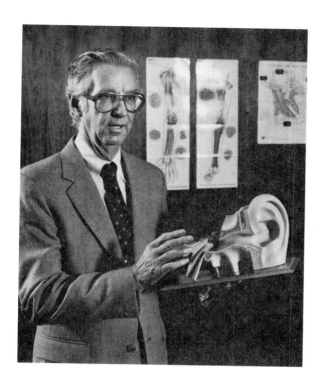

Models and drawings help a speaker communicate clear information.

movements in coaching a younger brother or sister on how to hit a softball or hockey puck.

A final type of visual aid is the ***listing of key words or statements*** for emphasis. For example, using the key words suggested by Jane Fonda for dealing with minor sprains (Rest, Ice, Compress, Elevate).[5] You could write these on the chalkboard as you talk. You could also give each audience member a small card with the words printed on it. Another approach would be to list the words on a poster and then point to each of the steps as you talk about it. Key statements should be short so that you do not need to stop your talk to write them.

Visual acronyms are another form of this type of visual aid and can be very useful for attention and retention. An acronym is a word formed from the first letters of other words. Notice how the first letters of the key words above for treating sprains form the word RICE. Sometimes the letters in an acronym form a new word like *United States Air Force* (USAF), sometimes they are selected to form an old word like *National Organization for Women* (NOW), and sometimes they form an unexpected word like Garrison Keillor's *American Shyness Society*, the organization which represents shy people.

With each type of visual aid you let the audience *see* what you are talking about, and thereby increase its attention, understanding, and retention.

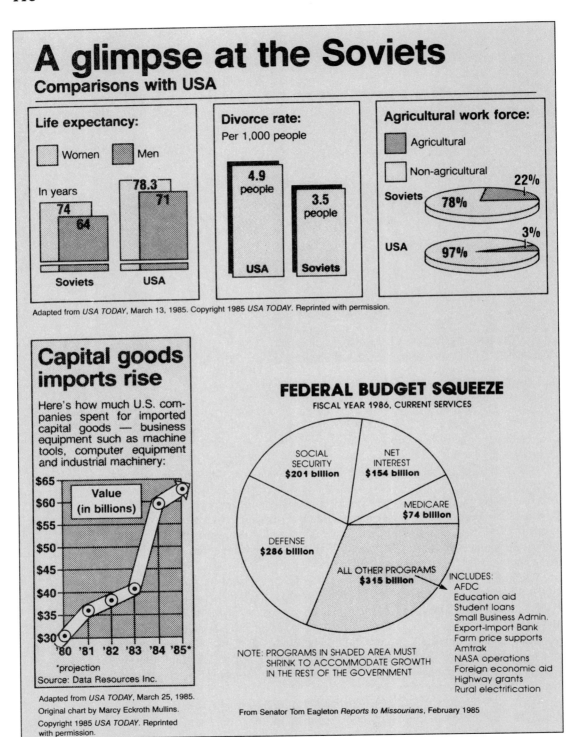

A glimpse at the Soviets
Comparisons with USA

Life expectancy:
Women   Men

In years
74
64
78.3
71
Soviets   USA

Divorce rate:
Per 1,000 people
4.9 people
3.5 people
USA   Soviets

Agricultural work force:
Agricultural
Non-agricultural
Soviets   78%   22%
USA   97%   3%

Adapted from *USA TODAY*, March 13, 1985. Copyright 1985 *USA TODAY*. Reprinted with permission.

Capital goods imports rise

Here's how much U.S. companies spent for imported capital goods — business equipment such as machine tools, computer equipment and industrial machinery:

Value (in billions)
$65
$60
$55
$50
$45
$40
$35
$30
'80 '81 '82 '83 '84 '85*
*projection
Source: Data Resources Inc.

Adapted from *USA TODAY*, March 25, 1985.
Original chart by Marcy Eckroth Mullins.
Copyright 1985 *USA TODAY*. Reprinted with permission.

FEDERAL BUDGET SQUEEZE
FISCAL YEAR 1986, CURRENT SERVICES

SOCIAL SECURITY
$201 billion

NET INTEREST
$154 billion

MEDICARE
$74 billion

DEFENSE
$286 billion

ALL OTHER PROGRAMS
$315 billion

INCLUDES:
AFDC
Education aid
Student loans
Small Business Admin.
Export-Import Bank
Farm price supports
Amtrak
NASA operations
Foreign economic aid
Highway grants
Rural electrification

NOTE: PROGRAMS IN SHADED AREA MUST SHRINK TO ACCOMMODATE GROWTH IN THE REST OF THE GOVERNMENT

From Senator Tom Eagleton *Reports to Missourians*, February 1985

Figure 6-1   Examples of Charts, Diagrams, and Graphs

LEARNING BY UNDERSTANDING

1. What are three reasons why visual aids are important means for developing your speech?

2. Match each type of visual aid with an example.

a. objects or models of objects

b. pictures, drawings, or photos

c. charts or graphs

d. body movements

e. listing of key words

an acronym

a skeleton of a human hand

a person demonstrating a good golf swing

a pie diagram of the college athletic budget

an artist's sketch of the proposed multipurpose athletic building

ANSWERS:

1. People pay more attention to visual stimuli, people understand better things they see, and people remember longer if they see as well as hear.

2. a. skeleton, **b.** sketch, **c.** pie diagram, **d.** golfer, **e.** acronym

How Do I Decide Which Type of Visual Aid Is Most Appropriate for My Speech?

A primary consideration in choosing a visual aid is the specific purpose of your speech. What specifically do you want your audience to understand, remember, and/or do as a result of your speech? If the individual steps of a process are crucial, then listing the steps visually with a reinforcing acronym would be helpful. If doing a procedure correctly is important, then having a model or demonstrating the procedure would be helpful. You might look at John Deeth's speech on spelling in Appendix B for numerous fine examples of visual aids which illustrate his main points.

A second consideration is the nature of your audience. An audience which already has some information about your topic may need a more specific or detailed visual aid. An audience that may be less motivated to hear your topic might need more stimulating and varied visual aids. Children are more likely to need large, simple visual aids, such as objects or movements, while college-age people are more likely to understand charts and graphs.

A third consideration is the physical setting in which you will speak. Three major physical setting concerns are your time limit, the shape of the room, and the lighting of the room. With a shorter time limit (from two to ten minutes), you would want to use fewer visual aids and to have aids which can be understood with little explanation. The shape of a room influences how well your audience will be able to see your visual aid; some rooms lend themselves more to one form of aid than another. Obviously, for your visual to catch attention and aid understanding and remembering, your audience must be able to see it. We strongly recommend that before your speech day, you place each visual aid where you will use it and walk to the far back of the room, the back corners, and the far sides to be sure it can be seen by all. The lighting is important because some mechanical devices used for showing visual aids, such as overhead projectors, depend on the lighting being dimmed. If the lighting only allows complete light or dark, or if windows cannot be shaded easily, you should avoid using these mechanical devices.

A final consideration is the level of your skill in using visual aids. Make sure your visual aid is one that you understand fully and can handle well. You could ask a person similar to your audience members to watch your use of the visual aid and to see if he or she understands. If that person is unsure, ask an expert to listen to your explanation and to improve it.

Overall, a visual aid should fit naturally into your speech. It should not draw excessive attention to itself or be the main focus of the speech. It is an *aid* to understanding and a means to accomplishing your desired communication goal.

Where Do I Find Already-Prepared Visual Aids for My Speeches?

One valuable source is to find professionals who use models or objects related to your speech topic. On college campuses many departments have large teaching models, charts, and other aids; these could be helpful for a speech related to that major. Mary Nielsen used a stuffed bat to visualize the similarities between the anatomy of bats and people in her speech "Hug a Bat—No Way" in Appendix B. Where might she have found that stuffed bat?

Another source for ready-to-use aids is the reading material you use to develop your speech topic. You can use most reading material directly with the opaque projector, while other material you may want to reproduce on poster board for easier use in your physical setting. You can use a whole book or magazine with the opaque project so please do not tear out a page. Most libraries also have vertical files which contain pictures, and some have curriculum sections for education majors which contain a variety of ready-made visual aids.

Although you will be able to find many already-prepared visual aids, some of the best will be created by you. Just as you develop and organize your ideas for your specific audience, so, too, you can customize your visual aids. The most obvious type you would make yourself is the list of key words or ideas. And while you would not typically make objects and models or photos and pictures, you *would* be likely to make graphs and charts. You often find relevant information but need to develop the bar graph or pie diagram that will make the point vividly with your audience.

As you know, a ***bar graph*** is a chart with bars, lines, or rectangles to show size, using a scale like one inch equals one unit of measure. The bars could also be implied as in the Capital Goods Imports Rise graph (see Figure 6-1). A ***pie diagram*** is designed to show percentages or relationships by dividing a circle into wedges or pieces of "pie."

Another reason for making your own graph or chart is that those you find in written material are often too complicated to use in a public speech. Consider the bar graph in Figure 6-2 which was taken from a written source. It has a great deal of valuable information for a reader who can take the time necessary to understand it well. But it would be much too complicated for an audience to understand.

How Do I Prepare My Own Charts and Graphs?

Figure 6-3 shows the key decisions for planning and constructing charts and graphs, as well as other visual aids. You might have access to computer software programs that will do the actual construction for you.

We will use the budget deficit bar graph (Figure 6-2) to visualize how the decisions guide the planning and constructing of a visual aid.

DECISION 1.

In terms of deciding what we want to communicate, let's assume that we wish to communicate the key concept implied by the title of the visual aid—that federal budget deficits are growing very rapidly, like a wave. Another possible point to communicate would be how the two political parties have compared in terms of debt increases.

DECISION 2.

In terms of deciding what data should be included to show the key relationship or concept, remember that charts and graphs as visual aids for speeches are less detailed than ones you will find in reading material. For the deficit graph, we only want to show the general trend. We could simplify the original bar graph by

Figure 6-2   Complex Bar Graph

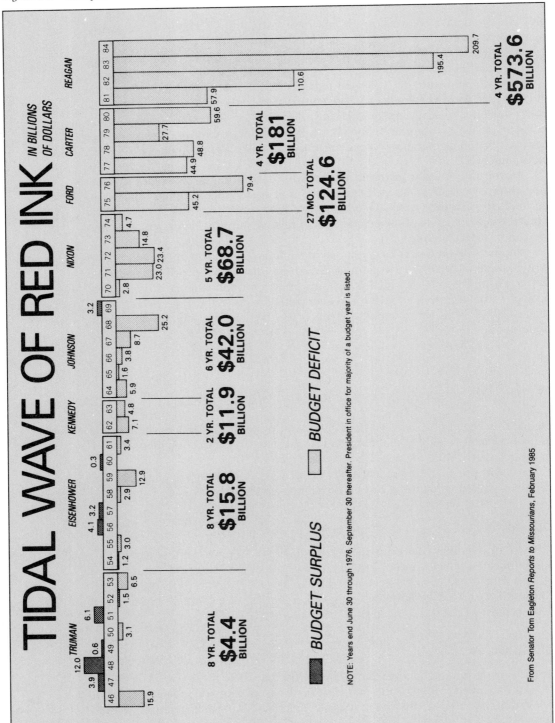

Figure 6-3   Key Decisions for Making Visual Aids

> Decide what is the key relationship or concept to be shown.
>
> Decide what data should be included to show the relationship or concept.
>
> Decide what sizes the letters, numbers, and other parts of the visual aid should be.
>
> Decide how to emphasize parts of the visual aid by colors and shapes.

representing the deficit or surplus totals for the four-year term of a president instead of year-by-year. Thus, President Eisenhower's first term would be the four years from 1954 to 1957, and his second term would be from 1958 to 1961. Then we would calculate each four-year total. President Eisenhower's totals are a $3.1 billion surplus for Term 1 and a $18.9 billion deficit for Term 2. Figure 6-4 represents this.

Figure 6-4   Planning Sizes in Visual Aids

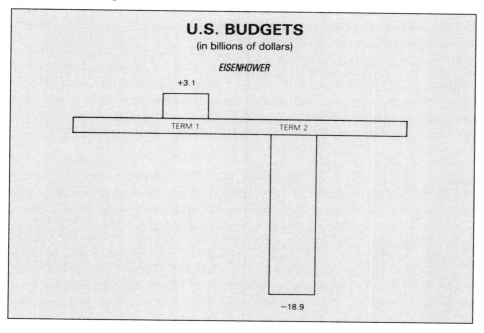

DECISION 3.

A third part of planning your visual aid involves decisions regarding the sizes of numbers, letters, and other parts, such as the length of the bars in bar graphs or the sizes of the pie slices in pie diagrams. Your goals here are to be sure that all parts of your graph or chart can be easily read and that they fit on backing you have chosen for your aid.

We usually recommend one-fourth-inch high letters and numbers as a minimum size for each ten feet of distance from the visual aid to the farthest listeners. Thus, if you have measured the distance from the visual-aid stand or screen to the farthest corner chair and found it to be forty feet, you would use one-inch high letters and numbers.

This approach also works for planning the printing of your posters. After deciding the height of the letters, use that size as an estimate for the width of the letters. Add a bit of space between the letters and an extra letter for each blank space between words. Given the width of your poster board, figure out how many words you can get on each line. Doing it this way, you won't have to erase a part of a word.

To lay out the sizes of the bars in our example, we find the biggest surplus (Eisenhower, Term 1 at $3.1 billion) and the biggest deficit (Reagan, Term 1 at $573.6 billion) and add them together (total = $576.7 billion). Then we measure the height of our poster board. Let's say it is 36 inches tall and we want to use about 30 inches for the chart and the remaining 6 inches for a title, numbers, letters, and border. To determine the scale we divide the number of inches available into the largest number (or total). Then we round this number up to the next largest round number. For our graph the number would be $19.2 billion (that is, $576.7 billion divided by 30 inches) rounded up to $20 billion per inch. Thus, in making our bar graph we would figure the four-year total and then divide by $20 billion to find out how many inches long to make the bar. A four-year deficit of $100 billion would be 5 inches, and one of $573.6 billion would be 26.7 inches long. Then with a ruler, we mark off that length and draw each bar. To check your understanding of this approach, you might prepare a bar graph (with $20 billion to an inch) for President Eisenhower's first and second terms and then lay it on top if Figure 6-4, which we constructed using that scale.

Now let's work on how to determine the sizes of the slices in pie diagrams. To make a pie diagram you have to figure out how to divide the circle into proportional parts to represent your data. First we have to find out the total amount the circle represents. For the budget-deficit data, we add up the budget-deficit totals (that is, $4.4 + $15.8 + $11.9 + $42.0 + $68.7 + $124.6 + $181.0 + $573.6 = $1022 billion total deficits since 1946). As always with numbers, it is important to double-check everything. You want to be correct, *and* it would be embarrassing if someone in your audience found a mistake in your diagram. Here, for example, starting with $1022 billion, we could subtract each president's total to see if we came back to zero.

Continuing with our budget-deficit pie diagram, we want to find what percentage of the whole each part is. To find percentages we divide the total into each part and multiply by 100. Let's use President Johnson's second term from 1966 to 1969 as an example. The second term had a budget deficit of $34.5 billion. We divide $1022 billion into $34.5 billion to get .0338. Since a percentage is a portion of 100, we multiply .0338 times 100. Thus, 3.38 percent of the total postwar deficit came from President Johnson's second term.

Next we need to find the length or circumference of our circle's border. To do this we multiply the diameter times 3.1416. Let's say for the budget-deficit circle we draw around the top of our wastepaper basket. The diameter of the basket is 20 inches. The length of our circle is then 62.8 inches (3.1416 times 20).

Finally we are ready to find out how much of the circle's length to give to each part. To do this we multiply the part, expressed in decimal terms, times the length of our circle. For President Johnson's second term, we multiply .0338 times 62.8 inches to get 2.12 inches. We draw a line from the center of the circle to the edge. From that point we use a string to measure 2.12 inches around the edge of the circle. We mark that point and draw a line from it to the center of the circle. We have now formed the wedge of the pie which represents the budget deficit of Johnson's second term. In the same manner, we proceed around the circle with the rest of the parts.

DECISION 4.

The final decisions you make relate to representing visually the various numbers, words, and parts of your aid to highlight the key relationship or concept you wish to communicate. The following suggestions will help you use color and shape.

GUIDELINES FOR HIGHLIGHTING KEY CONCEPTS

1. Use color to highlight parts of your visual aid.
   - Use darker colors for words and numbers.
   - Use colors which contrast with the background of your aid.
   - Use bright colors to emphasize important parts.
   - Use colors that your audience connects with the concepts shown.
   - Use different colors for different parts.
   - Use solid, primary colors.

2. Use shape to highlight parts of your visual aid.
   - Use thicker letters and numbers for important parts.
   - Use slanted letters and numbers to highlight important parts.
   - Use shapes (wavy or jagged edges for letters and numbers) that your audience connects with the concepts shown.
   - Superimpose your words and numbers on a drawing which represents something connected to the concept.

Again, you might benefit by seeing how *USA Today* innovatively and effectively uses these suggestions and others to represent relationships and concepts.

With these suggestions in mind, let's see how we can improve Figure 6-2. In Figure 6-2 a budget surplus is shown as a solid black bar above the line. A budget deficit is shown as gray and below the line. Remembering that the key concept is the increases in deficits, why not choose the darker color to emphasize deficits? What colors do people normally connect with surpluses and deficits? Also, since the original bar graph's title is "Tidal Wave," wouldn't you expect the increasing wave of deficits to be *above* the line?

When you list key words or ideas on a large poster, highlight the first letter (or word) of each line, especially if the first letters form an acronym. Use darkness, larger size, or contrasting color. We suggest that you keep individual ideas covered until you are ready to talk about each one. Use a piece of paper the width of the poster board and something to hold it in place which is also movable. Snap clips work best but large paper clips, small pieces of picture putty, or loops of scotch tape with the sticky side out can also work. If you are using an overhead projector, lay a sheet of paper over the not-yet-described idea. Revealing key words and ideas one at a time enables your audience to take notes, internally digest your point, and review previously discussed ideas without jumping ahead.

What Equipment Is Available for Presenting Visual Aids?

A variety of equipment is available for presenting pictures, charts, diagrams, and graphs and for listing key ideas or words. You will find most of the following items in classrooms and organizational meeting rooms. Your teacher or the audio-visual personnel at your school will be able to provide information about specific pieces of equipment. Most large organizations will have audio-visual personnel and equipment to help you use visual aids effectively in your professional talks. Written resources are also available to help you become skilled in using audio-visual equipment.[6]

A *flip chart and stand* are basic visual-aid equipment. If you have several visual aids, the flip chart keeps them in the appropriate order and holds them firmly while you talk. A flip chart stand can usually be borrowed from the audio-visual (AV) department on your campus or from your department or teacher. The flip chart visual aids are normally prepared using an artist's large sketch pad. Thick felt-tip markers or crayons will improve the attention given your flip charts.

Posters are also available for visual aids and are typically rested on a flip chart stand or on the chalk tray. Typical flip chart stands have clips on them to

A poster specifically prepared for a presentation focuses on the key concept of the speech.

hold a poster board securely in place. Poster board is thick, firm paper with one white side; you can buy it at the same stores as flip charts. Flip charts and poster boards are especially valuable for showing charts and graphs and presentations of key words or ideas for emphasis. They can also be used for drawings.

An *overhead projector* uses transparencies and requires that the front lights are dimmed. An overhead projector is often already a part of your classroom. If not, again either AV or your teacher will be a source for borrowing one. The transparencies are flexible, clear pieces of plastic-like material on which you can write or draw with a special felt-tip pen called a projection pen. These pens make the print less likely to smear while you handle the transparencies. You can buy commercially prepared transparencies. You can also make a transparency with a thermal copying machine from the following print sources: soft (#2) lead pencils, india ink, black printer's ink (book or newspaper), photo-copies, carbon-ribbon typewriters, and carbon-base computer printouts. Overhead transparencies are especially valuable for charts and graphs, key words, or pictures and drawings. Again, be sure to go to the back of your speech room to be sure you can see the writing on the transparency. If you can't, move the overhead farther from your screen and fine-tune the image again.

An *opaque projector* enlarges and projects printed material from books and magazines, as well as real objects like coins. It also requires that the lights be dimmed. This tool is helpful when you want to show actual objects that are small or photos and documents as they are. It is also helpful when using printed material that should not be torn apart. Opaque projectors are less common than overheads.

Slide and film projectors are useful in showing real events, people, and places that would be difficult to bring to the speaking situation. The equipment needed, the setup time, and the challenge of speaking fluently while using them lend these tools to longer speeches and more experienced speakers. The specific instructions for using individual slide and film projectors vary; they are typically printed on the inside of the hard cover which protects the lens area. For both slide and film projectors the important part is to have the machine properly loaded and adjusted ahead of time. When you are ready to use it, you will only have to dim the lights and switch it on.

What Are the Typical Problems Speakers Have in Using Visual Aids?

Good question! Beginning speakers usually have problems with visual aids. By considering the problems ahead of time you can generally avoid them. There are three stages in using visual aids: choosing visual aids, practicing with them, and presenting them during the speech. Let's review the problems associated with each stage.

First, the planning stage is important as you select or develop a visual aid. A key idea is to first develop your speech and then to search for visual aids that will best help your audience attend to, understand, and retain your message. We have found that student speakers often make the mistake of letting a visual aid become the dominant concern in a speech and work the message around it. We once assigned our students to describe an object in a five-minute informative speech. One student, who worked part-time for a local funeral director, decided to do his speech on the topic of caskets. For this speech he actually brought a full-size casket to the third floor of our building. The audience was overwhelmed and most members indicated they found it hard to focus on the speaker's information. Also, for a short speech, the time it took the student to "get the stage" was extensive, and five minutes was not enough time to deal adequately with the aid. Probably a picture or drawing shown by an opaque projector would have been a more appropriate aid. As recommended earlier, when choosing visual aids consider your specific purpose, the nature of your audience, the physical setting, and your own skill with a particular kind of aid. If you decide to make your visual aid, the guidelines in Figure 6-3 will help you avoid problems.

The practice stage will prepare you to use the aid naturally and effectively when you deliver the speech. Beginning speakers often practice only in their own rooms and then have difficulty adapting to the classroom itself. Because it is important to adapt to the physical setting in which you will talk, practice in the same (or similar) setting. Your main concern is that the audience can see your visual aid. A friend moving around the room as you practice can check on the aid's visibility, as well as your delivery. Based on your practice and your friend's feedback, we suggest you make notations on your outline, or speech notes, to remind yourself when to move or change your visual aid. Turn to Appendix B to see the "VA" places marked in John Deeth's speech text (and how well his chosen examples visualize his main ideas).

Finally, let's review the four suggestions made earlier for actually presenting the aid during the speech. They each correspond to typical problems a beginning speaker can have. First, *provide instructions* so that your audience can understand the aid. For example, if you are using a model which is proportional to the actual object but smaller, you could tell your audience that the actual object is "four times bigger." Second, *talk with your audience and not the aid.* It is appropriate to glance briefly at your visual aid, point to parts of it, and handle it; but your primary focus should be your audience. Third, *do not get between the aid and your audience.* This is especially challenging if you plan to write on the chalkboard and one of the main reasons why excessive board writing should be avoided. Repeated practice will enable you to move naturally as you use your aid. Fourth, *set your aid out of sight when it is no longer relevant to the part of the speech* you are delivering. You do not want the aid to distract your audience.

Careful planning and practice will enable you to present your visual aid effectively as you deliver your speech.

LEARNING BY UNDERSTANDING

1. What equipment for presenting visual aids requires dimmed lights?
2. What types of visual aids do speakers often make themselves?

3. For each of the following speech purposes, choose one of the types of visual aids and, if appropriate, the equipment for presenting it. Explain your choice.

   a. To have my audience be able to do a basic karate move
   b. To have my audience understand a new method of hulling sunflowers
   c. To have my audience understand the new year's car designs

4. List three sources for already-prepared visual aids.

5. What are two recommendations for preparing effective posters and flip charts?

ANSWERS:

1. Overhead projector, opaque projector, slide and film projectors
2. Charts, graphs, and listing of key ideas
3. Here are several possibilities. You might check your choices with another person in the class.
   a. To enable your audience to do the karate move, it would be helpful both to have a large picture of someone doing the move (or project a picture on an opaque projector) and to do a demonstration of the actual move. This would give the audience two realistic exposures.
   b. To enable your audience to understand how to hull sunflower seeds, a series of pictures would be helpful. This is an example of a situation where you might not want to construct the actual equipment just for the speech. An opaque projector or posters could be used.
   c. To enable your audience to understand the new year's car designs, pictures projected by an opaque projector are probably the most realistic. Include comparisons to enable accurate understanding of characteristics which can't be seen from a one-dimensional photo.
4. Your list could include books, magazines, vertical files, curriculum libraries, and models used by professionals.
5. Make sure the print is large and the information is clear and direct.

LEARNING BY INTERACTING

For one of the sample speeches in Appendix B, work with a small group to plan and develop visual aids to accompany the verbal message. Your plan should include:

1. What parts of the speech should be accompanied by a visual aid? Please indicate each part's key relationship or concept. (Note: Your decisions here could actually lead to additional verbal material in the speech. For example, the speaker may give statistics on the death rate from drunken driving in the nation. Your group might recommend a visual aid that shows the increase over the last ten years.)

2. What type of visual aid would be most appropriate for each identified part?

3. What equipment would be most appropriate for your choices in #2?

4. Where could you find already-prepared visual aids or additional information necessary to make the visual aids?

LEARNING BY SPEAKING

Prepare a three- to four-minute informative speech in which you introduce an object which is unfamiliar to your audience. In addition to using the actual object (or a representation of it) during your speech, use one other type of visual aid.

Your topic should meet the three guidelines specified in Chapter 4. Use the steps in preparation suggested in Chapter 5. Summarize your preparation by writing:

General Purpose
General Topic
Audience Analysis (use the Audience Analysis form from Chapter 4)
Specific Topic
Specific Purpose
Central Idea
Main Points

Include your visual-aid materials under the main points they are developing, clarifying, or supporting. Include a bibliography stating the sources for your visual-aid information.

REVIEW

Visual aids are usually considered the most important form of supporting, developing, and clarifying materials in a speech because they provide stimulation through the channel of sight. This is important because people tend to pay more attention to visual stimuli and understand and remember it better. There are five main types of visual aids: objects or models of objects, pictures or photographs, charts or graphs, bodily movement, and the listing of key words or statements.

Visual aids are especially important for longer speeches, speeches that deal with more complex information, and speeches that are intended to enable the audience to *do* something as a result.

NOTES

1. Robert Heinich, Michael Modenda and James Russel, *Instructional Media and the New Technologies of Instruction* (New York: Wiley, 1982), 11.

2. *Information Please Almanac*, 1985, 798.

3. Heinich, *Instructional Media*, 11, 63.

4. David Horton and Carol Mills, "Human Learning and Memory," *Annual Review of Psychology* 35(1984):381; also, Robert W. Finkel, *The Brainbooster* (Englewood Cliffs, N.J.: Prentice-Hall, 1983), 4.

5. Jane Fonda, *Women Coming of Age* (New York: Simon and Schuster, 1984), 92.

6. A source we have found to be very effective is Heinich.

7

DEVELOPING ORGANIZATIONAL SKILLS

In this chapter, you'll be . . .

LEARNING BY UNDERSTANDING

- Why organizing speeches is important
- The order in which parts of a speech are developed
- Guidelines for determining main points and subpoints
- Two principles for developing an outline
- Patterns for ordering the parts of the speech body
- How to develop introductions
- How to develop conclusions
- How to develop listening guides for audiences

LEARNING BY INTERACTING

- Developing alternative organizational plans for a speech topic

LEARNING BY SPEAKING

- A four- to five-minute informative speech that describes how an event in history could help your classmates understand a current situation they face

CHAPTER OUTLINE

I. Organizing a speech helps both the speaker and the audience.
   A. An organized speech helps audience members because it is easier to follow and it meets their expectations.
   B. An organized speech helps the speaker because it is easier to remember and it helps the speaker feel more confident.

II. Organization is a process of ordering the parts of a speech.
   A. The body of a speech contains the main points and is developed first.
   B. The introduction of a speech orients the audience to the body and is prepared second.
   C. The conclusion of a speech summarizes the body and is prepared last.

III. Outlining is an organizational procedure.
   A. An outline should follow a consistent notation system.
   B. Outlining helps you develop your ideas.
      1. An outline provides a means of seeing the relationships between the parts of a speech.
      2. An outline makes it easier to change and improve a speech.
      3. A keyword or phrase outline provides a visual aid for you during your speech delivery.

IV. The first step in preparing an outline for the speech body is using the principles of subordination and coordination to refine the chosen points.
   A. Subordination means that each point at one level of an outline should support, or be included within, the next higher point.
   B. Coordination means that all points at one level of an outline should be equally important and should not overlap each other.

V. The final step in preparing an outline for the speech body is ordering the main points of the speech.
   A. There are basic patterns for ordering the points of a speech.
      1. Points can be ordered the way people think—"first to last," "this to that," "problem to solution," "here to there," or "for versus against."
      2. Points can be ordered in patterns that are easy to follow.
         a. Order points from "easy to difficult," "simple to complex," or "acceptable to unacceptable."
         b. Order points inductively or deductively.
   B. The most effective pattern is chosen based on audience analysis.

VI. After the body of the speech is outlined, the introduction is developed.
   A. The first purpose of an introduction is to arouse interest in your speech, using approaches that are unusual and relevant to your audience.
   B. The second and third purposes of an introduction are to represent yourself in a positive way by developing rapport through reference to mutual concerns and by developing credibility with specific techniques.
   C. The fourth purpose of an introduction is to preview the speech's main points.

VII. After the introduction, a conclusion is developed to summarize the body of your speech.
   A. A conclusion reinforces the purpose of the speech.
   B. A conclusion also psychologically closes the communication experience.

VIII. Listening guides are developed for use in speech delivery.
   A. The purpose of listening guides, such as transitions and summary transitions, is to help your audience follow your speech and move with you from point to point.
   B. The purpose of listening guides, such as previews, reviews, and verbal emphasis, is to help your audience remember key parts of your speech.

IX. Introductions, conclusions, and listening guides are finally added to the outline of the body of your speech.

7

DEVELOPING ORGANIZATIONAL SKILLS

Every discourse, like a living creature, should be so put together that it has a body of its own and lacks neither head nor feet, a middle nor extremities, all composed in such a way that they suit both each other and the whole. —Plato

PREVIEW

You have worked on developing your skills in selecting an appropriate topic and developing and supporting your main points through five basic types of research. Now you are ready to organize these materials. Organization can be defined as a process of ordering or arranging the parts of a speech to develop an idea and enable your audience to understand it. This is done by developing an outline. The time you spend at this stage of preparation will pay off for you in increasingly effective speeches.

Organization has long been considered important. Some 2500 years ago, classical rhetoricians stressed organization as one of the five main parts of preparing speeches. The best organization was considered that which best fit the needs of the specific audience. Historically, long before what we now call the "information explosion," the discovery/research process was completed first, because virtually all information of importance on a particular topic was known. Now, because there is so much information available on any particular topic, you probably will find yourself moving back and forth between research and organization. As you refine your organization, you will discover you need more supporting data, and you might even change your main points. These two processes of speech development are closely intertwined.

Why Is Organization Important?

Because it is easier for an audience to follow an organized speech, the organization of ideas helps you attain your speech purpose.[1] People tend to use certain thought patterns when trying to understand, or change their minds about, something.[2]

That is, certain information or reasons, generally are considered first, followed by other information or reasons, and so on. Therefore, you will be working on skills that determine the most helpful ordering of points and subpoints. Research also supports the existence of strong expectations for organization in speeches.[3] A lack of organization will be distracting to most audiences and will minimize the attainment of your goal. Given these expectations, research also suggests that when an audience perceives a message to be disorganized, it tends to lose confidence in the speaker and, therefore, lose interest in the speech.[4]

A second advantage of organizing your speech is that it will be easier for you to remember. If you have a clear idea of where you are going with your speech, you will feel more comfortable while getting there. This improved confidence and quality of preparation will mean higher grades in this class and increasing success for you in your later personal and professional speaking opportunities.

How Do I Start Organizing the Materials I've Collected?

Organization means ordering or arranging the parts of your speech so that you can accomplish your speech purpose. A basic organizational pattern that speakers have used since classical times is introduction, body, and conclusion. The **introduction**, which is the first part of the speech, orients audience members to you and your topic and encourages them to be receptive to your message. The **body of your speech** contains your main points and subpoints and their developing, clarifying, and supporting materials. The **conclusion**, which is the last part of your speech, provides a summary and closing so that your audience will remember the important points.

We recommend that you first develop the body of the speech, then the introduction, and last the conclusion. It is best to develop the body of your speech first because it is important to know exactly what you want to communicate before deciding how to lead into and conclude it.

At this point, you have already developed skill in the first steps of organizing the body of your speech. These steps are shown in Figure 5-1 and Figure 5-2. You have selected a general topic; narrowed the general topic; selected a specific purpose and written a central idea; selected three or four main points and their subpoints; and chosen developing, clarifying, and supporting material for these points. To organize these materials, it is helpful to use an outline. A **speech outline** is a structured representation of the parts of a speech.

Why Is Outlining Used as an Organizational Procedure?

There are several reasons for using outlining to organize your speech. The first, and most important, reason is that it provides a clear visual means of seeing the parts of your central idea and how the parts relate to each other. You will be able to spot supporting points that overlap and main points for which you have little support. In other words, the outline helps you focus on the points you are trying to communicate. Occasionally, you may write out a speech, word for word. But, generally, you will focus on the overall idea development through the outlining procedure and add the specific words when you deliver the speech.

A second reason is that outlining will make it easier for you to work with your points—changing, adding, rearranging them until they are most appropriate for the topic, the content, and, especially, the audience. By having the parts of your message clearly before you, you will be able to reorder main points and subpoints more easily and quickly than if you had written out the exact wording.

A final reason for using an outline is that it will serve as a visual aid for you during your speech delivery. While you are giving the speech, the outline will aid your memory. Should you mentally lose your place, you can check the outline to find it quickly. This visual support will build your confidence and, therefore, improve your delivery.

How Do I Develop an Outline?

There are basically two types of outlines: a sentence outline and a phrase or key word outline. A *sentence outline*, composed of full sentences for each outline entry, is used mainly in speech preparation, because it helps you fully develop your central idea. The outlines at the beginning of each chapter in this book are examples of this form. A *phrase or key word outline* is composed of entries that consist only of phrases or single words. This type of outline is usually developed from the full sentence outline and is used as a delivery aid.

To develop an outline, you must visualize the relationships between the parts of your speech. There are three steps involved in developing your outline. The first is deciding the main points and subpoints you will use in your speech. The second is refining those main points and subpoints according to the principles of outlining. The third is determining the order in which you will present the main points and subpoints to your audience.

It is usually helpful to start your outline development with the major divisions of the body of your speech—that is, with your main points and their subpoints. You should write each of your main points and subpoints as full sentences, leaving plenty of space between each one for additional material. For each main point and subpoint, you will decide what supporting, developing, and/or clarifying (DCS) materials should be added so that your audience will fully understand or agree with it. When you have determined the needed additional materials for each main point, review each one to see if anything more should be said to have the audience understand or agree with it. Any materials added at this level would also be called subpoints, but they would develop, clarify, or support the next higher level of subpoints rather than the main points. (See the following outline pattern.)

Outlining helps you form a clear visual picture of all parts of your speech. Here is an accepted pattern of visualizing the relationship between main points and subpoints:

Main point one
  Subpoint one
    Subpoint one
    Subpoint two
  Subpoint two
    Subpoint one
    Subpoint two
  Subpoint three
Main point two
  Subpoint one
    Subpoint one
    Subpoint two
  Subpoint two
    Subpoint one
    Subpoint two

To make your outline visually clear you will use a consistent notation system in the left-hand margin to indicate which parts are related to which. The most commonly used notation system alternates numbers and letters in the following order:

Roman numerals (*I.*, *II.*, *III.*, etc.)
  Capital letters (*A.*, *B.*, *C.*, etc.)
    Numbers (*1.*, *2.*, *3.*, etc.)
      Lowercase letters (*a.*, *b.*, *c.*, etc.)
        Numbers followed by one parenthesis (*1*), *2*), *3*), etc.)
          Lowercase letters followed by one parenthesis (*a*), *b*), *c*), etc.)

We have illustrated this notation system for part of the first main point of an outline.

I. MAIN POINT
  A. Subpoint
    1. Subpoint
      a. Subpoint
        1) Subpoint
          a) Subpoint
          b) Subpoint
        2) Subpoint
          a) Subpoint
          b) Subpoint
          c) Subpoint
      b. Subpoint
        1) Subpoint
          a) Subpoint
          b) Subpoint
        2) Subpoint
          a) Subpoint
          b) Subpoint
    2. Subpoint

You could look at an outline using this notation system and know that all the main points follow a Roman numeral, all material supporting those main points follows a capital letter, and so on. The following rules for this notation system will help you develop an outline that makes the parts of your speech visually clear.

GUIDELINES FOR OUTLINE NOTATION SYSTEM

1. Use a consistent form of symbols that alternates numbers and letters.

2. Make the symbols stand out visually by starting each level of material at the same place at the left-hand margin. For typed outlines, indent each new level five spaces beyond the previous one. Also, if a point is longer than one line, do not begin the next line directly under the symbol; indent it as if it were a subpoint.

3. Assign a symbol to every element in your outline. These elements may be sentences, phrases, or single words. But do not have two sentences, phrases, or words after any one symbol.

4. Assign symbols of the same type at each level in your outline. For example, all your main points should have the same type of symbol.

Check the sentence outline at the beginning of each chapter for examples of these rules.

LEARNING BY UNDERSTANDING

1. Organizing your speech will help you achieve your specific purpose because _____ .

2. Because audiences expect speeches to be organized, which of the following may occur if your speech is perceived as disorganized?

   a. The audience will be distracted.
   b. The audience will be more sympathetic to your purpose.
   c. The audience will lose confidence in you as a speaker.
   d. The audience will become more interested as it tries to figure out what you are saying.
   e. The audience will take better notes.

3. List three reasons for using an outline to help you organize your speech.

4. Number the following parts of a speech in the order in which they are prepared.

   ____ introduction

   ____ body

   ____ conclusion

5. Describe the notation procedure used in outlining.

ANSWERS:

5. The notation system for outlines usually alternates numbers and letters, starting with Roman numerals, then capital letters, then numbers, then lowercase letters.
4. 2, 1, 3
3. It helps you see the parts of your ideas and how they relate to each other; it makes it easier for you to work with your ideas; and it serves as a visual aid for your speech delivery.
2. a. and c.
1. Your audience will be better able to follow your speech, and it will be easier for you to remember.

How Do I Improve My Outline?

Once you have determined which main points, subpoints, and additional DCS materials you will include in your speech, you will want to refine those points and subpoints, using the two principles of outlining—subordination and coordination. These principles will help you make any necessary changes to ensure that your ideas are fully developed, clarified, and supported. The principles of subordination and coordination are applied to each level of points in your speech. That is, they are first applied to your main points and then individually to the subpoints supporting each main point. If you have additional subpoints under any of those subpoints, the principles also would be applied at that level. Let's look at the principles of subordination and coordination as they apply to your main points.

Subordination means that everything included at one level in your outline should directly support, or be included within, the next higher level. Therefore, in terms of your main points, they should all work together to fully support your specific purpose and central idea. When you have clearly stated your specific purpose and central idea, the main points usually follow quite naturally from the intermediate step of the central idea. For example, if your specific purpose is "to have my classmates understand the four major characteristics in selecting a hiking boot" and your central idea is "the four major characteristics in selecting good hiking boots are that they should be comfortable, waterproof, insulated and pebble-soled," then your main points would be those four characteristics.

If you cannot easily determine what your main points are from your specific purpose, your specific purpose statement is probably too vague and should be refined further. In order for your main points to fulfill the principle of subordination, each would be one of the four major characteristics in selecting hiking boots.

Fine-tuning the outline is an important part of speech preparation.

If you include a main point on appropriate clothing for hiking, you would be adding something that is not included within your specific purpose or central idea; it would seem out of place and disorganized to your audience and would be harder for you to remember.

Let's look at another application of the principle of subordination to refine main points. In a lecture on the causes of the Civil War, the causes probably would be stated under main points such as "Economic causes," "Political causes," and "Social causes." Each of these three groups of causes relate to and are included within the specific topic "Causes of the Civil War." They support and clarify the specific purpose. If, however, the lecturer included a main point "Economic effects," we would probably feel that it did not fit. "Economic effects" would not be subordinate to the specific purpose of describing the *causes* of the Civil War. Let's look at how an outline can help you spot this lack of subordination.

Specific Purpose: To have my audience understand the causes of the Civil War

Central Idea: The causes of the Civil War were economic, political and social.

   I. Economic causes were . . .
     A. . . .
     B. . . .
     C. . . .
  II. Political causes were . . .
     A. . . .
     B. . . .
 III. Social causes were . . .
     A. . . .
     B. . . .
 IV. Economic effects were . . .
     A. . . .
     B. . . .

The outline helps you focus on the four listed main points, which are all preceded by roman numerals. You can quickly tell that there are more main points than the central idea indicates, and the wording indicates that the fourth one does not fit. The central idea referred to "causes," but the fourth deals with "effects."

The second principle, the principle of *coordination*, means that all points at the same level of an outline should not overlap each other and should be of equal importance. Basically, this means that each main point (or subpoint) should be about a different part of your specific purpose and central idea. If two of the points or subpoints overlap, then the second provides little additional support for the next higher level.

Let's imagine that your speech on the characteristics of hiking boots has four main points—"Comfortable," "Waterproof," "Insulated," and "Pebble-soled." Do you see overlap between the first three? Do you see overlap between "Comfortable" and "Pebbble-soled"? Probably not. Assuming there is some padding inside the boot, it would not matter what kind of sole is involved. However, the second and the third main points are a part of, and result in, comfort: If the boot is not waterproofed, you might get wet, and if it is not insulated, you might get cold.

Because the specific purpose talks about the characteristics of the boot, the first tentative main point would be dropped. If we were talking, instead, about the benefits of good hiking boots, then qualities like comfort and traction would support the central idea.

When we apply the principle of coordination to the lecture on the causes of the Civil War, we see that the three main points of economic, political, and social causes are equal and do not overlap. If we add a fourth main point "Not enough money for supplies," we would see that it does not fit, because it is not a separate and equal cause of the Civil War. It is a part of the first main point of economic causes and would probably be a subpoint listed under economic causes. In this context, *equal* means that points at the same level in an outline should be of approximately the same scope or size. In the last example, "Economic causes" is a much larger category than "Not enough money for supplies."

It will be more difficult for your audience to follow your idea if you treat points of different scope as though they are the same. We also worked on the principle of coordination when we talked about developing a clear central idea. You might check back to pages 79–81 for more examples of making sure that categories at the same level do not overlap and are approximately equal.

If you discover, as you outline your speech, that you have a main point or a subpoint that is not separate and equal, see if it fits under one of the other points you put on that level. Also check to see if it is unrelated and should be left out. The following list of rules will help you apply the principles of subordination and coordination:

RULES FOR APPLYING SUBORDINATION AND COORDINATION

1. Develop subpoints that are related to the main point above them.

2. Organize your materials so that the different subpoints under one point do not overlap.

3. Organize your materials so that the different subpoints under one point are equal or on the same level.

4. To clearly develop each point, subordinate at least two subpoints to it.

These rules ensure that each subheading supports a heading. Visually, this can be represented by the human pyramid in Figure 7-1.

In Figure 7-1 the cheerleader at the top (representing Specific Purpose) is supported by the cheerleaders on the second level (representing Main Points). They, in turn, are supported by cheerleaders on the third level (representing Subpoints), who are finally supported by cheerleaders on the bottom level (representing Developing, Clarifying, and Supporting Materials). For the pyramid to be solid, subordination is essential. There are at least two supports for each point on the next higher level.

Following is a student outline that uses appropriate outline symbols and follows the principles of subordination and coordination. The main points and subpoints in this outline are stated in parallel sentences. Writing out your points in similar sentences will help you clarify what you are saying, and the parallel form will help the audience follow your idea and remember your main points.

Specific Purpose: To have my audience understand the two personal advantages of assisting with the Special Olympics for the handicapped.

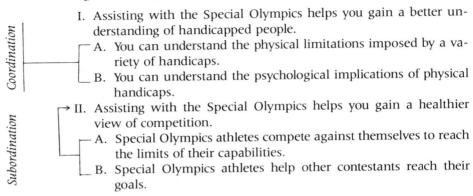

I. Assisting with the Special Olympics helps you gain a better understanding of handicapped people.
   A. You can understand the physical limitations imposed by a variety of handicaps.
   B. You can understand the psychological implications of physical handicaps.

II. Assisting with the Special Olympics helps you gain a healthier view of competition.
   A. Special Olympics athletes compete against themselves to reach the limits of their capabilities.
   B. Special Olympics athletes help other contestants reach their goals.

Coordination · *Subordination*

LEARNING BY UNDERSTANDING

1. Name and describe the two main principles used to select and refine the points in your outline.

2. Consider the following two speech outlines. Indicate where the outlines do not follow an appropriate notation system or do not apply the principles of subordination and coordination. Make the necessary changes to improve the outlines. Write out the central idea for each speech.

Outline 1

Specific Purpose: To have my audience understand the three benefits of teaching children to read before they start school.

Central Idea:

I. Knowing how to read before starting school improves student motivation.
   A. Motivation is important because the student is exposed to more information.
   B. Motivation will help the student with other skills.
II. Knowing how to read before starting school improves student concentration.
   A. Following the story in a book improves concentration.
   B. Reading the story to others improves concentration.
III. Knowing how to read before starting school depends on the encouragement of parents.
   A. Parental encouragement can occur directly through teaching.
   B. Parental encouragement can occur indirectly through exposing students to other facilities.

Outline 2

Specific Purpose: To have my audience understand the two main advantages of running as a means of getting into shape.

Figure 7-1   Principles of Subordination and Coordination

Central Idea:

   I. Running is an inexpensive sport.
      A. Running involves no special facilities.
      B. Running can be done in any weather.
  II. Running is the fastest way to get into shape.
      A. Running burns the highest number of calories per hour.
      B. Running involves more muscles of the body.

ANSWERS:

1. Subordination in outlining means that every point at one level of an outline should support, or be related to, the level above it.
Coordination means that every point at one level of an outline should be equal in scope and not overlap other points.
2. Here are the problems we see in the two outlines. Check with someone else in the class if you disagree.

ANSWERS:

Outline 1:

Central Idea: The benefits of teaching children to read before they start school are that it improves student motivation and student concentration.

— The outline does not use proper indentation. Each point that runs more than one line (IA, III, and IIB) should start the second line below the first word above, not below the number or letter.
— Neither of the subpoints to the first main point is subordinate to it. That is, they do not develop, clarify, or support the point.
— Main Point III is not subordinate to the specific purpose; it is not a benefit of knowing how to read. The subpoints to III, however, are somewhat subordinate to III and coordinate with each other.

Outline 2:

Central Idea: The two main advantages of running as a means of getting into shape are that it is inexpensive and the fastest way to get into shape.

— This outline uses appropriate notation and indentation.
— It would be helpful to the audience if the main points were stated in parallel form as follows:
 I. Running is a good means of getting in shape because it is inexpensive.
 II. Running is a good means of getting in shape because it is fast.
— I.B. is not subordinate to the main point of inexpensive. You should have improved the outline by adding another feature of running that makes it inexpensive.

How Do I Determine the Order of My Main Points and Subpoints?

After you select the main points and organize them according to the rules of subordination and coordination, you must determine the order in which you will present these points. Basically, you should use either a natural order or one that is easy for your particular audience to follow.

Natural patterns of order follow the ways people typically think about something. Table 7-1 illustrates these patterns for ordering. Examples of natural orders based on the way people think are "first to last," "this to that," "cause to effect," "problem to solution," "here to there," and "for versus against."

Patterns that are easy to follow but are not necessarily based on how people think would be "easy to difficult," "compare and contrast," or "simple to complex." The speaker making a persuasive speech must decide whether to choose an inductive pattern (parts leading to the whole) or a deductive pattern (whole followed by the parts). If an audience is familiar and/or agreeable to the whole idea, we recommend using the deductive pattern. In a sense, that is the pattern used to show the relationship between the central idea and the main points as we have developed it so far.

TABLE 7-1   ORDERING MAIN IDEAS

Inform	Persuade	Entertain	Special Occasion	Audience Characteristics	Name of Order	Pattern of Order	Example
				Type of Speech			
natural						**Natural Orderings**	
✓		✓	✓	Audience doesn't know or is uncertain about order of events or steps in a process; wants to learn more; likes suspense	Chronological	Time to time; usually first to last	I. We started at the foot of the hill at dawn. II. The ascent was gradual but steep. III. The peak loomed before us at sunset.
✓	✓			Audience is rational; topic is difficult to analyze; audience doesn't see relationship; doesn't see dimensions of the problem or consequences	Cause to effect or problem to solution or solution to benefits	This leads to that; cause or problem first	I. The family unit is breaking down in middle-class families. II. With less parental guidance, it is more difficult to maintain discipline in public schools.
✓		✓		Audience doesn't know a place, building, object; audience is disorganized; likes detail, can visualize well	Spatial	Place to place; usually here to there	I. The library circulation desk is by the main door. II. Periodicals are found on the first floor. III. Microfilm is on the second floor.
✓	✓			Audience is against speaker's preferred side; is uncertain; wants to learn more	Pro and con or both sides	Against before for	I. There are three reasons people oppose abortion. II. There are four reasons people support abortion.
	✓			Audience accepts problem, is uncertain about criteria and solutions; audience favorable to a solution, wants any solution	Criteria to solution	Criteria first	I. Marijuana is safe. II. Marijuana is inexpensive. III. Therefore, marijuana should be legal.
	✓	✓	✓	Audience had high initial interest; speaker desires change in audience attitude or action; audience is aware of problem, likes suspense	Climax	Least important to most important; weakest to strongest	I. The new tax bill helps the U.S. economy. II. The new tax bill helps this city's economy III. The new tax bill helps your personal economy.
						Easy-to-Follow Orderings	
✓				Audience is uncertain about topic; apathetic, uninformed; considers topic difficult	Easy to difficult	Easiest first; steps in increasing difficulty	I. Loosen the soil for planting. II. Determine plants appropriate for season. III. Understand complementary planting.
✓				Audience wants to learn; considers topic difficult; doesn't know topic; audience is apathetic; doesn't see the dimensions of the issue	Simple to complex	Simplest first; steps in increasing complexity	I. The molecule is the basic form of matter. II. Chains of molecules make substances unique.

TABLE 7-1 ORDERING MAIN IDEAS (CONTINUED)

Type of Speech				Audience Characteristics	Name of Order	Pattern of Order	Example
Inform	Persuade	Entertain	Special Occasion			**Easy-to-Follow Orderings**	
√		√		Audience has partial understanding; doesn't believe there is a common ground; the topic is difficult; audience is apathetic; likes examples	Comparison or compare and contrast	Familiar to unfamiliar	I. Families usually have two parents. II. Communes are families with many parents.
√	√	√	√	Audience is hostile to idea; doesn't see "big picture"; likes examples; speaker has low credibility	Inductive	Parts or reasons first	I. School busing is expensive. II. School busing breaks up communities. III. School busing should be eliminated.
√	√		√	Audience accepts conclusion but needs reasons for it; likes examples	Deductive	Whole or conclusion first	I. School busing should be eliminated. II. School busing is expensive. III. School busing breaks up communities.
√	√			Audience and speaker share common beliefs, values, or ideas; audience prefers to avoid the topic, uncertain, doesn't see problem as their own	Acceptable to unacceptable	Most acceptable first; steps in increasing unacceptability	I. Cooking is one household chore couples agree to share. II. Cleaning is one of the last chores couples agree to share.

LEARNING BY UNDERSTANDING

1. The two recommended patterns for ordering main points are _____ and _____

2. Identify the name of the order that the following organizational plans represent. Refer to Table 7-1 for names of orders.

   Type: Organizational Outline:

   _____   I.   The trip started out with a disaster.
                    II. The day went along slowly and uneventfully.
                    III. We returned home to find the morning's disaster had passed.

   Type: Organizational Outline:

   _____   I.   The Santa Barbara oil spill affects many local industries.
                    II. Cleanup methods tried in the past were unsuccessful.
                    III. "Firing" would be an effective way to clear the oil spill.

3. You are about to give a speech on your recent visit to the local art museum. You know that many people in the audience have visited the museum within the last year. Select an organizational plan for your speech from the pattern of order column in Table 7-1, and describe why you chose it.

ANSWERS:

1. A natural order; an order that is easy for the audience to understand
2. Chronological; problem to solution
3. Any number of plans would work well. However, "familiar to unfamiliar" might be more effective than "here to there" because "here to there" would include many features the audience already knows about, i.e., "old bricks."

What Further Support Might My Speech Need?

After you achieve the visual perspective of your speech that is possible by careful outlining, you probably will find that some points or subpoints need additional support. We call this step "re-searching" because you are searching again for just the right support for a particular point.

Here again, consider your audience when determining how much support each point needs. You will use more development and support if a main point is complex or is less familiar, less agreeable, or less interesting to your audience. If you are using a familiar-to-unfamiliar sequence, you would probably need less support and time for the first main point since the audience already understands it fairly well.

In Chapter 5, you learned about different kinds of supporting materials—details, examples, anecdotes, narrations, statistics—and where to find them. Now, using the principles of subordination and coordination, insert them into your outline. Use the principles of ordering for determining which pieces of support should be given in which order.

What About an Introduction for My Speech?

Cicero's advice to the young men of Rome on developing introductions was to "render your auditors well disposed and teachable." Today we might say, "Encourage your audience to be open-minded and ready to learn." To accomplish this overall goal, your introduction should do four things: arouse interest, develop rapport, raise your credibility, and preview the speech's main points. Together, these four accomplish the goal described by Cicero.

Let's consider how we normally **arouse interest**. Imagine that you have prepared a present for your family, and you want to arouse their interest or curiosity about it. Brainstorm how you would prepare or wrap the package to arouse interest. What did your brainstorming of possible approaches produce? As you analyze your list, you will find that ideas like "unusual size" or "unusual color" will be subordinate to the heading *unusual*. Other things that would arouse interest would be those that are relevant to your family.

In an introduction, we try to psychologically open the audience's concern for a particular topic. Attention, which fades quickly, is not enough. To involve the audience, an introduction should be unusual and relevant. That is why speeches often begin with humorous stories or startling statements. Other techniques include quotations, suspense, questions or references to the audience, and personal anecdotes. Take into account your specific audience as you make your choices. If, for example, you discover from your audience analysis that some members are not very interested in your topic, then you will need to do more to raise their interest.

The following is an example of an introduction for a publicity release about an author which really worked hard to arouse interest.

> One cold afternoon last spring, it was very silent at the country estate of Joni Evans, the publisher of Linden Press, and Dick Snyder, the chairman of Simon & Schuster. Suddenly there was a crack in the air, a roar approaching between the rows of linden trees.

The freshly laid expensive gravel sprayed out in fans like a water-skier's wake as a black Honda Nighthawk ripped up the driveway. Two giant schnauzers started barking and braying until Dick Snyder gave them a look. Riding the motorcycle was a small but otherwise ominous figure totally wrapped and zipped into black leather, with one of those all-black nightmare helmets that encase the entire face in menace.[5]

The second and third purposes of an introduction are intended to represent you in a positive way. This is done by **developing rapport** with your audience and **establishing your credibility**. In your speech introduction, you can develop rapport—a feeling of harmony and mutual concern—by indicating that you share common feelings and beliefs with your audience. For example, if you are talking to a group of coworkers at a monthly staff meeting about ways to solve the problem of unequal overtime assignments, you could begin by describing common experiences shared by most of your audience members. It is important to use such personal pronouns as "we" and "our," which include you and your audience, in developing rapport.

We suggest you avoid that overworked phrase, "Today I'd like to talk to you about. . . ." Just think of the combined effect of having all your classmates use this opening for each of their speeches. Another reason this opening is less effective

President Ronald Reagan is well known for establishing rapport with his audiences by referring to common interests.

is that a barrier is placed between you and your audience when you say "talk *to* you." In the interest of rapport, it is more effective to use words that stress mutual concerns, such as "Most of us have. . . ."

Credibility refers to your audience's perception of your qualifications as a speaker on your chosen topic. If the audience does not feel you are qualified to speak on this topic, it will be less likely to fully understand or accept your ideas. The four main factors an audience uses to determine your credibility—your competence, character, trustworthiness, and dynamism—will be discussed further in the next chapter. In the examples of introductions that follow, you will see a variety of ways speakers develop credibility.

The final purpose of an introduction is to **preview the speech content**. In general, previewing means directing your audience's attention to your central idea so that your listeners are mentally "on the same track" you are. In speeches to persuade and to entertain and in some ceremonial speeches, your preview may only be a general reference to guide your audience. For example, a professional salesperson selling door-to-door probably would not begin by saying, "Hi, my name is George. I'm here to sell you life insurance." Instead, he would provide some direction by saying, "Hi, my name is George. I'd like to talk with you about something that concerns you and your children." Thus, the listener is subtly oriented even though the speaker does not state a central idea. In informative speeches, however, a more explicit preview is effective. By previewing the speech's main points, you will help guide the audience and enable it to follow your main points more carefully. In addition, the preview provides listeners with one further repetition of your ideas to aid their understanding and memory.

Here is an introduction that effectively previews the content:

> Because of our mutual concerns and irritations about unequal overtime assignments, I've carefully researched the ways other companies have solved this problem, and I'd like to share three of these ideas with you.

At this point in an introduction you might state your central idea saying, "Three ideas to deal with unequal overtime are. . . ."

In summary, an introduction uses a variety of techniques to arouse interest, develop rapport, raise credibility, and preview your speech. Following are two examples of student introductions that illustrate how to accomplish these four goals. In the margin we identify the four goals of introductions and briefly how the speaker chose to attain them:

Arouse Interest (by a startling statement)

Raise Credibility-Competence (by showing research)

I think we all respect ex-President Carter, the American Bar Association, and the National Council of Churches. So it may surprise you, as it did me, that these three are among those supporting the removal of criminal penalties for possession of marijuana. Ten states have changed their laws to give only traffic-ticket-like citations and small fines instead of arrests and jail sentences for marijuana offenses. The *New York Times* reports that local justice agencies would

Preview of Main Points

save up to $25 million a year from unnecessary arrests. I believe that marijuana laws should be changed for three reasons: the recent court decisions, the social costs of arrests, and the medical data concerning marijuana. . . .

Arouse Interest and Develop Rapport (by stating a shared feeling)

Preview of Main Points

I'm sure many of you share with me a love for animals. During a course in biological science, I recently became aware of the many kinds of animals which are gaining the label ''endangered species.'' For that class, I did a project to identify endangered species in our area. I think you'll be surprised to learn what I came up with. I'd like to share my research with you and suggest three ways we can each help to resolve this problem. . . .

Develop Credibility-Competence (by stating previous project and research)

In the following two examples of introduction, the speakers were already introduced to their audience and, therefore, had their credibility established by the persons who introduced them.

Develop Rapport (by stating a similar interest)

Arouse Interest (by a story)

It was gratifying to be invited to join you today because, like everyone in this room, I am a seeker of answers, not a giver of advice. Giving advice is, at best, a precarious business. I remember the story about the school boy who was required to write an essay on the life of Socrates. Here is what he wrote:

> Socrates was a man who went around town giving everybody free advice, so they poisoned him.

Preview of Main Points

What I want to do is to share some thoughts with you on some of the changing aspects of our profession and how they may affect us in carrying out our responsibilities in the years ahead.[6]

T.C. McDermott, vice present,
Rockwell International

Arouse Interest (by suspense)

Develop Rapport (by stating a common concern)

Today, I want to talk about a subject which is attracting increasing and serious attention in the West . . . the manipulation of the media, and hence informed decision making in our democratic society. . . .

I have been studying this subject together with a colleague at the Fletcher School for several years, and we recently published a book. . . .

Preview of Main Points

What I would like to propose and submit evidence to support is the proposition that there is a massive attempt by the Soviet Union to influence and use the media as well as other important Western Governmental and private sector opinion leaders; that sometimes these attempts are successful; that the campaign is ongoing; and that by being aware of it, by speaking

Further Develop Credibility-Competence (by referring to book publication)

the truth about it, a free society can in large part neutralize its effects.[7]

Roy Godson, Professor of Government, Georgetown University

How Should I Conclude My Speech?

So far, you have developed and ordered the body of your speech and prepared your introduction. The third and last part of the speech you will communicate and the last part you will prepare is the conclusion. The conclusion usually has two purposes—to *reinforce your specific purpose* of your speech and to *psychologically close the communication*. One way to prepare a conclusion is to refer back to the introduction. If, for example, you are talking about the problem of unequal overtime assignments, you might show how your three researched ways would solve or minimize the problem. A second procedure is to summarize your main points and/or whatever other information you want your audience to remember. This is especially relevant for informative speeches in which your specific purposes are to have your audience understand and remember your main points. As we said earlier, repetition is the best way to help an audience remember parts of your speech. Another way to reinforce the specific purpose of the speech is to refer to yourself. Here you might describe what you learned or how you benefitted from doing the speech or research.

The other purpose of a conclusion is to psychologically close the communication experience. Why do people like to watch the last few moments of a close sporting event? Why do they feel uncomfortable if they do not figure out a joke or the solution to a puzzle? Because they like to have things concluded or completed.

There are various procedures for closing speeches. Quotations are often used at the end of a speech. If you have chosen a quotation to close your speech, be sure to stop when you have finished the quote; do not tack on irrelevant comments. Other procedures include predictions, rhetorical questions, and, for persuasive speeches, requests for action. The following speech conclusions effectively close the communication. The first three examples are conclusions from student speeches.

Reinforce Specific Purpose (by summary of main points) Closure (by rhetorical question)	In summary, a person should exercise every day to help his heart, ease fatigue, and enjoy life more. Only by exercising every day can you look good, feel good, and function at your very best. When are you going to start?
Reinforce Specific Purpose (by summary of main points) Closure (by quotation and by reference to story used in introduction)	In closing, I hope you'll remember that if you meet someone who is depressed, let them know that they shouldn't feel ashamed of that feeling. If one of your friends is depressed, try to help by: (1) being willing to talk, (2) drawing the person away from the illness, and (3) using encouragement. The old English proverb ''Misery loves company'' is not only true; it is a real cure. When you help someone who's depressed, you'll reduce the chances of having the person end up like Cindy.

Reinforce Specific
Purpose (by summary
of main points)

So remember, people who are always late aren't just disorganized. There are three possible reasons for repeated lateness: first, they could be trying to defy authority; second, they could be trying to gain power over the other person; and, finally, they could be trying to live up to stereotypes about groups of people. Could any of these reasons describe you?

Closure (by rhetorical
question)

Reinforce Specific
Purpose (by reference
to introduction and
summary of central
idea)

If we really hope to "Make America Smarter" in the coming decade, we must force the public to come to grips with the hard facts. Institutions of higher learning are in financial trouble, and they may not be able to fulfill their promise of developing our vital human resources without the generosity of their friends and alumni. Whether we will have a society shaped by high ethical standards, as well as sound professional skills, depends to a great extent on whether academics and society can fulfill their commitments to each other.[8]

Closure (by prediction)

John C. Sawhill, president,
New York University

Reinforce Specific
Purpose (by referring
back to introduction
and mentioning five
steps)

By keeping our eyes and ears open to these achievements, I believe we can satisfy a basic and legitimate public desire. And, in the process, we'll help restore the media's credibility and respect.

Well, those are the five steps—steps that, I believe, could help us plot a corrective course for our profession.

Closure (by general
request for action)

I hope you'll join me in that effort. I hope you, too, are concerned—that you want to turn public anger and outrage toward the media into admiration and respect.[9]

Gale E. Klappa, vice president,
Southern Company Services, Inc.

LEARNING BY UNDERSTANDING

1. Which of the following are not main purposes of an introduction?

   a. Developing rapport
   b. Summarizing your research
   c. Beginning to develop credibility
   d. Previewing your speech
   e. Providing an opportunity for audience questions

2. Which of the following speech types would most likely have an explicit preview of the main points?

   a. Persuasive
   b. Informative
   c. Special occasion
   d. Entertaining

3. List the two main purposes of the conclusion to a speech.

4. List several techniques to conclude a speech.

ANSWERS:

4. Summary, quotation, prediction, rhetorical question, request for action
3. Reinforce your speech's specific purpose and psychologically close the communication
2. b.
1. b., e. b is one way to raise credibility and is not always used.

How Can I Use Listening Guides in My Speeches?

By this point, you have developed all the skills necessary for putting together an organized speech. You are able to go from a general topic and narrow it to a specific topic. You know how to word your specific purpose and your central idea. Using subordination and coordination, you can choose main points to develop your idea and subpoints and support to clarify and develop your main points. Finally, you have developed the skills to prepare an organized introduction and conclusion to your speech. The final step involves using aids that will help your audience follow your speech and remember your main points. "Even when the speech is structured clearly, the audience needs help from the speaker in identifying the plan of development."[10]

The two main purposes of listening guides are to help your audience follow and to remember your speech. Transitions and summary transitions are listening guides which will help your audience follow you from point to point. Memory aids and verbal emphasis are types of listening guides which will help listeners remember your main points.

A **transition** is a word, phrase, or sentence that bridges two ideas or points to indicate that you have completed the development of one idea and you are moving on to another point of your speech. Transitions are primarily used between main points. A **summary transition** is a transition with a summary of the previous point(s). Some examples of transitions and summary transitions follow:

Next. . . . (*a transition*)

It follows that. . . . (*a transition*)

Now let's move on to. . . . (*a transition*)

Not only . . . but also. . . . (*a summary transition*)

Now that we've . . . let's look at. . . . (*a summary transition*)

Summary transitions are usually preferred to transitions because they have the advantage of including another repetition of your previous point. More examples of summary transitions are

After improving the residents' hall association by developing a newsletter and posting agendas for meetings, the next step is to develop a dorm court.

In addition to the residents' hall association which I have just described, we also could have a dorm court.

In addition to the residents' dorm association, we also could have a dorm court.

The second purpose of having your audience remember important parts of your speech, such as your main points, can be accomplished by using listening guides in the two categories of memory aids and methods of verbal emphasis. The preview, review, and summary transition combination are ***memory aids*** based on repetition. The ***preview*** tells the audience what is about to come in the speech; it is usually part of an introduction and is also used before each main point. The ***review*** summarizes what the audience has just heard; it is usually part of the conclusion and is often used after each main point. Summary transitions discussed above also help audiences remember by repetition.

Verbal emphasis involves either ***numbering your main points*** or ***using particular statements*** to repeat points and increase attention. If, for example, you told the audience that you were going to present three main points, when you reach your second point you could say, "My second main point is. . . ." The use of numbering will help the audience realize that you are moving into your second main point. Examples of statements that both increase attention and use repetition are "I believe this second solution is the best one" or "This one is really important" or "Maybe I should restate this because it's so important." In Chapter 11 we will describe nonverbal ways to emphasize.

How Do I Add These Additional Parts to My Outline?

Your introduction, conclusion, and listening guides are inserted in your speech outline at the place you will say them. Listening guides are usually placed in parentheses between the speech parts they are connecting. We will add these final parts to the outline for the following Special Olympics speech to illustrate the format for a complete outline.

Arouse Interest and Develop Rapport (by stating a shared feeling)	*Introduction* I. I'm sure we all have a great deal of compassion for the handicapped.
Raise Credibility (by mentioning research, major, and previous experience)	II. I've done a great deal of research on the handicapped because of my major in special education, and I've helped with the Special Olympics for four years.
Preview Content (by mentioning the number of personal advantages)	III. I'd like to share with you two personal advantages I discovered from helping with the Special Olympics for the handicapped.
	Body
Preview and Transition	(The first main advantage is) I. Assisting with the Special Olympics helps you gain a better understanding of handicapped people.
Numbering	(first)

Numbering

A. You can understand the physical limitations imposed by a variety of handicaps.
(second)
B. You can understand the psychological implications of physical handicaps.

Summary Transition

(I've explained some of the new ways you can understand handicapped people. Now let's look at another advantage of helping with the Special Olympics—getting a better understanding of competition.)

II. Assisting with the Special Olympics helps you gain a healthier view of competition.

Numbering and a Particular Statement

(first you'll be surprised to learn that)
A. Special Olympics athletes compete against themselves to reach the limits of their capabilities.
(second—even more surprising is that)

Reinforce Specific Purpose (by reviewing main points)

B. Special Olympics athletes help other contestants reach their goals.

Conclusion

I. I hope you now understand how assisting with the Special Olympics helps you gain a better understanding of handicapped people and a healthier view of competition.

Closure (by rhetorical question)

II. Can you take the time to grow a bit?

LEARNING BY UNDERSTANDING

1. What are the two main purposes of listening guides?

2. Identify each of the following types of organizational aids:

   ____ **a.** We've just considered why women tend to be more persuadable than men.

   ____ **b.** An extremely important point is that male role models seldom admit to feeling uncertainty.

   ____ **c.** Let's now look at the implications of the Equal Rights Amendment on relationships between the sexes.

   ____**d.** I've explained what I feel is the basis of homosexuality. Now let me indicate the impact I feel this group has on society.

ANSWERS:

1. They help people remember the important or main points, and they help the audience follow you from section to section.
2. **a.** review, **b.** verbal emphasis, **c.** nonverbal emphasis, **d.** preview, **e.** summary transition

LEARNING BY INTERACTING

Choose a general topic of common interest to the entire class—perhaps a campus situation or problem affecting everyone in the class. Then divide into small groups of two or three. Each group should choose one of the organizational patterns described in Table 7-1. Draw slips of paper with one of the patterns written on each so different patterns are used.

Using its organizational plan, each group should develop an outline for the body of a speech on the agreed-on topic. If the topic is chosen ahead of time, the groups could bring resource materials to class to use as supporting material. Check to see that your outline uses the suggested notation system and your entries apply the principles of subordination and coordination.

Share your outlines. Each group should be ready to briefly describe the choices it made in organizing. Discuss the variety of main points chosen. Does any one pattern seem best adapted to the particular topic? Which pattern would be most appropriate for a speech for your speech class? Decide what kind of audience each pattern would be most appropriate for.

LEARNING BY SPEAKING

Prepare a four- to five-minute speech that describes how a particular event in history could help your classmates understand a current situation they face. Prepare an audience analysis with information gathered from a direct source. Develop a full-sentence outline in which you include an introduction, body, conclusion, and listening guides according to the form suggested in this chapter. Use appropriate research types and sources to get background on the historical event and the current situation. Include a bibliography which lists these sources.

Add marginal notes by the introduction and conclusion which indicate where you have accomplished each of the goals for these parts. Also add marginal notes to show your listening guides. Include a paragraph at the end of your outline which describes why you chose the organizational plan you did for the body of the speech.

REVIEW

Organizing your speech involves ordering your main points and subpoints so that your idea is well developed and easy to understand. Organization helps your audience follow your speech, and it meets its expectations for organization. Outlining helps you see the parts of your idea. It makes it easier to work with your ideas. And it is a visual aid for delivery.

There are three steps involved in developing an outline. The first is deciding which main points and subpoints you will use in your speech. The second is refining those main points and subpoints, using the principles of subordination and coordination. The final step is determining the order in which you will present the main points and subpoints. Outlining consistently uses a notation system to clarify the relationship between the parts of your speech.

After outlining the body of the speech, prepare the introduction. The introduction should arouse interest, establish yourself in a positive way by developing rapport and raising your credibility, and preview the speech content. The conclusion, the last part of the speech to be developed, reinforces the speech purpose and psychologically closes the communication experience. Finally, listening guides are developed to help the audience follow and remember the important points. The introduction, conclusion, and listening guides are then added to your outline.

NOTES

1. Christopher Spicer and Ron E. Bassett, "The Effect of Organization on Learning from an Informative Message," *Southern Speech Communication Journal* (Spring 1976):290.

2. Robert W. Finkel, *The Brainbooster* (Englewood Cliffs, N.J.: Prentice-Hall, 1983), 151.

3. Judy Haynes, *Organizing a Speech: A Programmed Guide* (Englewood Cliffs, N.J.: Prentice-Hall, 1973), 156.

4. John A. Jones and George R. Serlovsky, "An Investigation of Listener Perception of Degrees of Speech Disorganization and the Effects on Attitude Change and Source Credibility," *SCA Abstracts* (1971):54.

5. Julie Baumgold, "Man Behind the Manuscripts: Michael Korda," (Baltimore: *The Sun*, Monday, April 15, 1985):1B.

6. T. C. McDermott, "The Human Dimension in Productivity," *Vital Speeches of the Day* 43(March 1, 1977):306.

7. Roy Godson, "Soviet Manipulation of the Media: Fact or Fiction," *Vital Speeches of the Day* 51 (April 15, 1985):405.

8. John C. Sawhill, "Make America Smarter: The Independent College," *Vital Speeches of the Day* 43(May 1, 1977):311.

9. Gale E. Klappa, "Journalism and the Anti-Media Backlash: Five Steps to Restore the Public's Respect," *Vital Speeches of the Day* 51(April 1, 1985):378.

10. Haynes, *Organizing a Speech*, 20.

8

DEVELOPING PERSONAL CREDIBILITY AND EMOTIONAL APPEALS

In this chapter, you'll be . . .

LEARNING BY UNDERSTANDING

- The role of credibility in audience decision making
- The components of credibility
- How credibility is determined
- How credibility is developed
- The role of emotion in audience decision making
- Basic needs, values, and desires of people in general
- How to determine appropriate emotions to use
- How to develop emotional appeals

LEARNING BY INTERACTING

- Developing a catalog of needs, values, and desires for basic audience types

LEARNING BY SPEAKING

- A four- to five-minute informative speech that describes an important decision you have made in an area of audience interest

CHAPTER OUTLINE

I. Your audience's decisions about your speech are influenced by its assessment of your credibility.
  - **A.** Credibility is your audience's assessment of your qualifications to speak on a specific topic.
  - **B.** There are four major components of credibility.
    - **1.** Competence is the most important component of credibility.
      - **a.** Your competence is determined by your expertise and composure.
      - **b.** Competence is developed by citing your sources and appearing confident.
      - **c.** Competence is especially important in informative and persuasive speeches.
    - **2.** Trustworthiness is the next component of credibility.
      - **a.** Your trustworthiness is determined by the safety and benefits of your ideas for your audience.
      - **b.** Trustworthiness is developed by telling your connection with the topic and describing its benefits to the audience.
      - **c.** Trustworthiness is most important in informative and persuasive speeches.
    - **3.** Character is the next component of credibility.
      - **a.** Your character is determined by your similarity to the audience and your sociability.
      - **b.** Character is developed by establishing rapport and using personal pronouns.
      - **c.** Character is important in all speech types.
    - **4.** Dynamism is the final component of credibility.
      - **a.** Your dynamism is determined by your extroversion and your nonverbal activity.
      - **b.** Dynamism is developed by describing your emotions and involvement in your topic.
      - **c.** Dynamism is most important in entertaining and special-occasion speeches.
  - **C.** Credibility can be established in the introduction of a speech.
    - **1.** Use a Credibility Analysis Form or your knowledge of the audience to determine your current level of credibility.
    - **2.** Decide which components to focus on in your introduction.
      - **a.** Use the Credibility Analysis Form or expectations of the audience as a guide.
      - **b.** Do a self-assessment to determine which components you must develop and how much for this speech situation.
  - **D.** Maintain credibility throughout the speech by continuing to develop the four components as needed.

II. Your audience's decisions about your speech are influenced by its emotional responses.
  - **A.** There are two main ways to develop emotional appeals for a speech.
    - **1.** You can develop positive appeals that connect needs, values, and desires of your audience to your ideas and recommendations.
    - **2.** You can develop negative appeals that focus on things your audience does not value or desire and that your ideas and recommendations will help them avoid.
  - **B.** You should be ethical in your use of emotional appeals.
    - **1.** It is ethical to use emotional appeals to encourage audience involvement in your topic.
    - **2.** It is unethical to use emotional appeals as the only basis for making an important recommendation.

C. It is important to relate your emotional appeals to the needs, values, and desires of your audience.
   1. You can use your understanding of people in general to decide which emotions to appeal to.
      a. Maslow's Hierarchy of Needs provides suggested needs.
      b. Values and desires are related to each level of human need.
   2. You can use your audience analysis to determine your specific audience's relevant emotions.
D. Emotional appeals are developed by using the twelve procedures of developing, clarifying, and supporting your ideas (DCS materials).
   1. The first step is choosing a procedure.
   2. The second step is using vivid language to express the appeal.
   3. The third step is using dynamic delivery to give the appeal.
E. You should encourage the audience to call up the appropriate emotion.
   1. If your information about the audience was based on a direct source, your chosen emotion probably will be called up.
   2. If your information about your audience was based on an indirect source or general knowledge, tell the audience how the appeal relates to its needs.

8

DEVELOPING PERSONAL CREDIBILITY AND EMOTIONAL APPEALS

Would you persuade—speak of interest, not of reason.   *—Ben Franklin*

PREVIEW

In the last four chapters, you worked on important skills in analyzing your audience, researching your speech topic, and organizing those researched materials. In this chapter and in Chapter 9, you will work on the key skills that will help you tailor your researched and organized materials to the particular audience you are preparing for.

As you learned in Chapter 3, thoughtful audience members will assess your speech in order to make decisions regarding your information, ideas, and suggestions for their behaviors. To make their decisions, audience members will ask themselves three important questions: (1) What qualifies this speaker to talk on this topic? (2) How does this speech topic involve me personally? (3) What reasons were given to support the speaker's ideas and recommendations? Their answers will be based on how they see you and your speech in terms of their frames of reference.

To have the audience answer those questions favorably, you can (1) develop your credibility based on audience expectations, (2) develop and use emotional appeals that connect your topic to the basic values and emotions of the audience, and (3) develop and use reasoned arguments based on parts of the audience's frame of reference. The sets of skills involved in handling these three key areas of speech development are called ***invention skills***. As described in Chapter 1, invention is one of the areas of speech preparation developed by Aristotle. The word invention highlights the creativity involved as a speaker develops the personal, emotional, and reasoned materials needed to accomplish a speech purpose with a particular audience. The new "invented" materials make use of the researched materials and supplement them in the speech. In Chapter 9, you will work on skills in developing reasoned arguments. In this chapter, you will work on skills in developing your credibility and developing emotional appeals.

How Important Is My Credibility?

Your credibility will greatly influence the final choices your audience will make.[1] **Credibility** is defined as your audience's assessment of your competence, trust-worthiness, character, and dynamism as a speaker on a particular topic. Audiences have been known to reject even well-researched and organized speeches because they did not accept the speaker as a credible source. You may have heard people say things like, "I wouldn't believe him if he told me that the sun would come up tomorrow." The greater your credibility, the more your ideas will be understood and accepted by your audience. In fact, people with high credibility are usually effective in terms of informing or persuading—even if their speeches are less carefully prepared.[2]

How Does My Audience Decide If I'm a Credible Speaker?

That is a difficult question. As we indicated earlier, your audience's opinion of you will be based on its frame of reference—the things it knows, believes, and is interested in. For example, if the audience members already know something about the topic, they will expect you to use information and reasons consistent with theirs. If they think research is important, they may determine your credibility by how much research you include in your speech. And if they are interested in a certain aspect of your topic, they may decide you are more credible if you also express interest in that aspect.

An audience's decisions will be influenced by what it already knows about you. Later in your life most of your speeches will be in an area of your expertise. Because of your position or reputation, you will be asked to talk about sales in your department for the last quarter, the effects of dumping toxic waste in the river, how to protect yourself against muggers, or how the passage of the school bond issue will help music students. The audience's opinions of you will greatly help its acceptance of you and your message. But here in class, very few are likely to know that you are president of the campus bike club or have been a bird-watcher since you were ten years old. So you tell them. And the first chance you have to build your credibility is in your introduction. Recent evidence indicates that credibility is mainly determined by the audience's perception of your competence to talk on the topic, and that this decision begins right from the start of the communication.[3] This and three other key factors, along with eight subfactors, that research has shown to influence your audience's decision about your credibility are summarized here.[4]

KEY FACTORS AFFECTING SOURCE CREDIBILITY

COMPETENCE
  Expertise
  Composure
TRUSTWORTHINESS
  Safety
  Benefits

CHARACTER
  Similarity
  Sociability
DYNAMISM
  Extroversion
  Nonverbal Activity

What Do These Terms Mean?

Competence refers to how qualified an audience thinks you are to talk on a particular topic and is based on your expertise and composure. Listeners are concerned with your *expertise* in the area you are talking about, especially in informative and persuasive speeches. When you explain how to do something or you describe something, your listeners may think you should have had some direct experience with the topic to become "expert." If you have never done it or experienced it, they might feel you are not qualified enough to tell them about it. For other topics, your audience might think you should have studied the topic by taking courses, reading articles or books, or talking to experts. Examples of such topic areas would be explaining the causes of a current problem or current trends or suggesting a solution for a complex problem. If you do not describe your research, audience members might feel you are not qualified to explain or recommend something to them. *Composure* refers to delivery behaviors that reflect a speaker's confidence. People expect a person to be comfortable talking in an area of his or her expertise. Therefore, if you show visible signs of being nervous, they

The reporting of current research on a topic will raise an audience's perception of the speaker's competence.

might feel you are not competent to talk on the topic. Because you have been working on your speaking skills, you are probably better at handling any feelings of nervousness.

The second major factor an audience considers is trustworthiness. ***Trustworthiness*** is a component of credibility that is based on listeners' perceptions of the ***safety*** and ***benefits*** of your speech for them. In addition to being concerned with your competence, the audience will consider if you are presenting only one side of an issue or making a recommendation that would be especially beneficial to you personally but not to your listeners. Their primary concern is how safe and beneficial your information, ideas, and recommendations are for them. Often, both factors are important. For example, in a speech that recommends a certain diet, your audience desires benefits but does not want to risk its health. Trustworthiness is especially important in informatve and persuasive speeches and if the speaker has something to gain from the decisions the audience will make. For example, when audiences listen to politicians or salespeople, they know that one primary goal of the speaker is to get their money or their votes. They realize that some speakers will lie or misrepresent to benefit themselves, even if it harms the listeners.

The third component of credibility is character. ***Character*** refers to your personal qualities and is based on your ***similarity*** to your audience and your ***sociability***. This component is important for all speech purposes. Audiences feel more open to your ideas if they see you as similar to them. They feel that you are more likely to know the information, ideas, and recommendations that are safer and more beneficial to them. Being sociable and friendly are helpful ways to communicate your positive character.

The fourth component of credibility is dynamism. ***Dynamism*** refers to your physical activity, which reflects your interest and involvement in your topic. It is based on your ***extroversion*** and ***nonverbal activity*** as a speaker. It is easy to understand how an audience would feel less open to your ideas if you appear indifferent or uninvolved with your topic. Audiences determine your involvement by the energy reflected in your voice and body language. They look for sustained eye contact and vocal variations, which indicate the importance of the points you are making, and body movements, such as gesturing, which suggest total involvement in the speech. The component of dynamism is more important in a speech to entertain or a special-occasion speech than in one to inform. If your audience felt you were highly qualified, trustworthy, and of similar character, a less dynamic delivery would not be a major problem. It will, however, have some influence on your audience. You will work on skills related to establishing this delivery-related component of credibility in Chapter 11.

Where Should I Include Specific Materials to Develop My Credibility?

Because your audience's perception of you will influence its perception of your speech, it is important to establish your credibility before you begin your main points. As we described in Chapter 7, this is a major goal for the introduction to your speech. During your introduction, you should tell your audience—directly by your words and indirectly by your involvement and sincerity—that you are a credible source on this topic. By the end of your introduction, your listeners should be saying to themselves something like, ''The speaker seems to be competent, likable, trustworthy, and dynamic. This speech probably will be valuable to me.''

After your introduction, it will be important to reflect your competence, trustworthiness, character, and dynamism throughout your speech to reinforce initial positive perceptions.

How Do I Develop My Credibility?

Before deciding how to raise your credibility, you must take two preliminary steps. First, you will want to determine what your initial credibility is with this audience and decide what parts of your credibility you want to raise. Use your knowledge of your audience to estimate what the audience already knows and thinks about you. Consider your listeners' knowledge, attitudes, and interests as they relate to each basic component of credibility. You can also use the Credibility Analysis Form (Figure 8-1) to determine your current credibility with any particular audience and to determine which subfactors should be changed to yield the greatest effectiveness.

The best way to use the Credibility Analysis Form is to apply the direct sources method for gathering information. Have each member of your class complete the

Figure 8-1   Credibility Analysis Form

Speaker's Name _____

Speaker's Specific Topic _____

	Speaker's Current Credibility Levels	**Speaker's Desired Credibility Levels**	**Differences**
	For this speaker on this topic, rate each subfactor from +10 (very positive) to −10 (very negative).	*For this topic, rate the desired level of each subfactor from +10 (very positive) to −10 (very negative).*	
Competence:			
Expertise	_____	_____	_____
Composure	_____	_____	_____
Trustworthiness:			
Safety	_____	_____	_____
Benefits	_____	_____	_____
Character:			
Similarity	_____	_____	_____
Sociability	_____	_____	_____
Dynamism:			
Extroversion	_____	_____	_____
Nonverbal activity	_____	_____	_____

form. Average your audience members' attitudes for each line in the first two columns and then subtract "Desired" from "Current" to determine if that subfactor needs development. (These averages could be Part V of your Audience Analysis Form as developed in Chapter 4.) What you have done is collected direct information on your audience's attitudes about subfactors of your credibility and also about what levels of attitudes would be ideal for those subfactors. The direction of the difference desired on each subfactor indicates the direction for credibility change. For example, if the desired level of expertise was more positive than your current level, you would want to develop your expertise. The amount of difference implies the amount of change needed and how much time would be needed to develop that needed change. If your expertise is viewed as only a point or two low, then a sentence or two might raise your expertise enough. You might have wondered about how to handle negative numbers to show audience members' negative attitudes. While it is unlikely that anyone in your class would have negative attitudes about you, in other situations people might be biased against you and that would mean a greater amount of change would be needed (e.g., to change -2 to $+8$ would need a 10 point raise.)

To see how this process works, let's imagine that your specific topic is "how to lose weight" and the "Current" and "Desired" levels for the first three subfactors are

	Current	Desired	Differences
Expertise	1.2	7.4	-6.2
Composure	3.2	3.8	$-.6$
Safety	-1.0	6.5	-7.5

This would indicate clearly and from direct sources that safety and expertise are strongly desired for your speech on this specific topic and that they should be developed significantly in the introduction and throughout your speech. Composure is much less important, down less than one point, and thus would not need much development.

You can also use the form with indirect sources. Even audiences that do not know you personally have some initial impressions about you. They may have heard something about you, or they may identify you with a specific group about which they have an impression. Let's imagine that you are going to talk to the Junior Chamber of Commerce to encourage action on placing a traffic light at a dangerous campus crossing. Even if the audience members do not know you personally, they are going to identify you in their minds as "college student" or "nonresident." In this case, you should consider how the Junior Chamber of Commerce views the competence, trustworthiness, character, and dynamism of college students or nonresidents. You might ask a typical member to fill out the form or to estimate what the average for the whole audience would be.

The second preliminary step is to determine which of the four major components will be most important to stress in your introduction. If you have direct or indirect sources of information on the credibility form, the highest numbers in the "Desired" column are the subfactors which are most important in the audience's mind. If you do not have direct or indirect sources, consider the audience's expectations for the speech and the choices it will make regarding your information, ideas, and recommendations. For example, if members of the Junior Chamber of Commerce invited you to speak at their weekly dinner meeting to describe the achievements of a committee you chaired on campus/town relations, they probably would accept your competence because of your position. You might have to work on your trustworthiness because they might feel that you, as a student, view things differently than they do; and on your dynamism in order to meet their expectations of an after-dinner speech. If you were speaking about the traffic light recommendation to the same group at a regular JC meeting, it might be more important to establish your competence by revealing the research and thinking that support your recommendation. Trustworthiness and character would be important for similar reasons to the after-dinner situation. Dynamism would be important, too, because it reflects your sincerity and involvement.

We suggest that for your speech class you work on all four components to develop all related skills. It would also be valuable to assess your own skill level in handling each of these components to determine those on which you will need to work hardest. The Inventory of Public Speaking Skills, which you worked on in Chapter 2, can be helpful here. For example, if you think you are not a very dynamic speaker, you could focus on ways to develop and reflect your dynamism.

TABLE 8-1   DEVELOPING CREDIBILITY

Credibility Components and Subfactors	Means of Developing	Source for Additional Material
Competence		
Expertise	Describe your training or experience with topic. Describe your research for the speech. Quote from respected sources and give sources.	Chapters 4, 5, 7 Chapters 7, 9
Composure	Use confident physical behavior. Avoid nervousness.	Chapters 2, 11
Trustworthiness		
Safety	Indicate your direct involvement. Explain away anticipated risks.	Chapter 4
Benefits	Describe audience benefits from the speech. Describe benefits for both you and audience.	Chapters 4, 7
Character		
Similarity	Develop rapport by referring to shared concerns, beliefs, or experiences.	Chapters 4 (audience analysis), 7
Sociability	Use humor about yourself. Use first names and personal pronouns.	Chapters 10, 14
Dynamism		
Extroversion	Use involved and varied vocal delivery. Visit with audience before the speech. Describe your emotions.	Chapters 10, 11
Nonverbal Activity	Use eye contact, hand gestures, and body movement to enhance your speech purpose.	Chapter 11

Table 8-1 indicates methods you can use to develop any of the components of credibility and the chapters that deal specifically with each skill.

For your introduction, you will want to focus on those parts of credibility you have determined are most important for a particular audience. Since competence is important to most audiences, this would be a logical one to work on in the introduction. The following are examples of statements or behaviors you might use in an introduction to establish your credibility for each of the four components.

COMPETENCE

(by Expertise)

Based on my five years of working with this organization, I've . . . .
After completing two major term papers on . . . .
My traveling opportunities to . . . have allowed me to observe . . . .
Three books I've read have led me to conclude . . . .

CHARACTER

(by Similarity)

We all want the best education for our children so . . . .
I'm sure you share with me a strong anger against . . . .

(by Sociability)

In talking with several of you earlier, I realized . . . .
I was so out of shape I got winded playing chess.

TRUSTWORTHINESS

(by Benefits)

I think you'll agree that knowing these three signs will help you . . . .
This will be a win-win situation; by your signing on the dotted line we will both win.

(by Safety)

I've invested my life savings in the same . . . .
I've committed myself to . . . .

DYNAMISM

(by Extroversion)

. . . and I've really become excited about the possibilities of . . . .
. . . and I'm sure you'll share my enthuriasm about . . . .
. . . each experience has been more exciting than the last . . . .

It is also important that your nonverbal behaviors reinforce each of these factors. You will work more specifically on these nonverbal skills in Chapter 11.

The following example of an introduction used by a student includes materials developed to establish each of the four major components of credibility.

CHARACTER (by similarity)

COMPETENCE (by expertise)

COMPETENCE (by expertise)

TRUST-WORTHINESS (by safety)

It was interesting to me to learn, in the last round of speeches, that most of us are concerned about health and physical fitness. I did a lot of thinking about these important goals when I came to school. I realized that my parents would no longer be making the major decisions that affect my health and physical fitness. I imagine this is true for most of you. Last semester, I had a course in nutrition during which I learned a lot of exciting information about the recent research on the importance of vitamins in our diet. Based on my research and thinking, I've made some changes in my diet that I'm convinced will be good for me. I'd like to share with you these three major changes. I think you'll agree with me that these are valuable changes, and maybe you will consider them for your own diet.

DYNAMISM (by extroversion)

CHARACTER (by similarity)

COMPETENCE (by expertise)

DYNAMISM (by extroversion)

The student delivered this introduction with a great deal of enthusiasm, confidence and composure, which added to her credibility. As you can see, she concentrated on developing her class's perception of her competence because she anticipated that the audience might question her qualifications to make recommendations in this area. She also knew that the decisions the audience might make would be in terms of personal benefits; thus, it would be concerned about her trustworthiness. Also check G. J. Tankersley's speech introduction in Appendix B to see how he developed his expertise.

LEARNING BY UNDERSTANDING

1. Define credibility.

2. List the four major components of credibility.

3. Name the major component of credibility that goes with each pair of subcomponents:
    a. Safety
       Benefits
    b. Extroversion
       Nonverbal activity
    c. Expertise
       Composure
    d. Similarity
       Sociability

4. Name the subfactor of credibility that is developed by each of the following statements:
    a. "I got so excited by my research that I'm going to change my major."
    b. "My trip to the local mental health agency gave me the background."

c. "You can see how this exercise plan has benefited me."

d. "We've all shared the experience of worrying about meeting a deadline."

5. Write down the specific topic you used for one of your earlier speeches. Assume that you are talking to your hometown parent/teachers association. Rank the subfactors of credibility for your introduction from most important to least important. Write one sentence you could use in your introduction to develop each component.

ANSWERS:

1. Credibility is the perception your audience has of your competence, trustworthiness, character, and dynamism related to a specific topic.
2. Competence, trustworthiness, character, dynamism
3. **a.** trustworthiness, **b.** dynamism, **c.** competence, **d.** character
4. **a.** extroversion, **b.** expertise, **c.** safety and benefits, **d.** similarity
5. Check your answers on this one with someone else in your class.

Why Are Emotional Appeals Important?

At each stage of your speech preparation, we have suggested that you adapt your information, ideas, and recommendations to the audience's frame of reference. This involves choosing and arranging materials so that they will be understood and accepted. This audience adaptation helps you accomplish your speech purpose. It is important to remember the large number of messages your audience receives. Think how many speeches you will hear in this class alone. Sometimes your credibility will be high and your speech reasonable, but your audience will not be personally involved enough to make positive decisions regarding your ideas and recommendations.

Emotional appeals are speech materials that call up your audience's emotions and relate them to your speech purpose. Emotional appeals go beyond audience interests to call up your audience's feelings about the topic and lead members to think, "This topic really is vital to my needs." Emotional appeals involve your audience personally in your speech. There are two basic approaches to using emotional appeals. First, you can call up positive emotions, which will lead your audience to react strongly toward your information, ideas, and recommendations. This approach involves connecting your materials to something the audience desires to have, needs, or strongly values. The other approach is to call up negative emotions, which will lead your audience to react strongly against something your ideas or recommendations will help them avoid. This approach involves associating your information, ideas, and recommendations with something the audience desires to avoid or does not need or value. These appeals are sometimes called *fear appeals*.

How Do I Use Emotional Appeals in My Speech?

In Chapter 1, we indicated that your ethics would be revealed to your audience by the *choices* you ask your audience to make and the *means* you use to encourage them to make those choices. Your use of emotional appeals will be based on ethical decisions you will make.

Parts of an audience's decisions—as most decisions—are based on emotional responses. For example, you may have chosen the school you are attending partly because of its academic reputation. And we imagine that part of your decision was more emotionally based, such as desiring to go where your friends went or liking the appearance of the campus. Advertisers take advantage of our emotional decision making every day. In fact, the basic principles of advertising have been described as follows:

1. Direct advertising toward selfish human desires and motives.

2. Appeal to emotions, not just (or even) reasons.

3. Repeat the message ad nauseam, or until it becomes a "household word."[5]

Because the emotional appeals in advertising are so strong, there are laws to promote truth in advertising. Such laws protect us from poor decisions based only on our emotional responses. Your ethical use of emotional appeals will help people make beneficial decisions about your speech topics.

Emotional appeals can be used ethically in your speech to increase audience involvement in your topic. Thus, the members will listen more closely to your speech and consider your information, ideas, and recommendations in their decision making. Most likely, you will use emotional appeals in your introduction to involve the audience, as developing material to encourage personal meanings for a main point, and in your conclusion to motivate your audience to use your information, ideas, or recommendations. It would not be considered ethical to use emotional appeals as the only, or main, supporting materials and then to ask your audience to make an important decision based on them.

To What Audience Emotions Should I Appeal?

Your emotional appeals will be based on what you know about your audience's frame of reference. To build both positive and negative emotional appeals, you should know what your audience needs and does not need, what it desires to have and not to have, and what it values and does not value. Knowing the basic emotions, values, and needs of people in general will help you make these choices.

Abraham Maslow's Hierarchy of Needs, which appears in Figure 8-2, describes basic human needs.[6] The specific terms within each category refer to things you would value if you felt that need strongly. The term *hierarchy* and the building-block structure suggest that some of our needs are more basic than others. The idea represented is that we can only be concerned with higher needs after our more basic needs are satisfied. For example, if you are really hungry, you probably would forget such higher needs as praise or financial security until you satisfied your need for food. Maslow's sequence goes from basic physical survival needs to self-actualizing or personal growth needs. To some degree, these needs are present at all points in everyone's life; but at different times, some things are more important than others.

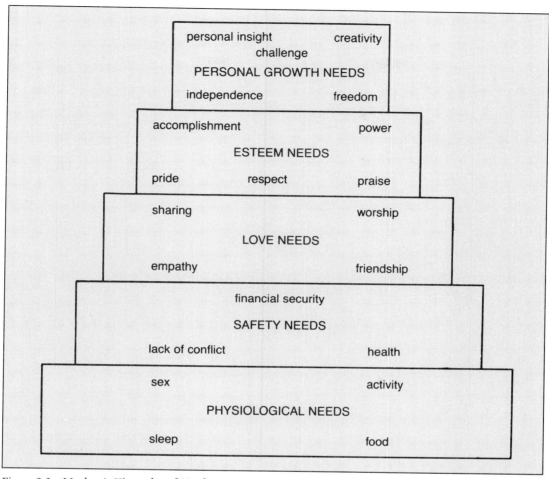

Figure 8-2 Maslow's Hierarchy of Needs

Figure 8-3 represents an estimate of this changing importance. For example, physical needs usually are most important in early years, and love and self-esteem are more important during adolescence. Human needs range from what people desire to what they wish to avoid.

HUMAN NEEDS

Desire to Have	Desire to Avoid
Security	Insecurity
Success	Failure
Acceptance	Rejection
Consistency	Inconsistency
Certainty	Anxiety/fear
Need satisfaction	Frustration
Order	Disorder
Completion	Incompleteness

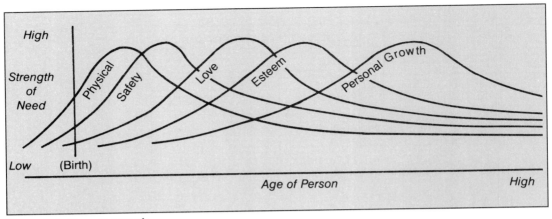

Figure 8-3 Changing Needs

You will be able to use your audience analysis to determine which of these basic needs, related values, and desires are important to your audience at this time.

How Can I Develop Emotional Appeals?

Emotional appeals are developed by using any of the twelve developing, clarifying, and supporting procedures described in Chapter 5 with materials that relate to the audience's needs, values, and desires. The emotional impact of these developed materials will be strengthened by your use of words that have strong connotative meanings for your audience and nonverbal delivery behaviors that reflect the emotion in the appeal. In other words, what makes materials emotional is the specific meaning they have for your audience and the meaning you convey through your language and delivery.

You will be working on choosing vivid language in Chapter 10 and on effective delivery in Chapter 11. At this point, we suggest you focus on developing emotional appeals by creating developing, clarifying, and supporting (DCS) materials that relate to the needs, values, and desires of your audience. The Learning by Interacting exercise for this chapter will help you build a catalog of specific needs for basic audience types. This will help you develop emotional appeals.

If you decide to include a negative emotional appeal, be sure you appeal to the emotion realistically. Research suggests that if your fear appeal is so strong that your audience considers it unrealistic, it will be ignored.[7] For example, if you were encouraging an audience of high school students to have regular dental checkups, vivid stories about people losing all their teeth due to lack of dental care probably would be too strong. Your appeal would be more effective if you described the suffering of a person who required extensive dental work.

Following are several examples of emotional appeals used in student speeches.

From a speech on drinking and driving:

We all have a tendency to think of our college years as free from control and a time to "sow our wild oats." Even our local police force admits to being somewhat lenient in penalizing students. This kind of thinking, however, leads to tragic results for thousands of college students a year. Statistics show that accidents which result from driving under the influence of alcohol lead to an average of 200 deaths and/or serious injuries a year for college students. Even those accidents which don't cause injury or go on a student's permanent record leave permanent emotional scars. We probably all know someone who made a careless decision about alcohol and driving and regretted it later.

Positive Appeal (to Independence)

Negative Appeal (to Avoid Physical Harm)

From a speech on organizing your time:

Positive Appeal (to Freedom and Independence)

Freedom of choice and flexibility are things that many college students desire. I'm sure one of the things you looked forward to when you began college was making your own decisions and not having the major portion of your day planned for you. Maybe you were like I was and thought that freedom meant no planning—kind of doing as you pleased hour by hour. I learned the hard way and my first semester grades showed it. I'd like to pass on to you how planning and budgeting your time can lead to greater freedom and flexibility rather than less.

Positive Appeal (to Personal Success)

Negative Appeal (to Avoid Failure)

From a speech on using biofeedback:

Positive Appeal (to Personal Growth and Insight)

Positive Appeal (to Curiosity)

Positive Appeal (to Freedom and Self-control)

One of the things I've learned from hearing many of you speak this quarter is that you share with me a real desire to learn more about yourself and explore new ways to grow. These desires probably brought us to college and lead us to new areas of reading and study. Sometimes we tend to forget that one of the greatest mysteries is that of our own bodies. Biofeedback is one of the new studies that enables us to grow in self-knowledge of our bodies. Through biofeedback we can not only grow in self insight but also gain greater control over our bodily reactions. This is similar to the greater control you gain over your emotions when you understand them better.

Also check Judith Barton's speech introduction in Appendix B to see how she used statistics and testimony to develop a strong negative appeal to avoid personal harm.

If your development of emotional materials was based on information about your audience from a direct source, your audience probably will experience the appropriate emotion when you present your emotional appeal. If you based your

Political candidates develop emotional appeals directed toward voters' needs, values, and desires.

development on information from an indirect source or from your knowledge of people in general, we suggest you tell your listeners how your emotional appeal relates to their own needs, values, and desires.

For example, imagine you have been invited to talk to a group of professionals who are about to retire. Your topic is using spare time constructively. After meeting several members of the group, you learn that they often discuss their concern about using their spare time because they value activity and productivity. If you then use a story in your introduction about a retired person who did not use his time well, you would be quite sure that your listeners would make the connections to their own needs and values. However, if you have been asked to talk about retirement and have not been able to do an audience analysis, we suggest that you tell listeners how the appeal relates to them. For example, after your story you could say, "You may have been so busy up to this time that you haven't thought much about your retirement. Joe's experience illustrates the importance of starting that thinking now."

LEARNING BY UNDERSTANDING

1. What are the two basic types of emotional appeals?

2. Name two safety needs that would be important to an audience of married businesspeople.

3. Identify an audience for which the following would be an effective emotional appeal.
   a. An illustration of the poor job schools do in teaching students to read
   b. A vivid narrative about an animal that gnaws off its foot to escape an animal trap
   c. Statistics showing the increase in food costs projected for the next year

ANSWERS:

1. Positive appeals and negative (or fear) appeals
2. Two possible answers are financial security and good health.
3. Possible answers are (a.) a parent/teachers association, (b.) supporters of the Humane Society, and (c.) a group of young married couples.

LEARNING BY INTERACTING

Work with others in your class to develop a catalog of needs, related values, and desires for the basic types of audiences you are likely to address. First, work together to decide what those basic audience types would be. Your list might include this class, business colleagues, senior citizens, and students (at various levels). Then divide the audience types so that each small group can work on two or three of them. Each group should write as many needs, values, and desires as it can that could be used as the basis for an emotional appeal for the types it is working with. An example might look like this:

Audience Type	*Needs, Values, and Desires*
College Class	Doing well on exams
	Meeting new people
	Being physically attractive

After each group has completed its list, exchange the lists so they are fine-tuned several times. Collect the final lists and make copies for the entire class.

LEARNING BY SPEAKING

Prepare a four- to five-minute speech that describes an important decision you have made in an area of audience interest. Your speech should help audience members understand why you made this decision, the implications of that decision, and what they can learn from your experience. Your brainstorming of speech topics in Chapter 4 probably included many topic areas which would be appropriate for this speech. Do an audience analysis which includes questions to help you build your credibility and develop emotional appeals. The Credibility Analysis Form may be helpful to you. Develop a sentence outline and use at least two research sources to support your decision. Include materials in your introduction to establish the basis for your credibility. Do this for each of the components of credibility. Include at least two emotional appeals which relate your topic to the needs, values, and desires of the class. In the margin of your outline identify the materials to develop each component of credibility and your emotional appeals.

REVIEW

A thoughtful audience asks itself three basic questions before making decisions about information, ideas, and suggestions in your speech: (1) What qualifies this speaker to talk on this topic? (2) How does this speech topic involve me personally? (3) What reasons were given to support the speaker's ideas and recommendations? To help the audience answer those questions favorably, you should: (1) develop your credibility based on audience expectations; (2) develop and use emotional appeals that connect your topic to the basic values and emotions of the audience; and (3) develop and use reasoned arguments based on the audience's frame of reference. In this chapter, you worked on skills in the first two areas.

Credibility is developed by establishing your competence, trustworthiness, character, and dynamism and is usually dealt with specificaly in the introduction of your speech. Emotional appeals are developed by using the twelve procedures for developing, clarifying, and supporting your speech. Using emotional appeals to increase audience involvement in your topic and to encourage consideration of your ideas and recommendations is considered ethical; but to use them as the only basis for making a recommendation is considered unethical.

NOTES

1. Stephen W. Littlejohn, "A Bibliography of Studies Related to Variables of Source Credibility," *Bibliographic Annual in Speech Communication* (New York: Speech Communication Association, 1972), 1–40.

2. N. H. Anderson, "Integration Theory and Attitude Change," *Psychological Review* 78(May 1971):171.

3. Joel Cooper and Robert T. Croyle, "Attitudes and Attitude Change," *American Review of Psychology* 35(1984):418.

4. Alice H. Eagly and Samuel Himmelfarb, "Attitudes and Opinions," *Annual Review of Psychology* 29(1978):532.

5. Howard Kahane, *Logic and Philosophy* (Belmont, Calif.: Wadsworth Publishing Co., 1973), 231.

6. Abraham H. Maslow, *Motivation and Personality* (New York: Harper & Row, 1970), 35–47.

7. Carl Hovland, Irving Janis, and Harold Kelley, *Communication and Persuasion* (New Haven: Yale University Press, 1953), 275.

9

DEVELOPING REASONED ARGUMENTS

In this chapter, you'll be . . .

LEARNING BY UNDERSTANDING

- Three main structures of reasoning available to a speaker
- When to use each structure in speech preparation
- Steps in preparing inductive reasoning
- Steps in presenting inductive reasoning
- Steps in preparing deductive reasoning
- Steps in presenting deductive reasoning
- Steps in preparing sequential reasoning
- Steps in presenting sequential reasoning

LEARNING BY INTERACTING

- Developing and assessing arguments that apply the three main structures of reasoning to an issue of common interest

LEARNING BY SPEAKING

- A five- to seven-minute informative speech that expresses your views and the reasons for your views on a current national problem

CHAPTER OUTLINE

I. Reasoning is an important speaking-related skill.
  A. Reasoning skills are valued by employers.
  B. Reasoning skills help you solve difficult problems.
  C. Reasoning skills help you express your reasoning to others.
  D. Reasoning skills help you adapt researched arguments to fit your audience and topic.

II. Three basic structures of reasoning are useful in your speech development.
  A. Deductive reasoning is one type of structure.
    1. Deduction often reasons from accepted generalizations to a conclusion about a particular situation or person.
    2. The important principle in deduction is inclusion.
    3. Deductive reasoning answers questions about particular instances or groups where a general rule applies.
  B. Inductive reasoning is one type of structure.
    1. Induction usually reasons from specific instances to a new generalization.
    2. The important principle in induction is the representativeness of each individual instance.
    3. Inductive reasoning answers questions where no general rule applies.
  C. Sequential reasoning is one type of structure.
    1. Sequential reasoning examines the relationship between specific instances, concepts, or generalizations.
    2. The important principle in sequential reasoning is establishing a sure relationship.
    3. Sequential reasoning answers questions about cause/effect, problem/solution, and solution/benefit relationships.

III. There are two basic uses for inductive reasoning.
  A. You can use inductive reasoning to develop arguments.
    1. The first step is to hypothesize a possible conclusion.
      a. Use creative thinking to develop a hypothesis.
      b. Use available knowledge to develop a hypothesis.
    2. The next step is to modify the conclusion.
      a. First, collect appropriate specific instances.
      b. Second, test the collected information—is it relevant, recent, from a credible source, consistent with other known information.
    3. The final step is to modify the scope or probability of the conclusion.
  B. You can use inductive reasoning to present arguments.
    1. The first step is to choose the information.
      a. Choose the most representative information.
      b. Choose the audience-needed number of instances.
      c. Arrange the information.
    2. The second step is to present the information.
      a. Include the dates and source in your presentation.
      b. Include unbiased or "reluctant" information.
    3. The final step is to present the conclusion.
      a. Qualify the conclusion in scope or probability.
      b. State the conclusion.

IV. There are two basic uses for deductive reasoning.
  A. You can use deductive reasoning to develop arguments.
   1. First, clearly state the specific instance or conclusion you want to prove through deductive reasoning.
   2. Second, from audience analysis determine related generalizations or rules that would be acceptable to your audience.
   3. Third, use the principle of inclusion to determine if your specific instance is included in the category.
   4. Finally, draw a conclusion by applying the appropriate characteristics of the major category to your specific instance.
  B. You can use deductive reasoning to present your arguments.
   1. Based on audience analysis, decide which parts of your reasoning you need to present to your audience.
   2. Determine the order in which to present these parts.
   3. Present the argument.

V. There are two basic uses for sequential reasoning.
  A. You can use sequential reasoning to develop arguments.
   1. Hypothesize the relationship between the elements, using research, brainstorming, and creative insight.
   2. Collect relevant information, possible effects, parallel examples.
   3. Use basic checks to determine if relationships exist.
     a. If the cause (solution) occurs, does the effect (benefit) always occur?
     b. If the cause (solution) does not occur, does the effect (benefit) not occur?
     c. If more of the cause (solution) is present, does more of the effect (benefit) occur?
  B. You can use sequential reasoning to present arguments.
   1. Identify the importance of the relationship to the audience by connecting it with a value or need.
   2. Demonstrate the relationship by presenting parallel examples and examples that show how basic checks establish the relationship.

9

DEVELOPING REASONED ARGUMENTS

People want answers, but they don't want to do the hard thinking it takes to get them.
—Harold Gordon

PREVIEW

In this chapter, you will work on some of the most important speaking-related skills—the skills of reasoning. These skills will enable you to make decisions, conclusions, and relationships. In Chapter 1, we said that reasoning was a speaking-related skill frequently mentioned by professionals as being important in their fields. Phrases like "able to argue logically" come up again and again in job interviews and performance appraisals. Your ability to reason will help you contribute to your audience's understanding of a particular topic area. It is easy to understand why having well-developed reasoning skills would make you a valuable asset in a job.

Reasoning is a specific type of thinking skill. In Chapter 5, you worked on skills in developing creative thinking. There you tried to avoid common ways of looking at something and brainstormed to get new insights about a problem or situation. Reasoned thinking is an approach that follows certain rules. Often people excel in one or the other type of thinking. For example, you might have been able to work through the creative-thinking problems in Chapter 5 with little difficulty; but perhaps reasoning will be more challenging to you. Both types of thinking are important and valuable skills.

Some people have difficulty using reasoning to solve problems, and others have difficulty expressing their reasoning to others. It is especially frustrating if you have reached a valuable conclusion but cannot make it sound "reasonable." In this chapter, you will use three basic structures for reasoned thinking that will help you achieve both purposes of reasoning—to think through problems and to present your thoughts effectively.[1] As you develop skills in these two uses of reasoning, you will do so in terms of using them with a particular audience to achieve a specific purpose. Through your research, you may find arguments that will work well for your audience. In many situations, however, you will need to develop your own arguments from researched data and generalizations. Or you will have to figure out how to relate a researched argument to your speech topic so that it makes sense to your audience.

What Argument Structures Can I Use in My Speech Development?

Three basic structures of reasoning will help you develop your speech content: inductive reasoning, deductive reasoning, and sequential reasoning. Each consists of basic steps that will help you determine reasonable answers, and each is useful for thinking through different types of situations. Let's look briefly at these three structures.

Deduction usually reasons from accepted generalizations to a conclusion about a particular situation or person.[2] If, for example, you were trying to determine what would happen if you did not pay your library fine, you could reason deductively by finding a generalization or rule that covers the specific situation and include your specific example in it. You could say, "The student handbook says that all students who don't pay their library fines will have their grades held at the end of the term until they pay them." After deciding that your not paying the fine is included in the general category of this school rule, you could then reason that your grades will be held if you do not pay your fine. The essential characteristic of deduction is that instances are included in, or covered by, the generalization. Deductive reasoning enables you to make decisions when you are faced with understanding or resolving a specific situation that is included in an appropriate generalization. While deductive arguments are constructed to guarantee or "prove" the conclusion, inductive arguments cannot "prove" conclusions.

Inductive reasoning is a procedure for discovering new conclusions from available data. It is also useful for testing generalizations. This kind of thinking becomes increasingly important as new discoveries and unusual situations occur in our complex world. Scientific studies often use observations, experimentation, and induction to develop new generalizations and principles or to support old ones. As you discovered while doing library research, there is a lot of information on almost all topics. Induction enables you to summarize that information to draw new conclusions. An example of using inductive thinking would be figuring out what would happen if you tried to raise attendance at your club meetings by rewarding attendance for those people who came. You could collect examples of what happened on previous occasions when other clubs had tried positive rewards for attendance. Then you could make an inference based on these instances. Because it is impossible to be sure you have collected all the instances related to your situation, the results of inductive reasoning are said to be supported, not proved. The strength of your support and, therefore, the essential characteristic of induction is the representativeness of your selection of instances.

Today, both induction and deduction are widely used and are often used together to clarify or solve a problem. As illustrated in Figure 9-1, reasoning using

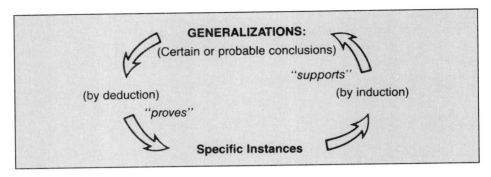

Figure 9-1   Cycle of Deduction and Induction

these two structures can be a continuous process. You can observe specific instances and, through induction, support generalizations. You can then apply those generalizations to other instances, through deduction, to prove a specific conclusion.

Sequential reasoning is the third structure that helps you think something through. Sequential reasoning examines the relationships between specific instances, concepts, or generalizations. We use this more general category of reasoning to identify: (1) the relationship between a cause and an effect; (2) the relationship between a problem and a solution; and (3) the relationship between a solution and the effects of implementing the solution. We treat it as a separate structure to focus attention on relationships as conclusions or arguments.

The following examples of arguments use each of the three types of reasoning:

DEDUCTIVE REASONING

MAJOR PREMISE:	All sophomores at this college are studious.
MINOR PREMISE:	All residents in Bookers Hall are sophomores at this college.
CONCLUSION:	Therefore, all residents in Bookers Hall are studious.

INDUCTIVE REASONING

SPECIFIC INSTANCES:	All the sophomore men I know at this college are studious. All the sophomore women I know at this college are studious.
CONCLUSION:	Probably all sophomores at this college are studious.

SEQUENTIAL REASONING

RELATIONSHIP CHECKS:	People who study get good grades. People who don't study don't get good grades. The more people study, the higher their grades are.
CONCLUSION:	Therefore, studying (probably) causes good grades.

Solving difficult questions involves deductive, inductive, and sequential reasoning.

How Can I Decide Which Reasoning Structure I Should Use for My Speech?

Each reasoning type answers different questions you may have about your topic. As we indicated earlier, the three reasoning structures will help you understand your speech topic and make appropriate decisions, conclusions, and relationships regarding the topic. For your specific topic, you might actually use all three types of reasoning at some point in your preparation. Let's say, for example, that you chose the specific topic "Alcoholism on This Campus." If you wanted to answer the question, What are the legal complications for students if they drink on campus?, you could use deductive reasoning by applying generalizations in the form of national, state, local, and campus rules covering drinking on campus. If you wanted to answer the question, How widespread is the problem of alcoholism on this campus?, you could use induction to gather specific information to draw conclusions about the seriousness of the situation. And if you wanted to answer the question, What are the main causes of drinking on this campus? or What are the effects of drinking on this campus?, you would be asking relationship questions and thus would use sequential reasoning. Answers to these questions could provide the basis for making a unique contribution to your audience's understanding of this topic. Table 9-1 lists examples of the kinds of questions that can be answered by each of the three types of reasoning structures.

In order to answer inductive questions, you will have to research representative information, which will be the basis for your conclusion. In order to answer deductive questions, you must research relevant generalizations. Both information and generalizations can answer sequential questions.

After answering your inductive, deductive, and sequential questions, it is important to consider how you will present your answers to your audience. To help you both develop and present your arguments effectively, we have outlined the information for each argument type (see Figures 9-2, 9-4, 9-6). Each outline has been divided into two parts: developing your argument and presenting your arguments.

TABLE 9-1   REASONING TYPES AND QUESTIONS ANSWERED

Reasoning Types	Kinds of Questions Answered
Inductive	What is the situation now? What is likely to happen in the future? What is the trend? When will something happen?
Deductive	How will a particular set of rules affect this situation? What are the characteristics of a particular instance? What decision is best?
Sequential	What is the cause of the problem? What will be the effects of the situation? What will solve the problem? What are the benefits of a particular solution? What will happen next?

LEARNING BY UNDERSTANDING

1. Define each of the three types of reasoning structures.

2. State the basic results you reach by using each structure of reasoning.

3. Name the type of reasoning that would be most helpful in answering each of the following questions.
    a. What will happen if I add sand to the clay soil in a garden?
    b. What causes divorce among student couples?
    c. What will the enrollment be at this school in five years?

ANSWERS:

1. Deduction reasons from accepted generalizations to a conclusion about a specific instance; induction reasons from representative instances to new generalizations; sequential reasoning examines the relationship between specific instances, concepts, or generalizations.
2. Deduction—proved decision; induction—supported conclusion; sequential—probable relationship.
3. **a.** deductive, **b.** sequential, **c.** inductive

INDUCTIVE REASONING

As indicated earlier, *inductive reasoning* is a procedure for drawing new conclusions. It usually moves from specific instances to a general conclusion. Figure 9-2 shows the steps for developing and presenting inductive reasoning.

What Are the Steps of Using Inductive Reasoning in My Speech Preparation?

The first step in applying inductive reasoning is hypothesizing a conclusion about the question you have asked. *Hypotheses* are guesses based on what you know

I. Develop inductive reasoning.
   A. Hypothesize a possible conclusion.
   B. Modify the possible conclusion after collecting information.
      1. Collect information.
      2. Test the information.
         a. Is the information relevant to the conclusion?
         b. Is the information recent?
         c. Is the information from a credible source?
         d. Is the information consistent with other available information?
      3. Modify the scope or the probability of the conclusion.

II. Present inductive reasoning.
   A. Choose the information to be presented.
      1. Choose the most representative and clearest information.
      2. Choose the appropriate number of instances.
      3. Select the order of the information.
   B. Present the information.
      1. Include dates.
      2. Include sources.
      3. Include unbiased or reluctant information.
   C. Present the conclusion.
      1. Qualify the conclusion in scope or probability.
      2. State the conclusion.

Figure 9-2   Using Inductive Reasoning

about the topic. The skills you developed in creative thinking as a research method in Chapter 5 will help you make your hypothesis. Brainstorming and What if? questions applied to your current knowledge are especially helpful. For example, you might be attempting to answer the question, When will the San Andreas Fault shift to the extent that western California will fall into the ocean? Your hypothesized conclusion might be that western California will fall into the ocean in 2005.

In step two, you modify your hypothesis by collecting information. Information collected by the research methods described in Chapter 5 will be helpful here. Many developing, clarifying, and supporting materials discussed in that chapter are examples of information in one form or another. Some information, such as statistics, are facts, and some, such as quotations, are opinions.

How Can I Test My Information?

Several tests of information have been developed that will help you reach the most reasonable conclusions.[3] The first and most important test—*relevance*—concerns the idea of *representativeness*. The accuracy of your conclusion will depend on how well each specific instance you chose was directly related to the conclusion. For example, if you are doing research on the extent to which the San Andreas Fault creates a hazard for homeowners in western California, you might find an excellent research study on the topography of the ocean floor off Los Angeles. But no matter how intriguing that information is, it is not directly relevant to the fault or to your hypothesis.

The second test—*recency*—is based on the premise that the most recent evidence is the most acceptable. In our rapidly changing world, facts are constantly changing as a result of new research. Thus, your audience will tend to regard the most recent information as the best.

The third test—having a credible source—includes mentioning both who said what and the context in which it was said. In Chapter 8, you learned the components of *credibility* that audiences use to judge you as a speaker. You can apply the same standards to your choice of sources for your inductive reasoning. The two most important standards for credible sources are those of competence and trustworthiness. A source's competence should be directly established in the area to which the information refers. For example, if you were looking for information to check your hypothesis about the San Andreas Fault, you would seek a person or agency whose expertise was directly related to faults.

Let's check your skills in determining the trustworthiness of a competent source. In your research about the dangers of the San Andreas Fault for western Californians, you see a brochure urging people to buy land in western California. The brochure contains a quotation from a geologist employed by the California Real Estate Association. The geologist says that the San Andreas Fault will not be a hazard until at least 2100. Do you think the expert may be somewhat biased? How about the real estate association? Now what do you think about the trustworthiness of the source on this topic?

There are three categories of evidence that will help you determine a source's trustworthiness on a topic—unbiased, reluctant, and biased information.[4] *Unbiased* information comes from a competent source who has nothing to gain from his or her statements. *Reluctant* sources of information are people or media who could gain from the issue but who provide information that either does not support or is actually contrary to their interests. For example, if the geologist says that the San Andreas Fault may be a problem by 1995, he would be giving reluctant testimoy because that statement would not help sell real estate in that area. Obviously, audiences believe unbiased and reluctant information more than biased information.[5] The *biased* category is from the source who has something to gain and who provides information to support his or her own interests. The geologist quoted in the brochure is an example of a biased source. Of course, just because a source has something to gain does not necesarily mean the evidence is biased. But it helps to keep this in mind to identify information that might be inaccurate and less acceptable to an intelligent audience.

Finally, the fourth test considers if all your information is *consistent*. If you check a variety of biased, unbiased, and reluctant sources and find information that consistently supports your possible conclusion, you will be in good shape. If, on the other hand, there are disagreements between the biased and the unbiased sources, these negative examples will narrow or change your possible conclusion.

After completing your research, you will modify the scope or probability of your inferred conclusion. For example, you might change the date of western California's falling into the ocean to 2020. Or you might say "probably will fall into the ocean" instead of "will fall into the ocean." This is important because generalizations only approximate reality. It is especially difficult to predict things that may happen in the future. Probability is important in induction for several reasons. For one, in your research you have only covered a fraction of the available examples or instances. For another, nothing is the same in all areas. For example, in the United States, crime (or bicycle sales) might be up 15 percent for a particular year; however, most of these increases in crime (or bicycle sales) might occur in certain states or cities. It is important to modify the scope or the degree of certainty of your conclusions.

How Can I Present the Results of My Inductive Reasoning?

As you prepare to communicate the results of your inductive reasoning, it is essential that you first select representative data to support your possible conclusion. The most helpful data will be clear and directly included in your generalization. Second, it is helpful to use information that you perceive to be psychologically important to your audience. If you are attempting to draw a conclusion about changing patterns in crime, statistics or quotations related to your audience's locale will be more effective than information about distant places.

We are assuming that your research will produce more examples than you could use in one speech. So, if your credibility is high and the audience is favorable, one or two examples may be enough. But these two situations are usually less true when you choose to use an inductive presentation. Generally, the lower your initial credibility or the more unfavorable your audience's attitudes are, the more support you will need. In this case, you should include as many supports as necessary to result in favorable, affirmative audience responses. If the audience is initially unfavorable to your position, data from a reluctant source would be best. Watch the audience for nods of acceptance that indicate you have provided enough support.

Your decisions on arranging your supports also will be based on your specific audience. It is probably best to arrange the data according to the audience's acceptance of your sources. Thus, you would give your best-known, least biased, most acceptable sources first. This will not only increase the audience's willingness to accept your induced conclusion, it will also raise your credibility. That is, the audience will think, "This speaker really has studied what important people have to say on this topic." We suggest that you save the data you decide not to use in the body of your speech for answering questions after your speech.

The final step is indicating the conclusion your data supports. You should mention any modification in scope or certainty of your conclusion. Because induction leads to probable, not certain, conclusions, your use of appropriately modified conclusions will communicate that you are a trustworthy person.

Can I Say I Have ''Proved'' Something by Using Inductive Reasoning?

No. The conclusions you make as a result of inductive reasoning are not proved; they are *supported*. In other words, you have "provided evidence for them." That is because it is impossible to find all specific instances related to the question you are asking. Support focuses attention on the audience's acceptance of the specific instances you have chosen and increases its willingness to accept the conclusion you have made from your collected information.

LEARNING BY UNDERSTANDING

1. List the two basic steps involved in developing inductive reasoning.

2. What principle is the most important check on inductive reasoning?

3. List the four basic tests used on information gathered for inductive reasoning.

4. Apply the four tests of information to the following examples gathered for a speech on the appropriateness of current marijuana laws. Indicate which examples do not meet any of the tests. The hypothesis is "marijuana should be legalized."
    a. A poll of people aged eighteen to twenty-one currently in prison for marijuana offenses revealed that 98 percent felt the laws were too strict.
    b. In a news conference on the results of laboratory tests done this year on the effects of marijuana, a professor of research physiology at a leading university stated, "The negative effects of marijuana have been greatly exaggerated."
    c. It is legal for American Indian tribes to use peyote, a hallucinogen, in tribal ceremonies.
    d. Americans are attending regular church services less frequently than they did five years ago.

ANSWERS:

1. Hypothesize a possible conclusion; modify the conclusion after collecting information.
2. The representativeness, or relevancy, of each item of information is the most important check on inductive reasoning.
3. Relevancy; recency; source credibility; consistency.
4. a. Would be biased information and, therefore, less acceptable to an audience (if you used it to support the need for change). b. Looks good. If it is consistent with other information, it would meet all the tests. c. Has possibilities. For most audiences, you would need to supply information to show that the substances were similar enough to be considered relevant. d. Is not directly relevant.

DEDUCTIVE REASONING

Deductive reasoning helps you understand specific situations by relating them to larger categories or generalizations that cover them. Essentially, deduction is the attempt to clarify a specific situation by stating a general rule that covers that situation. Just as the representativeness of each specific instance is the important principle in inductive reasoning, *inclusion* is the important principle in deduction. This principle involves determining whether the specific situation is "included in" the larger category. Figure 9-3 visualizes the principle of inclusion.

Almost all deductive reasoning can be developed and checked by using a form of logical demonstration called the *syllogism*.[6] A syllogism has three parts: a major premise, a minor premise, and a conclusion. The *major premise* is the generalization, or larger category, in the syllogism. It includes the specific instance with which you are working, along with a characteristic. The *minor premise* is the specific instance and is the second statement in the syllogism. The *conclusion*

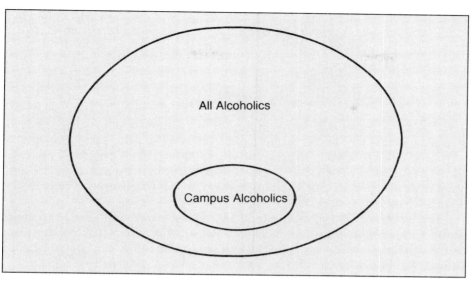

Figure 9-3   The Principle of Inclusion

applies the generalization in the major premise to the specific instance in the minor premise. Here is an example of a syllogism:

MAJOR PREMISE:	All true alcoholics have vitamin B deficiencies.
MINOR PREMISE:	Campus alcoholics are true alcoholics.
CONCLUSION:	Therefore, campus alcoholics have vitamin B_3 deficiencies.

"All alcoholics," the larger category in this syllogism, is stated in the first statement along with a characteristic and is called the ***major premise***. "Campus alcoholics," the specific instance in this syllogism, is stated in the second statement, which is called the ***minor premise***. As visualized, the specific instance of "campus alcoholics" is included in the larger category of "all alcoholics." Because what is true about the larger category applies to the specific instance, you can conclude that "campus alcoholics have Vitamin B_3 deficiencies."

How Can I Use Deductive Reasoning for My Speech?

You can use deductive reasoning to answer questions about your topic if your specific situation is covered by a more general category or rule. Examine Mary Nielsen's speech "The World Caste System" in Appendix B to see her use of deductive reasoning. She wants us to conclude that foreign diplomats living in the United States should be subject to United States laws. She works with inclusion when she argues that diplomats and their families who live in the United States are a specific instance of the larger category "People who live in the United States are subject to United States laws." If we agree that this category of people is included, then we must conclude that they should also be subjected to U.S. laws.

Figure 9-4 details the steps for developing and presenting deductive reasoning.

What Are the Steps of Using Deductive Reasoning in My Speech Preparation?

The first step in applying deductive reasoning to questions about your speech topic is to state clearly the specific instance or conclusion you are trying to understand or have decided to make a main point of your speech. For example, if you want to use "campus alcoholics have vitamin B_3 deficiencies" as a main point of your speech, deductive reasoning would be one way you could investigate or prove the soundness of that main point.

The second step in deductive reasoning would be to determine a major premise that covers or includes campus alcoholics and for which your conclusion is true. You want to be able to say, "Because this major premise is true *and* because campus alcoholics are included in that major premise, my conclusion is true."

The third major step in developing reasoning is using the principle of inclusion to determine if your specific instance is included in the major premise. This involves reasoning from the premise or generalization to your specific instance. Any of the developing, clarifying, or supporting procedures in Chapter 5 can be used to provide the link between your specific instance and your generalization. For example, you could use an accepted source that says it is included or a definition that shows it is.

The fourth step in developing deductive reasoning is to make the connection between the stated characteristics or part of the major premise you are interested in and the inferred characteristics of the minor premise. Thus, you can conclude,

Figure 9-4 Using Deductive Reasoning

I. Develop deductive reasoning.
    A. Clearly state the specific instance, decision, or conclusion you want to check through deductive reasoning.
    B. Determine related generalizations or rules which would be acceptable to your audience from audience analysis.
    C. Use the principle of inclusion to determine if your specific instance is included in the category.
    D. Draw a conclusion by applying the appropriate characteristics of the major category to your specific instance.

II. Present deductive reasoning.
    A. Decide which parts of your reasoning you need to present to your audience based on audience analysis.
    B. Decide in which order you want to present the needed parts.
    C. Present the argument.

"Because you agree that the major premise is true and that the minor premise is contained within the major premise, this particular characteristic of the major premise is true for the minor premise." In the campus alcoholism topic, you would be ready to conclude that campus alcoholics have vitamin B_3 deficiencies.

How Can I Determine Major Premises That Will Be Acceptable to My Audience?

Because you are using reasoned thinking to develop materials for a particular audience, it is important to start from major premises that will be acceptable to that audience. That is, you will want to begin your argument on a note of agreement between you and your audience. As Aristotle said, "We must not, therefore, start from any and every accepted opinion; but only from those . . . accepted by our judges or by those whose authority they recognize."[7] Major premises that are acceptable to audiences are usually those about which they know or feel something. In this example, your audience probably would accept the general statement, "All true alcoholics have vitamin B_3 deficiencies," if you supply appropriate information.

You can determine acceptable major premises by using the results of your audience analysis to determine what your audience knows and believes about

Understanding a listener's needs and values will provide major premises from which to reason.

your topic and related categories. If you cannot discover, from a direct or indirect source, the premises most acceptable to your specific audience, then you could use your understanding of people who are similar to your audience in terms of basic descriptive data.

Any of the needs and related values you and your classmates developed as part of the Learning by Interacting in Chapter 8 could provide the basis for a major premise. You could make an inference about the needs and related values that are most appropriate for your audience and build a premise from those concerns. For example, if you infer that your audience values good health, you could build the following deductive structure:

Good health is important.
A nutritious diet leads to good health.

Therefore, a nutritious diet is important.

Basic audience values are often stated in the form of *maxims*, which are short rules of conduct or general truths. Examples are "Necessity is the mother of invention," "Time is money," and "All things in moderation." So, if you are not sure of specific things your audience believes or knows about your specific instance, you could use a maxim as a major premise.

Because it is also important to represent ethically your own knowledge and beliefs about the topic area, you will want to consider what premises are acceptable to both you and your audience. Do you remember using the two intersecting circles to identify the selection of a speech topic by the overlap of your audience's and

Figure 9-5   Beginning Deductive Reasoning

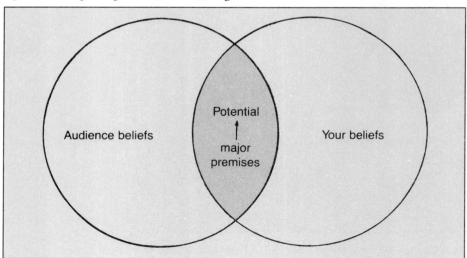

your own interests (see Figure 4-3)? You can use the same diagram to indicate the areas of overlap between your premises and your audience's premises. Figure 9-5 shows how these circles can help you find the beginning point for your deductive reasoning.

How Can I Present the Results of My Deductive Reasoning?

The first step is determining which parts of your reasoning you must present to this particular audience to have it accept the overall conclusion of your reasoning. Speakers usually express their deductive reasoning in an abbreviated form, without stating all the parts of that reasoning. This abbreviated form involves the audience by allowing it to supply the missing parts of the syllogism. Those parts of the reasoning the audience already understands or believes do not need to be stated in your speech. In fact, if you spend much time developing and supporting an idea it already believes, your audience might become bored. For example, if your audience strongly believes that campus alcoholics are similar to all alcoholics, your reasoning could be expressed as follows:

MAJOR PREMISE:	All true alcoholics have vitamin B_3 deficiencies.
CONCLUSION:	Therefore, campus alcoholics have vitamin B_3 deficiencies.

Or if your audience believes or knows that all alcoholics have vitamin B_3 deficiencies, your reasoning could be expressed by saying:

MINOR PREMISE:	Campus alcoholics are similar to all alcoholics.
CONCLUSION:	Therefore, campus alcoholics have vitamin B_3 deficiencies.

In either case, the audience members will provide the missing part of the reasoning structure in their own minds.

The second step in presenting the results of your deductive thinking is determining the order in which to present the premise(s) and conclusion. You will choose between giving a premise(s) first and then your conclusion, or the reverse. When starting with a premise, present the premise that is most acceptable to your audience first. Then present the rest of your argument. The two alternatives would look like this:

A premise first: "All true alcoholics have vitamin B_3 deficiencies as shown by . . . Because campus alcoholics are true alcoholics . . . Therefore, campus alcoholics have vitamin B_3 deficiencies."

A conclusion first: "Campus alcoholics have vitamin B_3 deficiencies because all true alcoholics have vitamin B_3 deficiencies and because campus alcoholics are true alcoholics."

LEARNING BY UNDERSTANDING

1. Name and describe the three parts of a syllogism.

2. Name the key principle involved in using deductive reasoning.

3. Apply the principle of inclusion to the following syllogisms. Indicate those in which the minor premise is not included in the major premise.
   a. All cars that are out of gas don't run. My car doesn't run. Therefore, it is out of gas.
   b. All students can attend free. I am a student. Therefore, I can attend free.
   c. No movie stars are CPAs. All CPAs are people with good business sense. Therefore, no movie stars are people with good business sense.

4. Assume you are working on a speech on the values of eating a balanced diet and you want to conclude that it is important to eat a balanced diet. Write three different major premises from which you could start your deductive reasoning. They should be acceptable to you and most audiences.

5. Imagine that you plan to speak to your local PTA. You want to conclude that "gay teachers should have equal job rights." What are two major premises that you believe? Is the audience likely to believe these premises would lead to your conclusion?

ANSWERS:

1. The major premise is the generalization from which you begin your reasoning. The minor premise is the specific instance included in the major premise. The conclusion is a statement of the characteristic of the major premise that you conclude is also part of the minor premise.
2. Inclusion
3. **a.** not included; **b.** included; **c.** not included. In a. and c., we have reworded the minor premise so that it is not included in the major premise. You will be able to see this clearly if you use the circle diagrams.
4. One possible answer might be "you are what you eat." Check your answers with someone else in the class.
5. One possible major premise is "privacy is a basic right of all people." Check your answers with someone else in the class.

SEQUENTIAL REASONING

A third reasoning structure you can use is sequental. Essentially, *sequential reasoning* involves establishing a relationship between two or more events, concepts, or generalizations. The main types of relationships speakers use are cause leading to effect, solution solving a problem, and solution leading to benefits. With sequential reasoning, you are investigating, or showing, that one thing *has* led to another or that one thing *will* lead to another. Sequential reasoning answers *cause/effect questions*, such as What is the cause of juvenile delinquency? substance abuse? cancer? poor test grades? divorce? It also answers *solution/effect* or *benefit questions*, such as What will be the effect of a Middle East settlement? a Central American dispute? an approach to a famine in Africa? You have probably heard people make inferences about the answers to these questions. By developing skills in sequential reasoning, you will be able to reason through such difficult questions and also be able to support your answers when you communicate them to others. Sequential reasoning is especially helpful in making predictions about the future.[8]

The key to using induction is establishing the representativeness of specific instances, and the key to using deduction is establishing the inclusion of a particular instance in a larger category. The key to using sequential reasoning is establishing a relationship between a hypothesized cause and effect or between a solution and an effect. Sequential reasoning will help you determine if such a relationship exists.

The steps involved in developing and presenting sequential reasoning are detailed in Figure 9-6.

What Are the Steps of Using Sequential Reasoning in My Speech Preparation?

The first step in using sequential reasoning is hypothesizing the relationship between a cause and an effect (or a solution and an effect). If you have already done some initial research, you may infer the realtionship from your research. You could also brainstorm to infer a connection. A hypothesis from any of these procedures will focus your later research on the most likely relationships. For example, from your reading, experience, and thinking, you may hypothesize that the emphasis on grades in American higher education is a cause of student alcoholism.

The second step in using sequential reasoning is collecting the information that will help you test the hypothesized relationship. If you are working with a cause/effect relationship, it is helpful to identify the symptoms of the problem first. If you repeatedly find similar symptoms, you may have found the key to discovering the cause. For investigating the relationship of grades to student alcoholism, you

Figure 9-6   Using Sequential Reasoning

> I. Develop sequential reasoning.
>   A. Hypothesize the relationship between the elements.
>   1. Use research.
>   2. Use brainstorming.
>   3. Use creative insight.
>   B. Collect relevant information.
>   1. Identify symptoms or possible effects.
>   2. Research parallel examples.
>   C. Use basic checks to determine existence of relationships.
>   1. If the cause (solution) occurs, does the effect (benefit) always occur?
>   2. If the cause (solution) does not occur, does the effect (benefit) not occur?
>   3. If more of the cause (solution) is present, does more of the effect (benefit) occur?
>
> II. Present sequential reasoning.
>   A. Identify an audience-relevant reason for the importance of the relationship.
>   B. Demonstrate the relationship.
>   1. Present parallel examples.
>   2. Present examples to show that basic checks establish a relationship.

would collect specific information about student alcoholism—what times during the school year is drinking heaviest and what are the grade averages of the students who drink heavily. If you are working with a solution/effect relationship, this step involves identifying possible effects of a solution. A second way to collect information is to research *parallel examples*, or those that are the same except for the aspect you want to compare. For example, it would be helpful to have information on student drinking at schools where competitive grading is used as opposed to schools where a pass-fail grading system is used.

The third step in sequential reasoning is applying checks to determine if the relationship between the two elements exists. John Stuart Mill, a nineteenth-century English economist, provided these three helpful checks on that relationship:

1. If the cause (solution) occurs, does the effect (benefit) always occur?
2. If the cause (solution) does not occur, does the effect (benefit) not occur?
3. If more of the cause (solution) is present, does more of the effect (benefit) occur?[9]

For example, in examining the relationship between emphasis on grades and campus alcoholism, you would use the information gathered in your research to answer these questions:

1. Where there is an emphasis on high grades in American higher education, does drinking always occur?
2. Where there is no emphasis on high grades in American higher education, does alcoholism never occur?
3. Does more drinking occur during times of grade-related stress?

This step helps you check your hypothesized relationships because most of the complex questions you will want to answer do not have single causes for a given effect or single effects resulting from a given solution. You probably will find several related causes or several related effects. For example, in the relationship of grade stress to student alcoholism, your research and basic checks probably will not show that grade stress is the *only* cause of student alcoholism. Thus, sequential reasoning is similar to inductive reasoning in that you do not reach absolute answers. You can, however, determine and then present the relative strength of a relationship, adding an appropriate qualifying statement to your conclusion to reflect the strength of the relationship. Your final results actually are probability statements about the likelihood of a certain effect resulting from the implementation of a solution. This kind of thinking resulted in the Surgeon General's office issuing a warning against cigarette smoking. The statement says that testing indicates that the effect of cancer occurs more often after the possible cause of smoking has occurred. The absence of an absolute causal relationship means that testing did not reveal a cause/effect relationship; that is, some people who do not smoke still get cancer. However, the more a person smokes, the more likely he or she is to get cancer.

How Can I Present the Results of My Sequential Reasoning?

The first step is to identify the significance of the relationship to audience members by relating it to a need or value that is important to them. You will then be able to apply your understanding of people in general to your specific audience as you did for determining major premises in deductive reasoning.

The last step in presenting the results of your sequential reasoning to your audience is to demonstrate the relationship by including enough parallel examples and information showing that the basic checks establish a relationship. If your credibility is high, fewer examples will be necessary. As with other forms of reasoning, you will choose examples that your listeners can understand and accept. This means talking about places, people, and situations with which they are familiar and in which they can see themselves involved. As you demonstrate the relationship, you should indicate any appropriate qualifications by using such phrases as "most likely leads to" or "in over half the cases, this effect results from this solution."

How Do My Reasoned Arguments Become Part of My Speech?

You will use the results of your reasoning mainly in the body of informative and persuasive speeches. Specifically, the conclusion of your argument could be your central idea, with the parts of your argument being the main points of your speech (e.g., premises for deductive, groups of instances for inductive, and basic checks for sequential reasoning). Also, if your central idea includes several arguments, the conclusion of each argument would be a main point, and the parts of that argument would be the subpoints.

For example, Mary Nielsen, a student at Northern Illinois University, used a deductive argument as the structure of her speech "The Dark Side of Freedom." She established as her major premise the American belief that freedom is important to all people. Then she argued, as her minor premise, that mentally ill people should *not* be considered a specific instance of this general belief. She concluded that total freedom is not the appropriate treatment for mentally ill people. To develop her minor premise, she used inductive reasoning. Nielsen provided specific instances to show that mentally ill people are unique in ways that make their inclusion in the generalization inappropriate. She supported her conclusion by arguing sequentially that total freedom for mentally ill people leads to societal and personal problems.

LEARNING BY UNDERSTANDING

1. List the two kinds of information you would research to establish a relationship between two factors.

2. Assume you were using sequential reasoning to determine if there was a relationship between

blondness and becoming a college cheerleader. Write three questions that reflect the three basic tests of a relationship described by Mill.

3. Give an example of parallel examples that could test the relationship between drinking at least ten cups of coffee a day and getting ulcers.

4. Here are three arguments about sending college students' midterm grades home to their parents. Fill in the type of reasoning each represents and name the parts of the argument.

   a. Type of argument (1) _____
   Parts

   (2) _____ As one of their major objectives, colleges promote the development of students as independent decision makers.

   (3) _____ Sending student's grades to parents is not a procedure that encourages independent decision making.

   (4) _____ Therefore, sending midterm grades to parents is not in agreement with one of the colleges' major objectives.

   b. Type of argument (1) _____
   Parts

   (2) _____ The estimated cost of teacher time in sending midterm grades is $___.
   The bill for keypunch time in sending midterm grades is $___.
   The bill for mailing midterm grades is $___.

   (3) _____ Therefore, sending midterm grade reports to parents is an expensive procedure.

   c. Type of argument (1) _____
   Parts

   (2) _____ Students whose parents push or praise them as a result of midterm grade reports do not necessarily do better.
   Students who receive no feedback from parents often do better the second half of the term than those who receive feedback.
   Across all students, grades did not go up any higher during the semesters when grades were sent home at midterm than during the semesters when they were not.

   (3) _____ Therefore, parental response to midterm grade reports does not necessarily lead to higher grades.

5. For each of the following arguments, identify the type it represents and apply the appropriate checks to determine if it meets the standards for that type.

   a. Coke Classic has less calories than Pepsi.
   Coke Classic sells more than Pepsi.
   Coke Classic has one-third less caffeine than Pepsi.
   The president of Coke prefers it.
   Therefore, Coke Classic tastes better than Pepsi.

   b. Some politicians are corrupt.
   Richard Moe is a politician.
   Therefore, Richard Moe is corrupt.

   c. Not every couple who loves each other has a lasting marriage.
   Some couples who do not love each other have a lasting marriage.
   More couples who love each other avoid divorce than couples who do not.
   Therefore, if two people love each other, their marriage will surely last.

ANSWERS:

1. Parallel examples, symptoms
2. When a blond tries out for cheerleading, does she/he always make it? When a non-blond tries out for cheerleading, does she/he never make it? Do more blonds who try out for cheerleading make it than non-blonds who try out?
3. Parallel examples would be two groups of people that are similar except that one includes people who drink at least ten cups of coffee per day and the other includes people who drink less than ten cups of coffee per day.

4. a. (1) deductive, (2) major premise, (3) minor premise, (4) conclusion
   b. (1) inductive, (2) specific instances, (3) conclusion
   c. (1) sequential, (2) relationship checks, (3) conclusion
5. a. Inductive Argument. While each of the specific instances is consistently positive for Coke Classic; no dates are given to check if the information is recent. Only the fourth instance is related to the conclusion regarding taste, and it is clearly biased toward the product.
   b. Deductive Argument. The argument does not meet the basic test of inclusion for deductive reasoning. Since the major premise states that "some" politicians, rather than "all" politicians, are corrupt, the minor premise does not necessarily fit into the major premise. Therefore, we cannot prove that Moe is corrupt by this argument.
   c. Sequential Argument. The structure of this argument does apply the three relationship checks, but you would want to check the support for the third one. This could be supported by inductive reasoning, but the specific instances chosen would be important. If the third relationship check is adequately supported, the argument would still not meet the standards. The conclusion is stated in an exaggerated way with the word *surely*. The relationship checks do not justify such a strong word.

LEARNING BY INTERACTING

Work with others in your class to develop and fine-tune examples of each of the three types of reasoning for a single issue of common interest. After selecting an issue, divide into small groups of four to five people. Each group will do the following:

For each type of reasoning: (1) develop two questions that type of reasoning could answer about the issue, and (2) develop and check one argument that meets the tests for that type of reasoning and that would be acceptable to your class. If possible, do the necessary research to prove or support your conclusion. If not, use your combined frames of reference to develop the most "reasonable" arguments. Be prepared to describe how you chose the parts of your arguments and how you determined their accuracy.

When each group has completed its arguments, have one person from each group report the arguments to the class. Discuss the different ways the issue was handled and which arguments would be most effective for this class.

LEARNING BY SPEAKING

Prepare a five- to seven-minute informative speech that expresses your views and the reasons for your views on a current national problem. Your written preparation should include an audience analysis and a sentence outline. Use at least two of the forms of reasoning to develop and present your arguments. Include a bibliography indicating your research. In the margin of your outline, indicate where you are developing all of the parts of your arguments.

REVIEW

Reasoning is one of the most important speaking-related skills. Three basic types of reasoning are inductive, deductive, and sequential. Each type of reasoning can be used for answering different questions related to a speech topic.

The essential test of effective inductive reasoning is the representativeness of the specific instance used to reason to a generalization. The essential test of effective deductive reasoning is the inclusion of the particular instance within a general category. And the essential test of effective sequential reasoning is the existence of a relationship between the hypothesized elements.

NOTES

1. Gerald M. Messner and Nancy S. Messner, *Patterns of Thinking*, 2d ed. (Belmont, Calif.: Wadsworth Publishing Co., 1974), 39.

2. Howard Kahane, *Logic and Philosophy* (Belmont, Calif.: Wadsworth Publishing Co., 1973), 231.

3. Robert P. Newman and Dale R. Newman, *Evidence* (Boston: Houghton Mifflin, 1969), 87–88.

4. James C. McCroskey, *An Introduction to Rhetorical Communication*, 3d ed. (Englewood Cliffs, N.J.: Prentice-Hall, 1978), 120–121.

5. W. E. Arnold and J. C. McCroskey, "The Credibility of Reluctant Testimony," *Central States Speech Journal* 18(May 1967):97.

6. Steven F. Barker, *The Elements of Logic*, 2d ed. (New York: McGraw-Hill, 1974), 76–78.

7. Richard McKeon, ed., *The Basic Works of Aristotle* (New York: Random House, 1941), 1417.

8. Newman and Newman, *Evidence*, chap. 3.

9. J. Stuart Mill, *A System of Logic* (London: Longmans, 1924).

10

CHOOSING EFFECTIVE LANGUAGE

In this chapter, you'll be . . .

LEARNING BY UNDERSTANDING

- The two types of meanings audiences call to mind
- The three principles of effective language use
- The relationship of clarity, appropriateness, and vividness to denotative and connotative meanings
- The three characteristics of clear language
- Specific words that can be unclear to an audience
- The basis for language appropriateness
- The characteristics of language vividness
- How to develop vivid language

LEARNING BY INTERACTING

- Developing alternative language choices for communicating an idea

LEARNING BY SPEAKING

- A four- to five-minute informative speech explaining a strong personal belief

CHAPTER OUTLINE

I. Language choices influence the meanings an audience will attach to your ideas.
   A. Symbols call up two kinds of meanings in the minds of your audience members.
      1. Denotative meanings are called up about the thing or idea to which the symbol refers.
      2. Connotative meanings are called up about the feelings associated with the thing or idea.
   B. Careful symbol choices will call up the meanings you intended from your audience.
   C. Language choices should be based on your analysis of the audience's frame of reference.

II. There are three principles of effective language use.
   A. Language clarity aids audience understanding.
   B. Language appropriateness reduces distraction, distortion, and loss of credibility.
   C. Language vividness gives impact to ideas.

III. Language clarity, the most important principle, limits the possible meanings an audience will attach to your words.
   A. Clear language is familiar.
      1. Choose words an audience could recognize immediately.
      2. Define unknown, but important, words early in the speech.
   B. Clear language is appropriately concrete.
      1. Concrete words refer to something that can be experienced through the human senses.
      2. Concrete words have more impact.
   C. Clear language is appropriately specific.
      1. Specific words are more exact, precise, and definite.
      2. Specific words add impact to your message.
   D. There are three types of clear language that may be specific but unfamiliar.
      1. Large numbers are specific but difficult to understand.
         a. Compare large numbers to something the audience knows.
         b. Round off large numbers.
      2. Technical language can be unfamiliar to some audiences.
      3. Slang terms can be unclear if the audience does not use them.

IV. Language appropriateness relates to the expectations of your audience.
   A. Appropriate language is that which meets the expectations of the listeners.
   B. Inappropriate language is distracting and lowers your credibility.
   C. Appropriate language calls up acceptable and familiar connotations.
   D. Appropriate language should be acceptable to the audience; the speaker's education, status, and profession; the situation; and the subject of the speech.

audiences would have connotative meanings for inflation, but some might not have an exact denotative meaning. It would be important, therefore, to define such words early in your message and also to use as many concrete and specific words as possible to compensate for the unfamiliarity.

Thirdly, the more specific a word is, the more likely it is to be clearly understood. Specific words are more exact, precise and definite. Some words and phrases have many meanings. For example, if someone told you that a football team had "a winning season," that phrase could mean that the team's record was six wins and five losses or that the team was eleven and zero and won the conference championship. The phrase "a winning season" is not clear, because it could refer to many different records. Your goal is to choose words that will reduce the number of possible meanings to the one you intend. In addition to clarifying your specific meaning, specific words also add impact to your idea. Consider the differences in the following:

General Words	Specific Words
fresh vegetables	sweet corn picked today
a winning team	a football record of six and five
daily exercise	exercising at least ten minutes a day
a hot oven	a 450-degree oven
several times	four times
a computer	an IBM PC Jr. personal computer

Are More Specific Words Always Better?

The words you choose should be both specific *and* familiar. There are three types of specific words you should use only if they are also familiar to the audience.

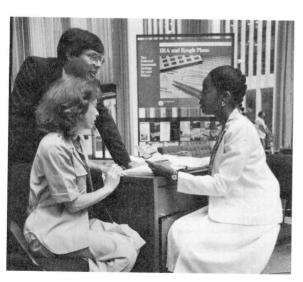

A speaker's message is most clear when word choice is adjusted to a level of concreteness the listeners will understand.

Many people have difficulty attaching a clear meaning to numbers, especially large ones. For example, you can tell an audience that 587 traffic accidents in your city last year were caused by drunken drivers. While your audience will realize that the number is large, it will be able to attach more meaning to it if you place the number in a ratio with something it already knows. You could, for example, compare the number of traffic accidents caused by drunken drivers with the number of students in your school. It is also helpful to round off large numbers, such as saying "almost 600." As developed in Chapter 6, using visual aids, such as charts and graphs, is another way to help audiences understand large numbers.

Technical terms also are specific words that have meaning only if they are familiar to the audience. For example, "VO_2max" is a specific phrase that probably would be understood only by someone in the field of exercise physiology. And the "Jacoby Two No Trump Convention" would have meaning only to people who play bridge.

A final type of language that can be specific but not familiar enough to have universal meaning is slang or jargon. Slang words can be meaningful to small groups of people but may have little meaning or different meanings for people who do not use them. For this reason and others, slang terms are usually inappropriate in public speeches.

LEARNING BY UNDERSTANDING

1. Name and define the two main types of meaning people attach to symbols.

2. Give your denotative and connotative meanings for the word *job*.

3. Identify each of the following as a denotative meaning or a connotative meaning.
   a. A chicken is a bird that lays eggs.
   b. Taking vitamin E will make me look younger.
   c. Police officers are friends of the people.

4. The three principles of effective language style are _____ .

5. Denotative meanings are most related to the language principle(s) of _____ ; while connotative meanings are most related to the principle(s) of _____ .

6. The three desirable characteristics of clear language are _____ .

7. Which of the following would be "clear" language for your public speaking class?
   a. Soccer
   b. Tort
   c. Diet cola
   d. Jerusalem artichoke

ANSWERS:

1. Denotative meaning refers to the idea or object that a symbol calls to mind; connotative meaning refers to the feelings that a symbol calls to mind.
2. Your denotative meaning may refer to agreed on work for which a person receives some compensation; your connotative meaning will be your own personal reactions to the work.
3. a. denotative, b. connotative, c. connotative
4. Clarify; appropriateness; vividness
5. Clarity; appropriateness and vividness
6. Concrete, familiar and specific
7. The answers here would depend on the people in your class. We would imagine that your audience would understand a. and c. and be less likely to understand b. and d. (Tort means a civil crime, and a Jerusalem artichoke is a vegetable.)

What about Language Appropriateness?

Language *appropriateness* refers to the expectations of your audience. When people listen to a public speech, they usually listen for the ideas, not the language. It is only when their expectations of appropriateness are not met that the language becomes noticeable and, therefore, distracting. If your language is noticeably inappropriate, your ideas and your credibility will suffer. Appropriate language typically calls up acceptable and comfortable connotations from a particular audience. Language that is inappropriate in most public speaking situations includes vulgar language, improper grammar, and language that negatively describes specific groups of people.

Language should be acceptable to the audience. In this respect, language appropriateness resembles clarity; appropriate language for a given audience is based on that audience's special interests, knowledge, and attitudes. However, appropriateness also has to do with the connotation or emotional meanings attached to words. Thus, the words *retirement, death,* and *old folks* would have more emotional meanings for senior citizens than they would for a group of high school seniors. Sometimes, words that are chosen by a speaker for their denotative meanings accidently distract the audience because of the emotional connotative meanings they call up.

The audience should perceive the language as appropriate to the speaker in terms of his or her education, status, and profession. This somewhat limits the extent to which the speaker should adapt his or her language according to the audience. For example, a bank president would not want to adopt the language of a rural farm community, nor would a radio disc jockey want to use extremely formal language. Such language would draw attention to itself and reduce the speaker's credibility.

Language should be appropriate to the situation. A rural audience will expect more exact and precise language if the speaker's purpose is to talk about the latest methods of applying herbicides to crops. On the other hand, the language of an entertaining after-dinner speech should be more vivid and colorful.

Finally, the subject you are dealing with suggests what language is appropriate. Your language choices for main points and conclusions should reflect the degree of probability suggested by your research and reasoning. Using such terms as *obviously, without exception, in all cases,* and *totally wrong* would be inappropriate for an issue subject to many possible interpretations. By appropriately qualifying your statements, you will increase your credibility and help your audience make reasoned choices about your speech context.

Because appropriateness, as well as clarity, is determined by the audience you are talking to, you should use the results of your audience analysis to guide your language choices.

How Can I Use Vivid Language?

Vividness of language is another characteristic that refers mainly to the connotative meanings an audience will attach to your words. Vivid language helps the audience form a strong mental picture of your idea and also helps them remember it. The quality of carefully chosen language that helps people form mental pictures is called *imagery*. Imagery helps an audience to experience your ideas by involving many of their senses.

In the following example, the speaker, a victim of hemophilia, uses vivid words to help his audience understand the nature of his disease:

> Medical authorities agree that a hemophilic joint hemorrhage is one of the most excruciating pains known to mankind. To concentrate a large amount of blood into a small, compact area causes a pressure that words can never hope to describe. And how well I remember the endless pounding, squeezing pain. When you seemingly drown in your own perspiration; when your teeth ache from incessant clenching; when your tongue floats in your mouth and bombs explode back of your eyeballs; when darkness and light fuse into one hue of gray; when day becomes night and night becomes day—time stands still—and all that matters is that ugly pain. The scars of pain are not easily erased.[2]

While most of your speeches may not involve communicating such an intense personal experience, your use of language to call up mental pictures can enhance the impact of your sales promotions, donation requests, or statements of personal belief.

Vividness also helps maintain the attention of an audience. This is especially important in speeches to entertain and speeches to persuade because, in both of these, you are working for impact as well as understanding.

How Can I Make My Language Vivid?

Before we suggest some things you can do, we would like to mention a language habit that makes your language *less* vivid—the use of clichés. A *cliché* is an expression that has lost its meaning because of overuse. The following phrases, for example, have lost most of their original impact because people hear them so often: *fit to be tied, sharp as a tack, dog tired, pretty as a picture, keep a stiff upper lip,* and *bite the bullet.*

There are several ways you can choose and combine words to make your meanings more vivid. First, you can choose individual words that stimulate the emotions because of the images they call up. In the speech about hemophilia, words like *pounding, squeezing, clenching,* and *explode* were used to describe pain. Look at the vivid language Mary Nielsen chose for the first paragraph of her speech "Hug a Bat—No Way" in Appendix B.

The following list contrasts stimulating words with those that are less so:

Less Stimulating	*More Stimulating*
hot	sizzling
soldier	war hero
damaged	devastated
torn	shredded
pretty	stunning

There are also ways you can combine words to add vividness to your ideas. You have already learned a number of ways to develop, clarify, and support your ideas. Any of the communication procedures described in Chapter 5 can be used to add vividness if you also include individual words that stimulate the emotions. In addition, there are three techniques often used in public speeches to add impact—parallelism, personalization, and rhetorical questioning.

Parallelism uses the repetition of a definite pattern of words, phrases, or sentences to add impact to the meaning. President Ronald Reagan, often called "the Great Communicator," used parallelism in his State of the Union message:

> New freedom in our lives has planted the rich seeds for future success.
>
> For an America of wisdom that honors the family, knowing that as the family goes, so goes our civilization.
>
> For an America of vision that sees tomorrow's dreams in the learning and hard work we do today.
>
> For an America of courage whose servicemen and women, even as we meet, proudly stand watch on the frontiers of freedom.
>
> For an America of compassion that opens its heart to those who cry for help.[3]

Check Judith Barton's excellent use of parallelism in the conclusion of her speech, "Deadly Discrimination: Testicular Cancer," which appears in Appendix B. Another student used parallelism concisely to conclude a speech urging more support for women's athletics: "We want it, we're going to fight for it, and we're going to get it."

Personalization involves using personal pronouns to refer to yourself and your audience. Words like *your, you, each of you,* and *I* will call up more personal

By using personal pronouns a speaker can better involve her listeners in her message.

meanings from your audience and make your ideas more memorable. It is much more vivid, for example, to say, "I'm sure *you* have all noticed the bright green box in front of the student union," rather than, "Most people notice the bright green box in front of the union."

Rhetorical questions are those that the audience is asked to think about but not answer directly. Lynn Weaver, dean of the School of Engineering at Auburn University, used rhetorical questions to highlight his conclusions about nuclear power:

> Is nuclear power a viable option today? Obviously no, in the context of its being considered for new capacity by any United States utility. Will it be before the end of the decade? The answer, I believe, is a guarded yes.

What If I Can't Think of Language That Is Clear, Appropriate, or Vivid?

As you continue to develop your language skills, it will become more natural to use more effective words. Using vivid language is perhaps the hardest skill to develop because it involves creativity. As you work on your own speeches and listen to the speeches of others in your class, focus on the ways ideas are expressed. While you are developing your own language skills, you can also borrow from the creativity of others. By using vivid language that others have developed, you will not only add impact to your ideas, you will increase your credibility if the source is acceptable to your audience. Representative collections of quotations from well-known speakers and writers include:

> Bartlett, John. *Familiar Quotations: A Collection of Passages, Phrases, and Proverbs Traced to Their Sources in Ancient and Modern Literature.* Edited by Emily Morison Beck. 15th ed. revised and enlarged. Boston: Little, Brown & Co., 1980.
> Henry, Lewis C., ed. *Five Thousand Quotations for All Occasions.* New York: Doubleday, 1945.
> Stevenson, Burton, ed. *The Macmillan Book of Proverbs, Maxims, and Famous Phrases.* 2d ed. New York: Macmillan, 1965.

A thesaurus is a special dictionary that gives a variety of words to express an idea. For example, if you looked up the word *speak* in a thesaurus, you would find these alternative words and phrases: *talk, patter, wag the tongue, mouth, gab, spiel, breathe, utter, deliver, emit,* and others. The most commonly used thesaurus is *Roget's International Thesaurus*, which can be found in your library.[5] Dictionaries also give alternative words or synonyms.

If Language Is So Important, Why Don't I Write Out My Speech and Read or Memorize It?

The main reason for not writing out a speech and reading (or memorizing) it is that your focus then would be on your wording rather than your audience's reactions. One unique advantage of oral communication is that you have direct eye contact with your audience and can watch, interpret, and adapt to its reactions.

A second reason for not writing out your speech is that oral style is quite different from written style. In fact, Charles Fox, noted British politician and orator of the nineteenth century, once said, "Does it read well? Then, it's not a good speech." Research has identified the following differences between oral and written language: oral language includes shorter and simpler sentences, less precise numerical words, words with fewer syllables, more personal pronouns, more rhetorical questions, and more incomplete sentences.[6] Each of these differences highlights the direct relationship you will have with your audience. Using an oral style will not only make your ideas clearer the first (and only) time your audience hears them; it will add impact by helping the audience feel personally involved. Following are examples of the two different styles:

Written Style	*Oral Style*
Traditionally, people who earn their living tilling the soil have healthier eating habits because of the availability and abundance of natural foods.	*Shorter and simpler*: Farmers usually eat better than other people. Good food is available, and there's lots of it.
The per capita income of United States sales personnel in 19___ was $35,177.	*Less precise*: United States sales personnel averaged an income of $25,000 in 19___.
The issue of abortion elicits diametrically opposed opinions.	*Shorter words*: There are strong opposing views on the issue of abortion.
This writer feels that any person who has never seen the opening of the local arts festival should make a point to go.	*Personal pronouns*: I urge you to see the opening of the local arts festival.
Many people have never considered the possibility of another economic depression occurring in the United States. Each reader could find himself penniless and jobless in an economic crisis.	*Rhetorical questions*: Consider the impact of an economic depression on you. How safe is your money? How safe is your job?
Many suffering people, when offered the choice of life as it is or death, cannot make the decision. It would be enlightening for each reader to consider *if*, *how*, or *when* he would make such a choice.	*Incomplete sentences*: If you were offered the choice of life with suffering or death, could you choose? *How* would you? When *should* you?

How Can I Remember the Language Choices I Make?

In the next chapter, you will work on effectively delivering your speech. We believe it *is* helpful to memorize small parts of your speech to give them added impact. The memorized parts probably will include your vivid language choices. You might also memorize the definition of a new word that is important to your idea or an exact quotation you found in your research. In the next chapter, you will also practice your speech, using steps that focus on your outlined sequence of ideas. Each practice will help you develop alternative words that are consistent with your overall language choices.

LEARNING BY UNDERSTANDING

1. List the four standards for determining the appropriateness of language for a speech.

2. Why is it inappropriate to use terms like *without exception* or *obviously* when talking about complex issues?

3. What is a language habit that makes your language less vivid? Give an example.

4. Tell a more vivid word for each of the following: cold, tired, colorful, happy.

5. Change the following written statements so that they will reflect a characteristic of oral language style.
   a. *Indications in representative media suggest that current patterns of inflation will get worse over the next thirteen months.*
   b. *This writer assumes the reader is familiar with statistics suggesting that the average age in the United States will be fifty-eight in 19____ .*

ANSWERS:

1. Acceptability to the audience; appropriate to the speaker; appropriate to the situation; and appropriate to the subject of the speech
2. There will be many interpretations of the issue by the audience, and your absoluteness will limit the audience's reasoned choices.
3. The use of clichés
4. There are many possible alternatives to the words listed. One list would be cold—numb; tired—exhausted; colorful—vivid; happy—thrilled.
5. Again, many alternatives are possible. Check your examples with others in the class.
   a. The federal debt will rise over the next year. You can learn the bad news from your radio or newspaper (shorter words).
   b. You probably know that the average age in the United States will be fifty-eight in 19____ . (personal pronouns).

LEARNING BY INTERACTING

Agree on one of the following statements that you and your classmates will use for this experience in language development:

Daily exercise is the key to a productive life.
Finding the right job is challenging for most people.
The federal debt is the most serious problem facing America today.

Divide into small groups of three or four. Each group should select three procedures and develop a speech, using clear, appropriate, and vivid language on the chosen topic. Each group may choose from the twelve developing, clarifying, or supporting procedures in Chapter 5 or from the procedures suggested in this chapter.

Fine-tune your language choices to make them as creative as possible. When all groups have completed their materials, share and discuss them with the entire class. Which of the developed materials would be the most effective for this class?

LEARNING BY SPEAKING

Prepare a four- to five-minute speech explaining a strong personal belief. Your goal is to have your audience understand how you feel about this issue. Develop an outline that includes researched material to develop, clarify, and support your personal idea.

Write a rough draft of your speech in which you focus on expressing your ideas, not on the specific words you use. Then rewrite your draft with emphasis on choosing words for clarity, appropriateness, and vividness. Apply each of the principles of language use developed in this chapter. If possible, check your language choices with someone else in the class before completing your final manuscript.

Practice your speech several times and memorize at least two brief parts for greater effect.

Turn in your outline and your rough and final drafts.

REVIEW

Language choices are important in public speaking because they influence the meanings your audience will attach to your ideas. The three principles of clarity, appropriateness, and vividness should guide your language choices. Using language that is clear to audience members will help them attach intended denotative meanings, and appropriate and vivid language will help them attach intended connotative meanings. Your language choices should be based on your analysis of your audience's frame of reference.

NOTES

1. Neil Postman, *Crazy Talk, Stupid Talk* (New York: Delacorte Press, 1976), 156–57.

2. Ralph Zimmerman, "Mingled Blood," in *Contemporary American Speeches*, ed. Linkugel *et al.* (Belmont, Calif.: Wadsworth Publishing Co., 1965), 200.

3. Ronald Reagan, "State of the Union," *Vital Speeches of the Day* 51(February 15, 1985):258.

4. Lynn E. Weaver, "The End of the Nuclear Power Option in the U.S.: and Its Beginnings," *Vital Speeches of the Day* 51(March 1, 1985):312.

5. Peter M. Roget, *Roget's International Thesaurus*, 4th ed. (New York: Crowell, 1977).

6. John F. Wilson and Carroll C. Arnold, *Dimensions of Public Communication* (Boston: Allyn and Bacon, 1976), 195–96.

11

DEVELOPING DELIVERY SKILLS

In this chapter, you'll be . . .

LEARNING BY UNDERSTANDING

▦ Four dimensions of speech delivery

▦ Two uses of memory skills in public speaking

▦ A procedure for practicing your speech

▦ The verbal delivery skills of articulation and pronunciation

▦ Behaviors that indicate speaking confidence

▦ Desirable nonverbal characteristics of a speaking voice

▦ Effective nonverbal use of facial expression and body behavior

▦ Effective use of notes and the physical setting

▦ Feedforward planning and use

LEARNING BY INTERACTING

▦ Practicing of assertive delivery behaviors

LEARNING BY SPEAKING

▦ A three- to four-minute informative speech that explains how to do something at which you are skilled

CHAPTER OUTLINE

I. Effective delivery skills are essential to the public speaker.
   A. Your delivery will affect the audience's understanding of your message.
   B. Your delivery will affect the audience's assessment of your credibilty.
   C. Effective delivery has four dimensions—memory skills, clear verbal delivery, effective nonverbal delivery, and planning and use of feedforward.

II. Memory skills are helpful to a public speaker.
   A. Total memorization of a speech is usually ineffective.
      1. When you memorize a speech, your focus is on remembering the words, not on the audience.
      2. Total memorization is very time-consuming.
   B. Memorization of your overall pattern of ideas will help your speaking.
   C. By memorizing specific parts of the message, you can add impact to those parts during delivery.

III. Verbal delivery skills are important to the public speaker.
   A. Clear articulation is important to a public speaker.
      1. Sound omissions are inappropriate.
      2. Sound substitutions are inappropriate.
      3. Sluggish articulation is inappropriate.
   B. Clear pronunciation is important to a public speaker.
   C. Poor verbal delivery skills can affect the audience's perception of your speech.
      1. Poor articulation and pronunciation can diminish the clarity of your speech.
      2. Poor articulation and pronunciation can affect your credibility.

IV. Nonverbal delivery skills are important to the public speaker.
   A. Assertive communication behaviors reflect confidence.
      1. Assertive communication promotes free audience choices.
      2. Assertive communication is typified by natural body movement, direct eye contact, and firm, even vocal stress.
   B. A speaking voice should be intelligible and pleasing.
      1. Intelligibility refers to loudness and speed.
      2. Pleasing qualities in a speaking voice include vocal variety and a lack of vocal pauses.
   C. Natural gestures can give emphasis.
      1. Emphatic gestures stress important points.
      2. Transitional gestures indicate movement in a speech.
      3. Descriptive gestures help define meaning in a speech.
   D. Natural body behavior should not draw attention from the speech itself.
   E. Notes should be clear, brief, and easy to read.
   F. The physical setting should be adjusted to enhance the communication.
      1. A pleasant environment enhances understanding.
      2. Eye contact with your audience should be maintained.

V. Feedforward is vital to a public speaker.
   A. Feedforward planning prepares you to handle audience feedback effectively and has four essential parts.
      1. The first step is setting goals at important response points.
      2. The second step is anticipating audience reactions at those important response points.
      3. The third step is determining the nonverbals that would indicate audience reactions.
      4. The final step is planning alternative message segments to handle audience feedback.
   B. Feedforward use allows you to adjust your delivery and has five essential parts.
      1. The first step is observing audience nonverbal responses at response points.
      2. The second step is interpreting audience responses.
      3. The third step is selecting an appropriate contingency message.
      4. The fourth step is using the selected contingency message.
      5. The fifth step is reobserving the audience's nonverbal reactions to see if the desired response has happened.

11

DEVELOPING DELIVERY SKILLS

Delivery, I say, has the sole and supreme power in oratory; without it a speaker of the highest mental capacity can be held in no esteem; while one of moderate abilities, with this qualification, may surpass even those of the highest talent. —*Cicero,* De Oratore

PREVIEW

Effective delivery skills are essential to the public speaker. How you present your message will affect not only the audience's understanding of your message but also its assessment of your credibility as a speaker. From the moment you begin to move toward the speaking podium, the audience is watching you. It continues to gather information about you from the way you handle yourself during the actual speech delivery and respond to questions and comments afterwards. Signs of nervousness, vocalized pauses, or mispronunciations not only leave a poor impression, they distract the audience. Feelings of empathy, embarrassment, or amusement may cause the audience to miss what you are trying to say. We want to stress at this point that effective delivery is not a substitute for having something worthwhile to say. But without it, a well-planned speech could fall short of your communication goal.

In this chapter, you will work on four dimensions of effective delivery skills—memory, verbal delivery, nonverbal delivery, and feedforward.

What Is Memory?

Memory was an important public speaking skill for the early Greek orators and teachers. At that time, speakers would memorize all or parts of their speeches in order to add impact to carefully chosen language. Because the orator was considered a performer as well as a communicator, the reading of manuscripts was considered inappropriate. Teachers of speech, such as Cicero and Quintilian, developed highly elaborate systems of memory based on establishing mental "hooks" on which to "attach" parts of the speech for later recall. Speakers skilled in the use of memory and other delivery skills often were hired to present the statements of those being tried in the Greek court, where people pleaded their own cases.

Since then, the performance aspect of public speaking has declined and, with it, the emphasis on total memory of speeches. A notable exception in the history of our country was the late nineteenth-century phenomenon known as the Chautauqua Circuit. Chautauqua speakers toured the country and gave the same speech several times for the entertainment, as well as education, of their audiences. For example, Russell Conwell memorized and delivered his speech, "Acres of Diamonds," more than 6000 times and earned more than a million dollars doing so. You might be interested in obtaining a copy of his speech and noting how his careful language choices gave impact to his ideas.

For most of the speeches you will give, total memorization would be inappropriate for two reasons. The first, and most important, reason is that if you concentrate on remembering the exact words you chose, you will not be able to interpret and adapt to the audience's responses during your speech. The second reason is that total memorization is very time-consuming.

Then How Do I Use Memory?

There are two ways memory skills will help you in your speech preparation. First, you can use memory to retain the overall idea and pattern of main points in your speech. And, secondly, you can actually memorize specific short parts of your speech for added impact when you deliver them to your audience.[1]

Look at the following brief notes a student prepared as a delivery aid. Which parts of this speech do you think the student might memorize to increase the intended communication effect?

> **Central Idea:** The best way to use your time effectively is to gather needed information, set up a timetable for completing behaviors, and monitor your completion behaviors.
>
> Introduction—story of procrastinator who lost job
> I. First Step—gather information
> II. Second Step—set up timetable
> III. Final Step—monitor behaviors
> Conclusion—summary and quotation from youthful millionaire

In this situation, the student chose to memorize her three-step organizational plan and this sentence in her introduction: "Time caught up with her as it could with you." She also memorized the quote in her conclusion so that, after briefly looking at her notes, she could maintain eye contact with her audience.

How Can I Remember the Organization and the Quotations?

To remember the overall structure of a speech, you can practice by focusing on that rather than on specific words.The following method will help you develop memory skills. But before you practice, we suggest you review the characteristics of oral style in Chapter 10 and use them to guide your language choices.

RECOMMENDATIONS FOR SPEECH PRACTICE

1. Read your speech outline silently, slowly, and thoughtfully from beginning to end. Do not backtrack for details or for any other reason. Get a feeling for the total speech.
2. Read the outline aloud thoughtfully, without hurrying.
3. Put away your outline and go through your speech from beginning to end. Do not stop or repeat, even if you realize you have forgotten a main point or a subpoint.
4. Reread your speech outline again silently.
5. Practice aloud again with your outline, without stopping or repeating.
6. Repeat steps 4, 5, and 6 several times until you feel in control of your speech. (Repeat steps 3, 4, 5, and 6 if you will be giving your speech without notes.)

After completing this procedure, repeatedly go over the short portions of your speech you want to remember exactly. Then integrate each portion into the overall practice sequence. Finally, jot your main ideas on a three-by-five inch note card. Most speakers write a brief phrase outline of their speech and then practice once or twice with that memory aid.

The majority of your speaking will be *extemporaneous*—that is, done after careful preparation but with a minimum of notes as delivery aids. The purpose of your delivery is to provide a vehicle for the audience's understanding of your speech. It is like an envelope for sending a letter—the contents are most important. Any procedures that limit your attention and adaptation to audience feedback could result in less understanding. This is why we suggest that memory be used only to help you get a general command of the sequence of your ideas (so that a brief outline of the main points on a note card will recall them for you) and for selected, brief portions of your message in which the meaning has been captured by specific language (yours or someone else's).

The suggested practice sessions also will help you polish and time your speech. By actually trying it out, you will be able to identify parts of your speech that you are not able to verbalize clearly and that might require more thinking and planning. The practice sequence will also provide a variety of effective phrasings for your idea. Incidentally, we suggest that you prepare for about one minute less time than you will actually have. Because the extemporaneous speaker supplies the specific wording at the time of the speech, the speech becomes somewhat longer than planned. If you plan for slightly less material than you think you will use, you probably will be closer to the time limit.

Plan to practice your speech in the same, or similar, physical setting you will actually use. You will find that an environment looks different when you are standing in front, instead of sitting and facing the front. Becoming familiar with

Practicing in the setting where the speech will be delivered helps a speaker feel comfortable during the speech.

this perspective will help you feel more comfortable during the actual speech. (Also review the suggestions in Chapter 6 for practicing a speech.)

What If I Forget Something When Giving My Speech?

Forgetting something while speaking is less likely when the speech is motivated by your own interests and is carefully thought out and developed. If you are using notes, your outline will direct you toward your developed thought pattern, and *feedforward* will help you cope with unexpected feedback.

If you have been asked to give a speech without notes, we suggest you adapt the suggested practice sequence to give more attention to step 3—giving your speech without notes. You might try using the steps in this order—1, 2, 4, 5, 3—and then repeat 4, 5, and 3 until you can give your speech without notes several times without forgetting parts. If you forget during early practice sessions, you will develop alternative ways of coping for the actual speaking situation. If you practice frequently, you probably will not forget the important parts of your speech, and you will be able to cover the absence of any developing, clarifying, or supporting materials.

LEARNING BY UNDERSTANDING

1. List the four dimensions of effective speech delivery.

2. List two disadvantages of totally memorizing a public speech.

3. Two ways memory skills can be used by a public speaker are _____ and _____ .

4. Which of the following would a public speaker be likely to memorize?
   a. The body of the message
   b. A short question
   c. A joke
   d. The overall sequence of main ideas
   e. A lengthy chronology of historical events

5. The physical setting in which a speaker practices should be _____
   _____ .

ANSWERS:

1. Memory, verbal delivery, nonverbal delivery, and feedforward
2. Your focus would be on the speech not the audience; memorizing takes a great deal of time for one speaking experience.
3. To remember the overall idea and pattern of main points and to memorize specific short parts for added impact
4. We would suggest memorizing b., c., and d.
5. As similar as possible to the one in which the speech will be delivered

What Verbal Delivery Skills Are Important to a Public Speaker?

In Chapter 10, you worked on selecting words that would effectively communicate your meaning and enhance its effectiveness. The verbal delivery skills of articulation and pronunciation will help you to clearly communicate those carefully chosen words. Both articulation and pronunciation deal with the production of the sounds of words. With both skills, you will choose the level of formality and correctness appropriate for your specific audience. Audiences usually have higher expectations for your use of language than would someone with whom you were conversing; but to use overly precise articulation or outdated pronunciations would call attention to your language and thus distract the audience. What is appropriate for the audience and context should determine the level of articulation and pronunciation. Your articulation and pronunciation choices influence both the clarity of your speech and your credibility as a speaker.

What Is Articulation?

Articulation skills refer to your use of your diaphram, vocal cords, tongue, and lips to distinctly produce the sounds of a language. Most of us learned the characteristic way we articulate by imitating the people we observed when we were learning to speak. That is why people can often tell the part of the country you are from or your family background by listening to you talk. Also, people usually change the distinctness of their speech according to the particular communication situation. A problem most beginning public speakers have is using overly casual articulation, which may be appropriate for everyday conversation but is not appropriate for a more formal speech. Such faulty articulation usually falls into one of three categories: omissions, substitutions, and sluggish articulation. The following chart indicates typical examples of each type:

> *Omissions* (not saying some parts of words)
> > Vowel omissions:
> > > 'cross (across)
> > > lible (liable)
> > > probly (probably)
> > > mou'n (mountain)
> > Consonant omissions:
> > > a'ready (already)
> > > f'aternity (fraternity)
> > > lib'ary (library)
> *Substitutions* (substituting other letters for parts of words)
> > lidle (little)
> > tomado (tomato)
> > doncha (don't you)
> *Sluggishness* (general lack of clarity)
> > "The subjec' of my 'dress is secur'ty f'm 'nvasion."

In their book *The Laughter Prescription*, Dr. Laurence Peter and Bill Dana include examples of humor using our tendency to speak sluggishly. While the following example is humorous, such sluggishness would be inappropriate for a speaking situation:

The act of mounting a horse—GEDDINON
The act of dismounting a horse—GEDDINOFF
Underachiever Cowboy (to his horse who got its hoof caught in its own stirrup): "Ay, if you're GEDDINON, I'm GEDDINOFF."[2]

How About Pronunciation?

While articulation refers to distinctness, *pronunciation* refers to standards of correctness. Incorrect pronunciations usually result from nervousness or lack of knowledge.

Your teacher and classmates will help you identify commonly used words that you mispronounce. For words that are new to you and necessary to our speech topic, check the correct pronunciation in a recently published dictionary; the preferred pronunciation is usually listed first. Practice the new word until you are comfortable with the pronunciation. You will build your oral vocabulary by learning the meanings and pronunciations of new words you encounter.

Reading aloud can help you improve both articulation and pronunciation skills. For practice, you could use part or all of one of the speeches in Appendix B. The first several times you read the material, exaggerate the articulation and check all words you cannot pronounce. Repeat this several times, until you are reading at a normal speaking rate. A tape recorder or some helpful listeners will help you identify any problems you are having. Before each speech, check again the pronunciations you are unsure of.

LEARNING BY UNDERSTANDING

1. The two verbal delivery skills important to public speakers are _____ and _____ .

2. The main standard for determining the level of articulation and pronunciation for any public speech is _____ .

3. Articulation and pronunciation affect both your _____ and _____ as you give a public speech.

ANSWERS:

3. Clarity and credibility
2. Appropriateness for audience and speaking situation
1. Articulation and pronunciation

How About Nonverbal Skills?

Nonverbal delivery skills include everything you do during a speech *except* speaking. These skills include vocal variety, gestures, facial expressions, and body movements. None of these should draw attention to the nonverbal behavior itself; but each should be a natural part of the overall communication. Before looking at some of the specific skills in each of these areas, let's consider the overall image your nonverbal behavior projects.

One of the most important overall meanings your nonverbal behaviors communicate is your confidence. As developed in Chapter 8, audiences will feel you are more credible if you are confident. Specifically, confident nonverbals will raise your credibility in competence, composure, and dynamism. As we described in Chapter 2, some feelings of anxiety are natural, expected, and desirable. Like the athlete, the public speaker must productively channel the extra energy provided by this anxiety. We suggest that you work toward the goal of *assertive communication*, which is self-confident and is typified by such nonverbal behaviors as natural body movement, direct eye contact, and firm, even vocal stress.

We probably all have seen speakers who have used nonverbal behaviors that could be described as either nonassertive or aggressive. The nonassertive speaker lacks confidence and displays such nonverbal behaviors as muscle tension, lack of eye contact, flushed skin, and hesitant speech. The aggressive speaker uses a strident voice tone, threatening eye contact, and excessively forceful gestures. Audiences often question the competence of the nonassertive speaker and argue with the aggressive one.

An assertive speaker, on the other hand, reflects thoughtful choices by means of confident delivery and allows the audience to make personal choices without feeling pressured. Effective use of your voice, gestures, facial expressions, and body movements will increase your assertiveness.

How Can I Use My Voice Effectively?

The two desired nonverbal characteristics of an effective public speaking voice are intelligibility and pleasantness. *Intelligibility* means that the voice is loud enough to be heard comfortably and the pace is low enough to be understood. Your early messages in class will help you get a feeling of how loudly you must speak in order to be heard by everyone in your audience. Remember, in a large room full of people your voice will be absorbed, so it will be necessary to speak louder. If you know you have a soft voice, your teacher will be able to suggest exercises to practice projection without straining your vocal cords. The practice sequence we suggested earlier in this chapter will enable you to limit the length of your speech to the allotted time. If you discover that speaking too fast is a problem for you, you might try the following:

1. Take a moment or two to get settled before talking; get your breath and do not feel rushed.

2. Make written notes to yourself on your outline to *slow down*.

3. Mark your outline for places to breathe deeply and pause briefly. You can plan your pauses to emphasize important points in your speech.

The other nonverbal characteristic of an effective public speaking voice is pleasantness. *Pleasantness* is usually associated with the effective use of vocal variety and the lack of vocal pauses. *Vocal variety* refers to the natural changes in pitch and inflection that people usually make in normal conversation. We tend to raise our voices at the end of questions, speak more slowly when making an important point, and stress certain words to clarify our meaning. Consider how differently this statement could be interpreted with different vocal variety: ''Come here and show me what you mean.'' For example, try emphasizing different words. As public speakers become more comfortable in the situation, vocal variety comes naturally. But if this is a difficult skill for you, you may wish to practice this aspect of your delivery by reading aloud.

Vocalized pauses—that is, the addition of such sounds and phrases as *um* and *you know* between points and subpoints—are distracting to the audience. They are also perceived as less assertive. This habit, often a carryover from everyday conversation, can be broken with the help of a friend who calls attention to each verbalized pause. You can learn to anticipate these verbal pauses and avoid them. Remember, silent pauses effectively emphasize important points.

What About Using Gestures?

Most of us gesture naturally in our everyday conversations, and you will begin to do so in your public speaking as you become more experienced. The use of occasional appropriate gestures can add interest and emphasis to your message.

The main kinds of gestures used in speeches are emphatic, transitional, and descriptive. **Emphatic gestures**, which include pointing with the index finger, raising one hand with palm up, and making a fist, give emphasis to points and aid your listeners' memory. **Transitional gestures**, such as placing both palms on the podium or using fingers to enumerate the points being made, indicate that you are moving from one main point to another. Finally, **descriptive gestures** specify meaning by actually showing with your hands and arms the size or scope of an object or concept.

For your earlier speeches in class we suggest that you concentrate on developing an effective message and practice having full control over your ideas. Seek feedback from class members about your gestures. If they say that your lack of gestures lowered your credibility because you did not seem committed to your idea, you might plan to use any of the three kinds of gestures suggested. Then, practice in front of a mirror, or ask your teacher to videotape you. Videotaping is better. You will be able to concentrate on your nonverbal behaviors while you view the tape rather than try to be conscious of them while you talk. Keep in mind that any new behavior will seem somewhat awkward at first. Videotaping will also be helpful if feedback indicated that you used too many gestures. It will also give you an opportunity to check your facial expressions and body behavior.

How Should I Use Facial Expressions?

If your audience is paying close attention to you, its members probably will be looking at your face, which should reflect interest and complement the tone you are setting with the speech. If you are interested in your topic and in communicating it to your audience, your facial expressions will indicate this naturally.

Eye contact is an important part of facial expression that can enhance your meaning. It not only communicates your interest and assertiveness, it is the main channel through which you will receive feedback from your audience. It is helpful to maintain eye contact with a small portion of the audience for several seconds and then to move on to another portion. Because eye contact is so important, the audience should be arranged so that all members are within the speaker's visual range. Be careful, though, not to sweep the audience with your eyes in a mechanical way.

What Is Effective Body Behavior for a Public Speaker?

Effective body behavior is natural and does not draw attention to itself; in other words, it should not be a noticeable part of the speech. If you are relaxed, prepared, and sincerely interested in communicating your message, body behavior, like other aspects of nonverbal speaking behavior, will come naturally. Two specific procedures can help you feel more comfortable during your speech—checking out the physical setting ahead of time and planning for your use of notes. Make certain that you will be able to see all your audience members and they will be able to see you.

Remember, your audience will begin forming perceptions of you the moment you appear. Your movement *to* and *from* your speaking position should also be relaxed and natural. You might review the body behaviors you worked on in Chapter 2 to reflect speech confidence and those you looked for in Chapter 3 as a member of a speech audience.

How Can I Use Notes Effectively during My Speech?

Notes are often a problem for beginning speakers. We have all suffered along with speakers who got their note cards out of order, dropped them, or lost their place. As we indicated earlier, totally memorizing your speech limits your flexibility to adapt to audience feedback. We suggested that you become familiar with your overall sequence of ideas and let the wording be spontaneous at the time of delivery. Most speakers will use some brief form of notes, such as a brief phrase outline, as a visual reminder of the points they want to make. The notes should contain only enough information to call back to your mind the point to be made. The only material that should be in front of you word-for-word would be statistics or a longer direct quote you chose not to memorize. Figure 11-1 shows a sample note format. You may want to use a highlighter or underline to further focus your attention, and you might type your notes to be sure they are legible.

Specific Purpose: Understand people's lateness

Introduction: Bill story
                My research
                Preview

Body:
    I. Defy authority
       "Research shows that 39,000 ..."
    II. Gain power
       Story—15 case studies
    III. Fulfilling stereotypes
       Women
       Busy

Conclusion: Summary
             Challenge

Figure 11-1   Sample Note Card

LEARNING BY UNDERSTANDING

1. List three characteristics of assertive speaking behavior.

2. List the four basic components of nonverbal speaking behavior.

3. Which of the following procedures would help a public speaker develop assertive behaviors?
   a. Taking several deep breaths before speaking
   b. Not looking at the audience while speaking
   c. Consciously relaxing muscles before speaking
   d. Walking calmly to the front of the room
   e. Telling the audience how you feel

4. An effective public speaking voice is _____ and _____ .

5. To be intelligible, you must speak _____ and _____ .

6. A pleasant public speaking voices uses _____ and avoids _____ .

7. The three types of gestures used in public speeches are _____ , _____ , and _____ .

8. Describe a procedure you could use to maintain eye contact with an audience.

ANSWERS:

1. Natural body movements; direct eye contact; firm, even vocal stress
2. Vocal variety, gestures, facial expressions, and body movements
3. a., c., d.
4. Intelligible, pleasant
5. Loudly enough, slowly enough
6. Vocal variety, vocal pauses
7. Emphatic, transitional, descriptive
8. Establish eye contact with a small portion of your audience and then move on to another portion; avoid a sweeping pattern of movement.

What Else Is Involved in Delivery?

Through the nonverbal communication of your voice, gestures, facial expression and body movement, you will establish the tone for your speech and develop and maintain rapport with your audience. In addition to those nonverbal behaviors, your physical appearance and use of the physical environment also will influence your audience's responses. As with your other nonverbal behaviors, your physical appearance should seem to be a natural part of you and be appropriate to the speaking situation. For example, if your clothing draws attention to itself, your audience will be distracted from your message.

In your public speaking experiences, you will have different amounts of control over the physical setting in which you speak, but you should always see that all parts of your audience have easy visual contact with you. For example, it is easier to see people at the extreme left or right if they are far away from you. If the audience is too close to you and spread from extreme left to right, you will have difficulty making eye contact with those in the extreme corners of the front. You might try designing an audience seating arrangement that would be optimal for audiences of different sizes.

Be sure to check out the physical setting ahead of time, and do not hesitate to suggest changes that will enhance your delivery. A pleasant environment, without major distractions and with chairs that are neither too soft nor too hard, is most conducive to critical listening.

What If My Audience Doesn't React the Way I Expect?

This is a crucial question because the accomplishment of your specific purpose depends on the audience's responses to your speech. These responses will be revealed by feedback, which you must interpret and adapt to. The final key to effective speech delivery—*feedforward planning and use*—will help you plan for and handle unexpected audience reactions.

Feedforward planning helps you cope with what could go wrong during your speech. By planning ahead to handle problems, you will be more confident of attaining your speech goal. Feedforward planning, as shown in Figure 11-2, has four essential steps.

Figure 11-2   Feedforward Planning

Determine Response Points	Plan Expectancies	Predict Audience Nonverbals	Plan Contingencies
Identifying important points in the speech for specific purpose attainment	Anticipating possible audience responses at the important points	Determining nonverbal behaviors that will indicate each possible response	Planning what to say to cope with each response

First, you determine the important response points in the speech where audience understanding, laughter, agreement, and so on are necessary to achieve your overall specific speech purpose. These feedback response points usually occur at the end of your introduction, main points, and conclusion. For example, before leaving your introduction you want your audience to be interested, and before leaving Main Point I you want to be sure that your listeners clearly understand it. Second, you anticipate how the audience might react at each response point. You should plan for both positive and negative responses. Third, you predict the nonverbals that will indicate each response. For example, frowns might mean confusion, diminished eye contact might mean disinterest, and leaning forward with eye contact might show interest. Fourth, you plan what you will say to adapt to each response. The goal of these contingencies is to bring the audience back to the desired response. Contingencies might take the form of an interesting story, additional logical support, additional indication of the relevance of support to audience members, or a request for interaction with the audience after the speech. Different responses require different contingencies.

Figure 11-3 is a sample of feedforward planning for the first major point in a student speech. The student has planned for three possible audience responses to his main point. When the student speaker sees the nonverbals showing Expectancy 3, then he infers understanding of his first main point has happened and he goes on with his speech.

How Can I Actually Use Feedforward Planning as I Deliver My Speech?

For an example, let's use the Sample Feedforward Planning for Main Point I in Figure 11-3 below. If, as you come to the end of Main Point I, you observe

Figure 11-3 Sample Feedforward Planning

Response Points:	Expectancies:	Nonverbals:	Contingencies:

I. Late people are trying to defy authority.
A. Use of excuses
  1. To escape punishment
  2. To shed responsibility
	(1) "I think you're exaggerating."	Disbelieving look, shaking head	Give specific research sources; call to their mind other examples.

B. Based on childhood experiences
  1. Defying parents
  2. Defying teachers
	(2) "I disagree. Why would they take it out on friends?"	Firm head shake, arms crossed	Explain research study which found that motivation for lateness is subconscious.

	(3) "I understand."	Nodding head up and down	State summary transition to Main Point II.

unbelieving looks among some people in your audience, and other people shaking their heads slowly, you can interpret their nonverbals as showing the planned-for reaction of exaggeration. No problem, since you had thought that some people might think your point on defying authority was an exaggeration and had planned Contingency 1 to handle it. So you move into Contingency 1 as planned and say,

> I can see that some of you think that I'm exaggerating when I say that my research strongly indicates that defying authority is one of the three main reasons for lateness. Well, while you're right that the latest research findings indicate that there can be other reasons, an article in last year's *Annual Review of Psychology* by _____summarized all studies of tardiness for the last three years and stated that over three-fourths of. . . .

After saying Contingency 1, carefully reobserve the audience nonverbals—especially the people who were showing the exaggeration reactions. If, based on your contingency message, they are now nodding their heads up and down, you can go on to Contingency 3, the summary-transition to Main Point 2. Note that while you plan the predicted audience nonverbals *after* you forecast the expectancies, when you actually use them in a public speaking situation you observe and interpret the nonverbals *before* you infer the expectancy and choose the appropriate contingency. Figure 11-4 shows the five parts of feedforward use during the speech.

This kind of feedforward planning is beneficial in numerous other communication and living situations. How many of you have thought, "If my mother's first reaction to my going to Florida for Easter break is . . ., I'll say. . . ." Or, "If Dick keeps inching in on my second (tennis) serve, I'll lob the service return over his head."

Effective use of feedforward presents two challenges. First, feedback will be essentially nonverbal and often difficult to interpret accurately. Second, given the number of people in any audience, there will be varied responses to any given point.

Figure 11-4 Feedforward Use

Observe Audience Nonverbals	Interpret Audience Nonverbals	Select Contingency	Say Contingency	Reobserve Nonverbals
Observe audience's nonverbal responses at selected response points	Interpret audience's nonverbals to infer which expected response is occurring	Select appropriate contingency	Say the chosen contingency	Reobserve audience's nonverbal responses

Interpreting audience feedback is a challenging part of feedforward use.

What If the Audience Does Nothing to Clearly Indicate a Response?

If you are unsure about how to interpret the feedback from your audience or if you seem to be getting no clear feedback, you may need to encourage audience feedback. We suggest that, early on, you let the audience know its feedback is important. You can accomplish this by acknowledging responses openly and adapting to them, by letting the audience members know you are interested in their reactions. Comments early in your speech, such as "By the looks on your faces, it seems that many of you have had a similar experience" or "It seems as though you, too, are shocked by this information," will encourage later feedback. You might also specifically ask for responses by saying, "Does that seem as unfair to you as it does to me?" Such a rhetorical question does not demand an oral answer, but your listeners may respond nonverbally by nodding or leaning forward. These procedures will help you avoid the frustrating situation of having little or no clear audience reaction.

How Might I Use Feedforward in My Class Speeches?

Most audiences you will address will have some interest in or attitude toward the topic of your message, and you will be able to plan accordingly. But your class speeches may be exceptions. Unlike most audiences you will address, your classmates are not drawn together because of you or the specific issue you will talk about but because they share a common interest in developing speaking skills. Therefore, each speech will stimulate a variety of responses.

Sometimes, a small number of people will be sending feedback of disagreement while the majority of the audience will be agreeing. In such cases, you might choose to use a planned contingency to acknowledge this disagreement. You could then ask the audience to listen to the rest of the speech and to express any disagreement afterward. Your audience will appreciate your acknowledging the negative response, and listeners who agree with you will not have to listen to lengthy alternative message segments that are inappropriate to them.

LEARNING BY UNDERSTANDING

1. What is feedforward planning?

2. When is feedforward planning done?

3. What are the four parts of feedforward planning?

4. What are the five parts of feedforward use?

5. Which part of feedforward planning does each of the following represent?
   a. The audience may doubt the credibility of certain information.
   b. I want the audience to sign my petition for a local school bond issue.
   c. Some of the audience may feel uncomfortable with my use of data regarding local lawbreakers.
   d. Frowning might indicate disagreement.
   e. If the audience gets bored, I will share the example of the wealthy actor who moved to Texas.

6. What are two methods of encouraging audience feedback?

7. Which of the following might be effective ways to handle listeners who disagreed with a point you were making?
   a. Ignore them
   b. Acknowledge the disagreement
   c. Give an alternative message segment to get their agreement
   d. Arrange to talk to them later
   e. Ask them to leave

ANSWERS:

1. The preparation a speaker does in order to handle the feedback received from the audience
2. Before the speech
3. Determining response points; planning expectancies; determining nonverbal indicators; planning contingencies
4. Observing nonverbal feedback; interpreting nonverbal feedback; selecting appropriate contingency; using chosen contingency; reobserving nonverbal feedback
5. **a.** expectancy; **b.** response point; **c.** expectancy; **d.** nonverbal indicator; **e.** contingency
6. Acknowledging nonverbal responses and using rhetorical questions
7. We would suggest considering **c.** if a large number of people showed disagreement; **b.** and **d.**, in that order, if a small number disagreed; **a.** might be used if only a very small segment of the audience disagreed.

LEARNING BY INTERACTING

In small groups, take turns reading the following passage. After reading it to yourself, have each person in the group read the passage in a nonassertive, an aggressive, and an assertive manner. See what each feels like as you communicate and what each looks and sounds like as other members of the group read the passage. Talk about how each type of delivery felt. Repeat the experience until you can physically feel the difference between the three delivery types. Work to include effective verbal and nonverbal delivery.

> **"I've taken a great deal of time thinking about this issue and feel strongly about my decision. I'm willing to listen to other points of view but would need very strong evidence to change my mind."**

LEARNING BY SPEAKING

Prepare a three- to four-minute informative speech in which you explain how to do something at which you are skilled and in which your audience is interested but unskilled. Prepare an audience analysis using information from direct sources. Prepare a sentence outline and feedforward planning for your introduction, conclusion, and each main point of your speech.

Plan to practice several times, using the practice sequence suggested in this chapter. In your practice and actual speech delivery, focus on your delivery behaviors. You will be able to do this more easily because you are talking about a familiar topic.

After your practice sessions, prepare a word or phrase outline to use in your speech delivery. During your speech, use as many contingencies as your audience's feedback demands.

REVIEW

Your delivery behaviors will influence your audience's understanding of your message and its perception of your credibility. We have considered delivery behaviors in four main categories: memory, verbal delivery, nonverbal delivery, and feedforward planning and use. Memory skills help you to remember the overall pattern of ideas in your speech and to memorize small portions of your speech in order to add impact by maintaining eye contact with your audience. Verbal delivery skills of articulation and pronunciation depend on what would be appropriate for a specific audience. Nonverbal behaviors of vocal variety, gesture, facial expression, and body behavior should be natural, assertive, and not draw attention to themselves. Feedforward planning and use help you interpret and adapt to audience response.

NOTES

1. Robert W. Finkel, *The Brainbooster* (Englewood Cliffs, N.J.: Prentice-Hall, Inc., 1983), 152–53.

2. Laurence J. Peter and Bill Dana, *The Laughter Prescription* (New York: Ballantine Books, 1982), 120. (Note: excerpts were made from *The Cowboy/English-English/Cowboy Dictionary*, Ballantine Books.)

12

DEVELOPING INFORMATIVE SKILLS

In this chapter, you'll be . . .

LEARNING BY UNDERSTANDING

- How informative speaking differs from other types
- Principles to use in informative speaking
- Main types of informative speeches
- Steps in preparing an informative speech
- Barriers to audience understanding
- Methods for checking accomplishment of purpose

LEARNING BY INTERACTING

- Analyzing and improving a lecture

LEARNING BY SPEAKING

- A ten-minute speech to enable your audience to understand new information

CHAPTER OUTLINE

I. An informative speech is one with the primary purpose of conveying new information to an audience.
   A. Communicating new information to others is an important professional skill.
   B. Developing skills in informative public speaking will improve the clarity of your informal explanations.

II. Speakers help audiences learn new information by applying three basic principles of learning.
   A. People learn best through organized material.
   B. People learn best if they can visualize the new information.
   C. People learn best when they connect new information with information they already understand.

III. There are three main types of informative speeches.
   A. The demonstration speech is a format in which you show an audience a new procedure.
      1. When you want your audience to be able to do the process, the sequential organizational pattern is most helpful.
      2. When you want your audience to understand, but not do, the process, you may choose from other organizational patterns.
   B. The oral report is used to provide specific information in a concise way.
      1. There is a basic organizational plan for oral reports.
         a. Review the purpose of the report.
         b. Tell the findings or conclusion.
         c. Cover the three or four main points which provide the information.
         d. Summarize the information and draw a conclusion.
      2. Graphs and charts are often used in oral reports.
      3. There is often a question-and-answer period after an oral report.
   C. The lecture is a longer speech for the purpose of increasing the audience's knowledge of a particular subject.
      1. Lectures should include a great deal of high-interest material.
      2. Lectures are ordered around key subtopics and use a variety of organizational plans.

IV. There are thirteen basic steps to preparing an informative speech.
   A. Choose a topic of interest and value to you and the audience.
   B. Analyze your audience to determine its frame of reference.
   C. Narrow your topic to a meaningful part for this audience.
   D. Research additional information.
   E. Consider the time limit when choosing information to include.
   F. Decide the order in which you want to give the information.
   G. Select or develop materials that will aid understanding and keep interest high.
   H. Develop or discover visual aids for your speech.
   I. Decide important places in the speech to actively involve your audience.
   J. Plan feedforward.
   K. Develop notes for use in delivering your speech.
   L. Practice several times.
   M. Determine how to assess results.

V. There are three typical barriers to audience understanding.
   A. Lack of interest can lead to lack of understanding.
   B. Lack of background information can lead to lack of understanding.
   C. Lack of active processing by the audience can lead to lack of understanding.

VI. There are procedures which can help you determine the success of your informative speeches.
   A. Observe audience speech-related behaviors after the speech to check the amount of understanding.
   B. Check for nonverbal reactions during your speech.
   C. Listen to the questions the audience asks after the speech.
   D. Use delayed postcommunication assessment.
      1. Questionnaires and rating scales can reveal audience understanding.
      2. Testimonials by listeners can reveal audience understanding.

12

DEVELOPING INFORMATIVE SKILLS

Not only is there an art in knowing a thing, but also a certain art in teaching it. —*Cicero*

PREVIEW

Among top managers in major organizations, being able to communicate new information to subordinates is typically perceived as one of the most important skills of a promotable manager. Accurate communication of new information is also important to teachers, lawyers, financial consultants and numerous other professionals. Being able to effectively communicate information is a valued skill, not only in your professional life but also in your personal life. In this chapter you will work on communication skills to help your audiences understand important information. These skills are basic to all other types of speaking and will allow you to fine-tune those skills which you have already developed.

Aren't All Speeches Informative?

Yes, in the sense that in every speech there is usually something new you want your audience to understand. However, an informative speech is different from other speeches because its *primary* purpose is helping people understand something that they did not understand before the speech. Remember that the focus on a specific purpose for your speeches is essential because it not only guides your choices as you develop and deliver the speech; it also helps determine your success after the speech is over. For example, in a persuasive speech your purpose might be to get audience members to contribute money to a worthy cause. Then the amount they contribute would determine the degree of your success. Even if you decide that it would be valuable for them to understand the nature and size of the cause involved, you could be successful in your specific purpose without their complete understanding of the problem.

This question is a good one, however. Achieving the purpose of most speeches—informative, persuasive, or entertaining—depends on your audience's understanding of the key points you are making. Therefore, the skills you work on in this chapter will be helpful to accomplish other speech purposes.

When Will I Use Informative Speaking?

Actually a great deal of informative speaking occurs every day. Parents explain new information to children. Spouses explain daily activities to each other, and friends explain feelings and problems to each other. Managers explain new procedures to individual employees. People use a public speech when they want to explain something to a group in a more organized way than is typical in a one-to-one conversation. Many professionals use public speaking to share information efficiently. Typical examples include department managers making oral reports in monthly meetings, nurses making oral reports on their patients at staff meetings, teachers lecturing to classes, and home economists demonstrating new procedures to community organizations. Professionals increasingly use modern media, such as teleconferencing, for communicating new information with people in different locations. In each example the primary purpose is helping the audience understand new information.

In the future you will be asked to speak on a general topic because of the overlap between an audience's needs and interests and your expertise. This would be the case in the examples of professionals' speaking that we gave earlier. You would then use your brainstorming skills to focus on the specific topic that would be most valuable for your particular audience. For example, we are often asked to speak on our work with individual learning skills. We first consider the specific

Managers use public speaking to communicate important information to their staff members.

audience, especially what its background is and why it wants to know about individual learning skills. We would choose one specific topic for an audience of parents of high school students and a different one for an audience of professors in a university's education department. Depending on the audience, the presentation might be a lecture overviewing the significance of individual learning skills, or an oral report on the latest research on individual learning skills.

For your in-class speeches, you must do the work to discover a specific topic which overlaps between your audience's needs and interests and your own knowledge and interests. You will feel most comfortable if you work on a topic with which you already have some expertise and experience. It will be helpful to refer to the list of general topics typically of value and interest to college students (see Chapter 4, page 58).

The skills involved in conveying new information in a public speaking setting will be valuable to you. As a side benefit, you will find that your informal explanations to others will improve in clarity. Effectively communicating new information is one of the most challenging communication goals and requires an understanding of how people learn.

How Can I Help an Audience Understand Something New?

Research and experience in teaching indicate that people learn best through visualization of concepts, connection or comparison of new information with information they already understand, and organized material.[1] Each of these principles is important to effective informative speaking. To apply these principles about how people learn, we suggest the following:

1. Help audience members visualize key ideas in their minds or through visual aids. As we indicated in Chapter 6, the visual memory is much stronger than the verbal memory. Therefore, it is important to help your audience *see* what you are talking about. For instance, Randy Larsen helped his audience understand how a laser works (see his complete speech in Appendix B) by using two inflated balloons, one inside the other. He explained that a laser could move through the body without harming it to destroy a growth inside, much like bursting the inside balloon without harming the outer one. We encourage you to use the variety of visual aids described in Chapter 6 in your informative speeches. It will also be valuable to ask audience members to picture for themselves certain concepts and ideas. For example, you could ask them to visualize how green the grass and trees look in early spring. Each audience member's own imagination will be a powerful tool to understand and remember your key ideas.[2]

2. Help audience members to associate the new information with information they already understand by making meaningful connections for them. People gain new information through one of their senses: sight, sound, smell, taste, and touch. Once they have experienced something, it becomes part of their sensory memory. This kind of memory disappears in less than a second unless they pay conscious attention to the experience. If they pay attention to the experience, it becomes part of their short-term memory. As discussed in Chap-

ter 3, short-term memory itself only lasts about thirty seconds unless meaningful connections are made to place the new information into long-term memory.[3] By doing careful audience analysis to determine related information audience members already understand, you will be able to help them make those important connections. For example, in Michael Stolts' speech on new techniques of eye surgery (see Appendix B), he explained the cutting technique involved in radial keratotomy surgery by comparing it to the audience's understanding of the placement of spokes in a wheel.

3. Organize your material to enable your audience to easily follow the development of your idea. In addition to the recommendations given in Chapter 7 for choosing the best organizational plan, consider the speech content itself. For example, if you are demonstrating how to do something well, there is usually a necessary, or best, order for listeners to follow if they want to remember and be able to do the desired procedure well. If you have nothing else to guide you, the most effective organizational pattern might be the easy-to-difficult pattern.

What Are the Main Types of Informative Speeches?

The informative speeches most often used are the demonstration, the oral report, and the lecture. The demonstration is a format in which you show an audience a procedure. The purpose is to enable the audience to *do* (or understand) something new as a result of your speech. The oral report is a brief speech designed to inform your audience about new information in a concise format. The lecture is a more detailed speech designed to have your audience more fully understand a new concept or subject. Let's look at each of these main types more closely.

The *demonstration speech* focuses on a process: how to do something, how to make something, or how something works. A key distinction is that you are talking about something that can be visualized or is real to the senses. For example, you might give a speech on how to write a résumé, how to build a bookcase, or how a cordless phone works. In the first two examples your purpose would be to enable your audience to later *do* the process. In the example of the cordless phone, your purpose is to have your audience understand the process. This distinction determines how you order the information in your speech.

When informing your listeners about a process you want them to be able to do, you will usually order the steps sequentially from start to finish. The steps are the essential behaviors that the listeners need to do to complete the process. Consider the following ordering of steps or main points in two speeches:

Specific Purpose: To enable my audience to teach a dog how to sit.
Main Points:
    I. Slip a leash over the dog's head.
   II. While holding the leash, press on the dog's rump and say "sit."
  III. Give the dog a reward while it is in the sitting position.

Specific Purpose: To enable my audience to make a transparency for an overhead projector.

Main Points:
    I. Prepare a master on plain white paper using carbonaceous markings.
    II. Place a sheet of thermal acetate on top of the master; the missing corner on the acetate should be at the upper right.
    III. Set the dial for the type of thermal acetate you are using.
    IV. Feed the two sheets into the thermal copy machine.
    V. Separate the two sheets.

If there are more than five steps in the process you are explaining, it will be helpful to group the steps into stages. This is because people understand and retain information better if it is organized around a smaller number of parts.[4] Look ahead in this chapter to the thirteen steps in preparing an informative speech. Work to group the steps into three or four stages so you could communicate them effectively in a public speech.

When presenting a demonstration speech to enable your audience to *do* a process, visual aids like objects or models or objects, a series of photos, movements, or presentation of key words are important. At minimum, have the main steps visually listed so the audience can see the order. In some speaking situations you might also provide a copy of the steps for your listeners. For example, when demonstrating a new machine to an office staff, the salesperson would give the listeners a copy of the essential steps in the operation or maintenance of the machine.

When the purpose of your demonstration is to have your audience understand rather than do a process, you have more choices in the way you order the information. You might use easy-to-difficult, known-to-unknown, or a chronological order. To make this choice it is necessary to know the audience's level of understanding and interest. Following is an example of the main points of a demonstration-speech outline ordered from least-preferred to most-preferred:

Specific Purpose: To have my audience understand three ways to thaw frozen water pipes.
Main Points:
    I. Heat the pipe with a propane torch.
    II. Pour boiling water over rags wrapped around the frozen pipe.
    III. Wrap the frozen pipe with electrical heat tape.

The ***oral report*** provides specific information in a concise way for listeners. Professionals use this format extensively to keep up-to-date on matters which affect them. Oral reports usually occur at regular meetings. Such meetings allow efficient updating of information and the opportunity for questions and comments about the interrelationships among reports.

The following organizational pattern allows for efficient sharing of information:

ORGANIZATIONAL PATTERN FOR ORAL REPORTS

1. Tell the audience the purpose and scope of your report.

2. Tell the audience the conclusions you are drawing.

3. Cover the three or four main points which provide the necessary information.

4. Summarize the information and relate it to the conclusion.

The following is an example of an outline for a typical oral report.

Specific Purpose: To have my department understand the benefits of the new government contract for our company.

Introduction: This report reviews a four-month study designed to determine the potential value of the proposed government contract.
The results of the study lead me to recommend the contract.
There are three basic reasons for the recommendation.

Body:
    I. The new contract will lead to more take-home pay from overtime.
    II. The new contract will lead to larger profit-sharing revenues.
    III. The new contract will lead to larger stock dividends.

Conclusion: The overtime pay, revenues, and dividends lead me to recommend the government project.

Visual aids are valuable in an oral report. Graphs and charts especially make information more understandable. Each main point in the previous example involves numerical data which could be quickly and clearly visualized by bar graphs.

Often a question-and-answer period follows an oral report. This enables a speaker to focus concisely on information in the report based on audience analysis and then provide additional information as requested. The more important the oral report, the more likely the speaker will carefully prepare for the question-and-answer period. We will work on the skills involved in handling questions in Chapter 14.

Lectures are longer speeches for the purpose of increasing the audience's knowledge of a particular subject. Examples are classroom lectures, program talks at club meetings, and paper presentations at conferences. Because of the extended time period—usually from twenty to fifty minutes—lectures put more demands on both the speaker and listener to maintain interest. No matter how high the initial interest, it will be important to choose verbal and visual material which is interesting and stimulating to the audience. This material will be especially helpful in the middle of the lecture. A lively delivery style throughout is also necessary, not only to maintain interest but also to enhance your credibility.

Lectures are organized around various subtopics and use a variety of organizational patterns. Outlines for lectures include more detail than those for oral reports or demonstrations. The chapter outlines in this book are notes for a lecture on the topic of the chapter. We prepare these outlines to teach you to do something; the organizational patterns for the chapters are sequential on a need-to-know basis.

What About the Other Parts of an Informative Speech?

We have been talking about ordering the main points in an informative speech. But you should also review in Chapter 7 the objectives of the introduction and conclusion. For almost all informative speeches you will want to begin with a focus on the "big picture" and an orientation to audience needs and interests.

Most people understand new material better if they grasp the overall principle or end product before looking at the specifics.[5] If you conclude with a review of the specifics and a connection to the overall principle or product, the audience will remember the new information better.

Your teacher may ask you to prepare each type of informative speech. You may also be asked to develop an informative speech which focuses on one of the procedures of developing or clarifying, such as a speech of definition or a speech of comparison. The materials in Chapter 5 will be helpful for this. For each of these assignments you will have the opportunity to introduce new topics to your audience. And just think of the new ideas you will learn as you listen to your classmates' speeches.

LEARNING BY UNDERSTANDING

1. In which of the following situations are you likely to use informative speaking? Give an example of a speech topic and setting.
    a. Professional
    b. School
    c. Personal
    d. Family

2. Which of the following principles is likely to aid people's learning?
    a. Organized material
    b. Visualized concepts
    c. Connection or comparison with already-known information
    d. All of the above

3. Which type of informative speech is implied by each of the following topics?
    a. Handling the rattlesnake safely
    b. The causes of the stock market crash of 1929
    c. How to improve your test scores by eating better

ANSWERS:

3. **a.** demonstration, **b.** lecture, **c.** oral report
2. **d.**
1. You could use informative speaking in each situation. Share your answers and examples with someone else in the class and talk about the reasons behind your decisions.

What Are the Steps in Preparing an Informative Speech?

In Chapter 2 we suggested seven basic steps in preparing a short speech. The purpose then was to get you started on public speaking skills. Now we expand on those seven steps for preparing an informative speech. These thirteen steps represent suggestions from Chapters 4–11.

STEPS IN INFORMATIVE SPEECH PREPARATION

1. Choose a specific topic of interest and value to you and our audience (if one has not been chosen for you).

2. Analyze your audience to determine its current level of knowledge and interest in your topic.

3. Narrow your topic so that you are providing new and interesting information about a meaningful part of the topic for *this* audience.

4. Research additional information (if you do not know enough about the topic to talk to this particular audience).

5. Consider the time limit when you decide what new information you will provide.

6. Decide the order in which you want to give the information.

7. Select developing, supporting, and clarifying materials that will aid understanding and keep audience interest high.

8. Discover or develop aids which will help your audience visualize what you are describing in words.

9. Decide important places in the speech where you can involve your audience (see page 256 in this chapter).

10. Plan for feedforward.

11. Develop notes (not a script) to which you can refer during the speech.

12. Practice several times with a focus on:
    —reflecting your own strong interest nonverbally.
    —using visual aids effectively.
    —staying within your time limit.

13. Decide how to assess the results of your speech.

> *What are the Barriers which keep
> an Audience from fully Understanding a Message?*

Three barriers to understanding are (1) lack of interest, (2) lack of background information, and (3) lack of active processing by the audience. By understanding these barriers, you can more effectively work to overcome them. Sometimes these barriers are related. Sometimes they cause each other. For example, lack of background information could lead to lack of interest.

To avoid the first two barriers, do a careful audience analysis prior to your speech preparation and also observe carefully audience reactions as you speak. Use your audience analysis to focus on a topic which is within the audience's needs and interests and to build on what the audience already knows. Recognize the nonverbal indicators for disinterest or confusion as you talk. Figure 3-2 will help you review audience nonverbal responses and their meanings.

This speaker encourages her listeners to actively process new information by involving them in her message.

The third barrier is an important one to consider. We know that people understand something better and retain it longer if they actively think about it rather than passively hear it.[6] As we discussed in Chapter 3 this barrier is typical in public listening, where it is easy to become a passive member of a large group which discourages oral involvement.

To avoid the third barrier, encourage the audience's active involvement. You can invite physical participation. Ask audience members to raise their hands in response, write something individually, or try a new behavior in unison. For example, you could ask your listeners to close their eyes for a moment to experience blindness. This will encourage them to process the information they hear. These behaviors could be done without interfering with your format.

You can also invite active mental participation. Choose examples and comparisons which are important to your audience and communicate them with personalized language: "We all know how it feels . . ." or "Most of us have had the experience . . ." If you ask your listeners to imagine their own most embarrassing moment and give them five to fifteen seconds to call up and think about that image, it will help them to understand your point on a more personal level. You will also encourage active involvement if *your* nonverbal behaviors reflect your strong interest in the topic. Your excitement will be catching! Without such involvement, a public speaking audience can become passive observers of your speech and get little from the experience.

How Can I Tell If They Really Understood My Message?

An excellent question! Effective public speakers are concerned with results. This is especially vital for informative speeches, when you are trying to teach your audience something new. For professional contexts, the focus is clearly results-oriented. In the last chapter we discussed how you can interpret and adapt to audience response during your delivery. Now we want to suggest how you can measure audience response and understanding after your delivery.

For many of your informative speeches, you will have an opportunity to observe audience behaviors which will tell you if you have accomplished your specific purpose. For example, if you are a teacher, you could check the results of paper-pencil tests or students' usage of the material in class. If you are a manager explaining a new procedure, you could observe your listeners correctly completing the procedure. If you give an in-class speech on how to troubleshoot a car which won't start on a cold day, you could ask questions at the end or wait for compliments from classmates who are able to get their cars started.

For in-class informative speeches our students prepare two open-ended questions that their audience would not have been able to answer successfully without having understood the speech. The questions are asked orally or in written form. Audience members answer these questions in writing to give the speaker feedback on the level of their understanding. You could score audience answers to get a percentage for communication accuracy: (1) compare audience answers with answers you wrote before you gave your speech; (2) score each answer as *correct* (1 point), *not correct* (0 point), or *half correct* (½ point); (3) total the scores for both answers and divide by the total possible points or twice the number of listeners.

For some of your informative speeches, however, you will not have the opportunity to directly check audience understanding. The following procedures will be helpful in measuring your success in these situations:

1. Plan feedforward carefully for important points in your speech. This process was described in Chapter 11. The important points would most likely be the steps in the process you are demonstrating or the main points of your speech. If you see nonverbal signs of misunderstanding (see Figure 3-2 for a review), you would use a planned contingency to increase understanding. The contingency might involve another verbal example or the use of an additional visual aid.

2. Listen carefully to the questions that audience members ask after your speech. If the speaking situation permits a question-and-answer period, let your audience know this at the beginning of your speech. Having audience members hold their questions is usually a better approach than allowing them to interrupt you, particularly if your time is short or if it is a one-time-only speaking event. Audience questions might be answered by later information, or the question could be off the subject and confuse other listeners. Delaying questions encourages the listeners to be actively involved as they take notes for reference in the question-and-answer period. We encourage effective questions

by a statement such as, "You might want to ask yourselves if you could explain this process to another person. If not, you'll probably have some questions for me when I finish."

3. Attempt to do a delayed postcommunication assessment. This is especially important if you are giving your speech as part of an organization, or as a consultant to an organization, and you will be accountable for the results. Typical methods of postcommunication assessment include questionnaires, rating scales asking about the use of your information by the audience, testimonials by listeners, and assessment of change by the listeners' supervisors.

LEARNING BY UNDERSTANDING

1. What are three barriers to audience understanding?

2. For each of the following specific topics, infer which of the three barriers would be most likely with a college audience.
   a. Handling a Rattlesnake Safely
   b. The Causes of the 1929 Stock Market Crash
   c. How to Improve Your Test Scores by Eating Better

3. Briefly explain how you would recognize the three barriers you inferred for the specific topics in #2, and how you would resolve them.

4. How would you directly determine an audience's understanding of your informative speech?

ANSWERS:

1. Lack of interest, lack of needed background information, lack of active processing
2. a. Lack of interest, b. lack of needed background information, c. lack of active processing
3. Your answers here would focus on recognizing the nonverbal behaviors of your audience. One solution is using planned contingencies, such as additional verbal or visual material. Check your answers with another person in class and review the suggestions on pages 255 and 256.
4. Have the audience take a test or answer a few written or oral questions. Observe listeners do a process.

LEARNING BY INTERACTING

With four or five others from your class, attend a twenty- to fifty-minute lecture. Take notes and do individual thinking so that you will be able to discuss the following together:

1. What pattern of ordering main points did the speaker use? How well did the speaker's choice work? What other choices would you have made and why?

2. What developing, supporting, or clarifying materials were helpful for your understanding? What additional materials would you have used if you had been doing the lecture?

3. What visual aids were most helpful, or problematic, for your understanding? What additional visual aids would have increased your interest, understanding, and retention?

4. At what points in the lecture did you face one of the barriers to understanding? (Given the number of people in your group, it will be interesting to compare the different barriers experienced and the

reasons for them.) Share with your group how you expressed that barrier nonverbally to the speaker. Discuss what the speaker could have done to overcome the barrier.

5. How did the speaker relate new information to what the audience already knew? Give examples. What other opportunities could the speaker have used to make these important connections?

6. How did the speaker actively involve the listeners? What other opportunities could the speaker have used to get the audience involved?

LEARNING BY SPEAKING

Prepare a ten-minute speech on a topic on which you are well informed and which would enable your class audience to understand or do something new. Narrow your topic based on a careful audience analysis so that you enable the audience to use effectively the information you provide.

Prepare a sentence outline and feedforward planning for each main part and point of your speech. Practice several times, focusing on communicating enthusiasm, using your visual aids effectively, and keeping within the time limit. After your practice sessions, prepare a word or phrase outline to use in your actual delivery. Plan and use two methods to determine the degree you accomplished your speech purpose.

REVIEW

In this chapter you have been developing skills in effectively communicating new information to an audience. The key skills are organizing the material for a particular audience, using material to help audience members visualize the material, connecting the new material to that which they already know, and working to actively involve the listeners in the processing of the information. The three main types of informative speeches are the demonstration, the oral report, and the lecture. There are definite steps for preparing informative speeches. Barriers to audience understanding can be anticipated and you can measure the accomplishment of your informative goals.

NOTES

1. Robert W. Finkel, *The Brainbooster* (Englewood Cliffs, N.J.: Prentice-Hall, Inc., 1983), 178.

2. Ibid., 15–16.

3. David Horton and Carol Mills, "Human Learning and Memory," *Annual Review of Psychology* 35(1984):368.

4. Finkel, *Brainbooster*, 131–32.

5. Ibid., 180–81.

6. Horton and Mills, "Human Learning and Memory," 368.

13

DEVELOPING PERSUASIVE SKILLS

In this chapter, you'll be . . .

LEARNING BY UNDERSTANDING

- The three parts of an attitude and their relationship to behavior
- How to set a specific behavioral goal
- How to determine an attitude that will lead to the desired behavior
- Barriers that limit people from doing suggested behaviors
- How to change attitudes and behaviors
- How to determine if a persuasive attempt has succeeded

LEARNING BY INTERACTING

- Preparing and assessing alternative approaches to attitude/behavior change

LEARNING BY SPEAKING

- A six- to eight-minute persuasive speech to change an attitude or behavior

CHAPTER OUTLINE

I. Persuasive speeches are designed to change the attitudes and/or behaviors of audiences.
   A. Attitudes, which tend to lead to certain behaviors, are learned combinations of thoughts and feelings about something.
      1. The thinking part of an attitude is called the cognitive part.
      2. The feeling part of an attitude is called the affective part.
      3. The combination of the cognitive and affective is the behavior tendency of an attitude.
   B. Behaviors are observable actions done by a person.

II. Attitude and behavior change are based on the relationship between attitudes and behaviors.
   A. Attitudes with strong cognitive and affective parts will lead to expected behaviors.
   B. Behaviors will reinforce related attitudes.

III. Changing an audience's attitudes or behavior is difficult.
   A. Audience members associate with other people who reinforce their current attitudes and behaviors.
   B. Audience members filter new information in terms of their current frames of reference.
   C. An audience's attitudes are interconnected and support one another.
   D. Time, embarrassment, or money barriers often prevent your audience from doing a recommended behavior.
   E. Sometimes an audience's cognitive or affective attitude parts are not developed well enough to lead to the desired behavior.

IV. There are five steps in planning for a persuasive speech.
   A. The first step is setting an attainable goal.
      1. Consider the time limit and the audience's current attitudes.
      2. Determine a specific behavior to be done.
   B. The second step is determining an audience need(s) that will motivate change.
   C. The third step is determining what attitude(s) would lead this audience to do the desired behavior.
   D. The fourth step is determining if the audience already holds the cognitive and affective parts of the attitude(s).
   E. The final step is determining what barriers exist to limit the audience from doing the behavior.

V. A persuasive speech consists of four steps.
  A. The first step is providing motivation to change.
    1. You should visualize current audience needs that are not satisfied.
    2. You should show the undesirability of the current situation.
  B. The second step is developing the attitude that will lead to change.
    1. Use reasoning to develop the cognitive part of the attitude.
    2. Use emotional appeals to develop the affective part of the attitude.
    3. Relate the new attitude to currently held audience values.
  C. The third step is urging audience commitment to do the behavior.
    1. Relate the suggested behavior to satisfaction of current audience needs.
    2. Overcome barriers to doing the behavior such as lack of time or low self-confidence.
    3. Provide a concrete plan for doing the behavior.
  D. The fourth step is helping the audience resist counterpersuasion.
    1. Provide a handle within the audience's common experiences to remind it of the behavior.
    2. Preview and refute counterarguments.
    3. Summarize support for the new attitude.

VI. It is important to determine if you succeeded in your persuasive goal.
  A. You can determine your success by using audience feedback during the speech.
  B. You can determine actual change after the speech.
    1. Check attitude change by a shift-of-opinion ballot.
    2. Check attitude and/or behavior change by asking or observing the behavior later.

13

DEVELOPING PERSUASIVE SKILLS

"Does everyone just believe what he wants to?"
"As long as possible, sometimes longer." —Isaac Asimov

PREVIEW

Persuasive speeches are designed to change the attitudes and/or behavior of audiences. These are the most difficult of all types of speeches because it is very difficult to change people. People see their current attitudes and behaviors as sensible, and they tend to be friends with people who agree with them. You can, however, encourage others to change by: (1) providing a personally important motivation for them to change; (2) developing favorable attitudes toward the suggested change; (3) overcoming barriers to doing the behavior; and (4) developing resistance to counterarguments. These four steps should follow a careful study of your audience's knowledge, attitudes, and needs. The skills of audience analysis, message preparation, and delivery are especially important in persuasive speaking. It is critically important to have a clear purpose in mind and to base your speech choices on information about your particular audience.

Isn't Most Speaking Persuasive?

Almost all communication has the *potential* for influencing people. Similarly, almost all communication also has the potential for informing and/or entertaining people. The audience's interpretations and responses determine the main outcome of a speaking situation. The designation of a type of speech clarifies the expectations of the speaker and audience. It helps the speaker set a clear speaking purpose and helps the audience set personal listening goals. Clear goals for both will make it more likely that the goal will be accomplished. Any speech, however, can include material designed to inform, entertain, or persuade to accomplish the specific speech purpose. For example, if you want to persuade your audience to vote for you in the upcoming student senate election, you might include material to inform your listeners of your genuine interest in student government. You might also reveal your sense of humor, as well as communicate materials more directly designed to motivate them to vote for you.

Why Did You Say ''Attitudes and/or Behavior''?

Researchers have been trying to understand the relationship between attitudes and behaviors for a long time.[1] Before we explore that relationship, let's define the two key terms. An *attitude* is a learned combination of thoughts and feelings about something that tends to lead to certain behaviors. *Behavior* has been defined in a variety of ways. We use the word to refer to an observable action done by a person.[2] This definition helps the public speaker because it provides a visible goal to work toward and also a means of checking the accomplishment of the communication goal.

An attitude can be thought of as having three basic parts: the thinking, or cognitive, part; the feeling, or affective, part; and the resulting behavior tendencies.[3] The following sample attitude on exercise includes the three parts:

Cognitive part (thinking): ''Regular exercise leads to a healthy body.''
Affective part (feeling): favorable personal feelings toward exercise (+ 6).
Behavior tendency: very likely to run for thirty minutes every day.

The cognitive part of an attitude is based largely on personally meaningful information and reasons and can be expressed in thoughts and then in words. Many times, this part of an attitude results from hearing other people's ideas. The affective part of an attitude is often based on reactions to personal experiences and can be expressed in a description of the direction and strength of feelings.[4] The behavior tendency of an attitude is the action part. For any given combination of cognitive and affective parts, one or more behaviors or actions are likely, as shown in Figure 13-1, and some are more likely than others.

We tend to express the cognitive part of our attitudes by what we say or write. Thus, if you asked a member of your audience her opinions, her answers would reflect the cognitive part of her attitudes. To be as accurate as possible in recording the cognitive parts of attitudes and to show whose they are, we recommend putting quotation marks around the person's statements. This is also important because

Figure 13-1   Parts of Attitudes

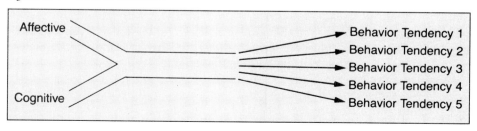

the strength of people's thinking is expressed in the words they choose. The person in the example who said, "Regular exercise leads to a healthy body" would have a weaker mental commitment than a person who said, "I'm definitely going to start on a regular exercise program today to have a more healthy body."

In terms of persuasion, the feeling, or affective, part of attitudes is at least as important and probably more so. We probably all know people who want to stop doing something, such as smoking or overeating, but they have not done so. These people may have expressed positive cognitive parts of their attitude; for example, they have said, "Right! I know there are definite health hazards from smoking cigarettes" or "Right! I sure would like to lose weight." Why, then, haven't they lost weight or stopped smoking? Probably because the affective part of their attitude is not strong enough to produce commitment to the change. Usually the strength of people's feelings can be inferred from how strongly they express the cognitive parts of their attitude or from the absence of probability in the cognitive statement of the attitude. However, for speech purposes it is better to directly ask audience members to express their feelings and then measure the feelings. One way would be to have each audience member select a number (as done in #2 of the following Learning by Understanding exercise) between +10 for "very favorable" and −10 for "very unfavorable" to represent the direction and the degree of their feelings. You could then average those numbers to learn the audience's feelings.

The behavior tendencies stem from the combination of the cognitive and affective parts.[5] The stronger the statement of the cognitive part and the more favorable the affective part, the greater the likelihood of doing any particular behavior. But regardless of the strength of the cognitive and affective parts of the attitude for the audience, some behaviors are more likely than others. For example, simple behaviors are more likely than complex behaviors. Ones which are enjoyable are more likely than ones that are not. Behaviors to be done immediately are more likely than delayed behaviors. And behaviors leading to immediate results are more likely than behaviors producing delayed results. Accordingly, to maximize the likelihood of the audience doing your suggested behavior, the behavior should be simple, enjoyable, immediate, and have immediate results. Thus, returning to our exercise example, the speaker's goal of getting listeners to run for thirty minutes every day is much less likely than a goal of doing their favorite sport for ten minutes every day. See #2 in the following Learning by Understanding exercise for more specific examples.

Often a speaker has a specific behavior in mind that he wants listeners to do. He works with their attitudes to increase the likelihood that the behavior will be done. The attitude, which could be changed in terms of the thinking or feeling parts, provides the motivation to do the behavior. In speeches where the goal is to change an attitude, the suggestion of a definite behavior will support the development and/or strengthening of the desired attitude. For example, if an audience chose to sign a petition against an upcoming bill to legalize abortion, that behavior would reinforce and strengthen the attitude that abortion is wrong.

Because attitudes and behavior are closely interconnected, we suggest that you work for changes in both attitudes and behaviors in your persuasive speeches.[6] Check Judith Barton's speech, "Deadly Discrimination: Testicular Cancer," in Appendix B for an excellent example of a speech that works to change both attitudes and behaviors.

LEARNING BY UNDERSTANDING

1. The cognitive part of an attitude is the _____ part; the affective part of an attitude is the _____ part; and the behavior tendency of an attitude is the _____ part.

2. As you can tell, we believe in exercise, and we have used this subject as an example for understanding the nature of attitudes. Write out word-for-word two or three beliefs you have about exercise under "Cognitive Part." Check your current attitude from +10 to −10 to indicate direction and strength toward those belief statements under "Affective Part." Then, given your thoughts and feelings, check the degree of likelihood of your doing the various proposed behaviors.

A DAILY EXERCISE PROGRAM FOR ME

Cognitive Part:	Daily Behaviors	*and*	Behavior Tendencies		
			very unlikely		very likely
			10%	50%	100%
1. _____	1. Yoga for 30 min.				
2. _____	2. Yoga for 10 min.				
3. _____	3. Yoga for 5 min.				
	4. Calisthenics for 30 min.				
Affective Part:	5. Calisthenics for 10 min.				
	6. Calisthenics for 5 min.				
very favorable +10	7. Running for 30 min.				
	8. Running for 10 min.				
+5	9. Running for 5 min.				
	10. My favorite sport for 30 min.				
neutral 0	11. My favorite sport for 10 min.				
	12. My favorite sport for 5 min.				
−5	13. (List your own:)				
	14.				
very unfavorable −10	15.				

ANSWERS:

1. Thinking, feeling, action
2. There are no right answers to this question. Your cognitive statements might be placed in quotation marks to represent your thinking; the affective—how strongly you feel; and the behaviors—what you are likely to do and how likely. We recommend you check your responses with someone else in the class.

Why Is It Difficult to Change an Audience's Attitudes and Behavior?

Although some changes in attitude and behavior seem to make good sense, people continue current behaviors. For example, millions of dollars in advertising have been spent to try to persuade people to stop smoking cigarettes, fasten their seat belts, vote for a candidate, and drive fifty-five miles per hour; yet evidence indicates that many, many people do not do these desired behaviors. That is because attitudes and behaviors tend to remain stable.

FACTORS LIMITING ATTITUDE AND BEHAVIOR CHANGE

1. Your audience associates with other people who reinforce current attitudes and current behaviors.

2. Your audience filters new information in terms of its current frame of reference, based on its current needs and attitudes.

3. Your audience's attitudes become interconnected so that they support each other.

4. Time, embarrassment, or money barriers often prevent or weaken the doing of the recommended behavior.

5. Sometimes an audience's cognitive or affective attitude parts are not developed well enough or strongly enough to lead to the desired behavior.[7]

Let's say, for example, that you want to persuade a friend to begin a regular exercise program, but you aren't having much success. Perhaps one or more of the following examples of the above five factors are limiting your friend's success. (1) Your friend spends time with people who don't exercise regularly and who reinforce contrary behaviors, such as overeating, drinking, and sitting around. (2) Your friend doesn't listen to information about the values of exercising and tends to distort information he hears about health hazards. (3) Your friend has

Changing a listener's attitudes is often a difficult task.

supported his nonactivity with other attitudes, such as "Studying is more important now" or "I don't see myself as a jock." (4) Your friend says he lacks the time and money to get involved in an exercising program. (5) Your friend either doesn't think that exercise is important (weak cognitive part of the attitude) or doesn't have a strong personal feeling that exercise is important (weak affective part). Probably several of these factors are working against your desired change.

If Persuasion Is That Difficult, What Can I Do in One Speech?

Although bringing about significant change in the course of a single persuasive attempt is difficult, significant changes can occur as a result of public speeches. We would like to share two very different examples of this happening. Irving S. Shapiro, chief executive of DuPont and chairman of the Business Roundtable (a group of corporation presidents personally involved in issues confronting the business community), described such a speech that he made:

> One Sunday morning I was in a Washington hotel room reading the *New York Times* book review section . . . There was a review of somebody's book concerning corporate governance . . . When I came back to Wilmington, I tried to clarify my own thinking on this subject and wound up putting together a speech. The speech struck a responsive chord in the business community. It got people talking about the subject, and led to the judgment at the Business Roundtable that we ought to put together views that would reflect the consensus of the business community. So the Roundtable created a task force to do the work of gathering the views.[8]

Clearly, one speech can be an important influence. This example also reflects the use of the two research skills of reading and thinking as preparation for speaking.

The second example involves a speech given by a student in a public speaking course similar to yours. The speech vividly described the physical abuse suffered by certain students on campus and concluded with the speaker's urging her audience to do an immediate behavior—sign a petition to be sent to the state governor expressing concern about the students' lack of protection. After submitting the petition, the speaker received a letter from the governor, in which he wrote: "I would be interested in working with you and other interested students, as well as with the city and county . . . to determine what additional security measures can be taken. My administration is committed to being of all possible assistance in this regard."

How Can I Move My Audience to Change Its Attitudes and/or Behaviors?

As indicated earlier, you will use all the skills you have developed thus far—invention, organization, style, memory, and delivery—for persuasive speeches. The additional skills involved in persuasive speaking include planning for persuasion and developing a persuasive speech.

PERSUASIVE SPEAKING SKILLS

Planning for a Persuasive Speech
1. Set an attainable goal, including a specific behavior to be done.
2. Determine an audience need(s) that will motivate change.
3. Determine what cognitive and affective parts of an attitude(s) would lead this audience to do the desired behavior.
4. Determine if the audience already holds the cognitive and affective parts of the attitude(s).
5. Determine what barriers exist to limit the audience from doing the behavior.

Developing a Persuasive Speech
1. Provide motivation for change.
   a. Visualize current audience needs that are not fully satisfied.
   b. Show the undesirability of the current situation.
2. Develop the attitude leading to change.
   a. Use reasoning to develop the cognitive part of the attitude.
   b. Use emotional appeals to develop the affective part of the attitude.
   c. Relate the new attitude to currently held audience values.
3. Urge audience commitment to do the behavior.
   a. Relate the suggested behavior to satisfaction of current audience needs.
   b. Overcome barriers to doing the behavior.
   c. Provide a concrete plan for doing the behavior.
4. Help the audience resist counterpersuasion.
   a. Provide a "handle" within the audience's common experiences.
   b. Preview and refute counterarguments.
   c. Summarize support for the new attitude.

Let's look at each of the skills and component steps in more detail, using the example of urging your speech class to follow a consistent exercise program.

The first step in planning for a persuasive speech involves setting an attainable goal. Beginning public speakers often try to accomplish too much in a short speech. By focusing on a specific behavior, you will be able to decide if your goal is attainable for this audience. To be sure you have the information to help you accomplish each of the skills in persuading, use the skills you developed in Chapters 4 and 8 for analyzing your audience. With our example, a goal of doing calisthenics for five minutes a day would be more realistic for a college audience than would running for thirty minutes every day. The latter would be a goal for someone training for the spring intramural track meet. Again, it is best to choose specific behaviors with immediate benefits.[9]

The second step also involves knowing important things about your audience. With your class audience, as with others, you would focus on the similarities of experiences, knowledge, and attitudes. For example, we might assume with a college audience a felt need to lead a productive and successful life. You may also have learned from your interaction with classmates that most share a common desire to improve themselves personally and to do well on final exams. All these safety and esteem needs could be helped by the good health resulting from consistent exercise. So you might concentrate on those needs at this stage in your preparation.

The third step focuses on the parts of the attitude that would be most likely to produce the desired behavior of five minutes of daily exercise. Choose this attitude based on what you know about this audience's frame of reference including the needs the audience has at the time. The attitude should provide the connection between the need and the suggested behavior.[10] One attitude that might lead this audience to do the behavior could be

> Cognitive: "I'm definitely convinced that daily exercise will help me do better on final exams."
> Affective: strongly positive (+8)

The fourth step builds on knowledge about the audience's attitudes to determine how strongly each of the components of the chosen attitude is already developed. Perhaps the audience "knows" the cognitive dimension but does not "feel" the personal impact strongly enough to do the desired behavior of daily exercise. Or perhaps the audience does not fully believe and accept the attitude. By determining what the audience already knows and feels, you can use your speech time to the best advantage to develop one or the other part. This kind of audience analysis could be done by the direct method used in #2 of the last Learning by Understanding.

Finally, the fifth step suggests that you analyze what specific barriers (sometimes called "excuses") might keep the audience from doing the desired behavior. The following are potential barriers that prevent people from doing suggested behaviors:

- lack of time
- lack of money
- lack of self-confidence to do the behavior
- negative reinforcement by friends or reference groups for doing the behavior
- related interfering attitudes
- habits that interfere with doing the behavior
- former negative experience with the behavior
- the publicness of the behavior
- the time lag between your speech about the behavior and doing the behavior[11]

If you can anticipate the reasons why an audience might not follow through and do the behavior, you can suggest ways to overcome them in your speech. Because of the variety of audience members, it is often helpful to make suggestions regarding several typical barriers to doing the behavior. For example, students might feel they lack the time to do daily exercise, have related interfering attitudes (for example, "It isn't ladylike"), or are embarrassed to exercise in public.

LEARNING BY UNDERSTANDING

1. For each of the following goals for a persuasive speech, write a specific and attainable behavior the class audience could do.

Goals	Specific Behavior
a. To study more	**a.**
b. To donate time to a charity	**b.**
c. To be active in campus politics	**c.**

2. For each of the above goals and behaviors, write the cognitive and affective parts of the attitude that might motivate your class members to do the specific behaviors.

3. For each of the above goals, behaviors, and motivating attitudes, indicate two barriers that might keep the class from actually doing the behavior.

ANSWERS:

There are several possible answers for each question. For example, for goal b:

1. b. Specific behavior: To spend two hours helping pass out cookies and orange drink this Saturday at the Red Cross blood drive.

2. b. Cognitive attitude: "I promise to go to the student union from ten o'clock to twelve noon this Saturday to work for the Red Cross blood drive."

Affective attitude: Moderately favorable (+5)

3. b. Barriers: Lack of time; previous negative experience in giving blood.

How Do I Actually Develop the Speech?

The steps indicated earlier suggest a general outline for a persuasive speech. You will also use your skills in choosing and ordering main points to arrange your speech parts. For example, if your audience was generally positive toward doing the behavior, you might use a *deductive* approach. If it was negative, you might use an *inductive* approach as you develop the appropriate parts of the desired attitudes before urging the behavior. But please remember, here we are working on the body of the persuasive speech. Do not forget to use the parts of an effective introduction, *especially* the expertise and trustworthiness factors of credibility. Research shows these to be most valuable for judgment and persuasive situations,[12] particularly when the audience is not highly motivated.[13] Personal attractiveness developed through similarity and sociability are also important in oral persuasion.[14]

The first step urges that you provide a motivation for the audience to change. You do this by visualizing needs that the audience has that are not now fully satisfied and by showing how undesirable this state is. For example, you might remind your fellow students of their personal desires to do the best they can in college. Then point out to them that, by not being in good physical shape, they limit their ability to achieve that need. It is not enough to *tell* an audience about an unfulfilled need; you must help the audience *feel* that unfulfilled need enough to want to change. After this step, the audience members should be believing, "I really want to change!" They should be open to new ideas. Your skills in developing emotional appeals and using vivid language will help you develop a strong need.

In persuasive speaking effective delivery is as important as a well-developed speech.

To encourage the audience members to do the behavior, encourage them to believe and feel that it is important to start meeting that need *now*, rather than at some vague time in the future. In a speech to encourage daily exercise, you might use positive appeals to good health by having them imagine being able to run up the stairs to third-floor classes or being able to play full-court basketball with their younger brother or negative appeals to avoid falling asleep while studying for final exams.

In the second step, remind the audience of, or develop, the attitude that will lead to the change. This attitude will provide the link between audience need and behavior. Your audience analysis will indicate if you have to develop the cognitive part, the affective part, or both. If you have only one speaking opportunity, it is helpful to use an attitude for which the audience already holds, or partially holds, the cognitive part and then further develop it.

Use reasoning and evidence to establish the cognitive part of the attitude and emotional appeals to establish a strong affective part. By relating these attitudes to values the listeners already hold, you will encourage them to add the new attitude to their current attitude structure. For example, a standard pitch by life insurance salespeople is, ''You are buying security and protection for your loved ones.'' What needs and values are being appealed to? If you were developing the attitude ''daily exercise makes me feel better'' and had provided reasoning and emotional appeals to prove it to your classmates, you could connect that attitude to the existing belief that ''the way you feel about yourself influences the way you behave.'' Thus, you help the audience use its frame of reference as a positive filter in understanding your message. After the second step, you want your audience to be thinking, "It makes logical and personal sense to change."

The third step involves urging the audience to commit to do the behavior. Now you are ready to suggest your specific behavior—doing five minutes of exercise a day. Again, you would use a combination of logical and emotional proofs to support the suggestion that this behavior will satisfy the identified audience needs. You would suggest specific ways to overcome the barriers identified during the fifth step of your planning stage and suggest how the behavior can be done. You might encourage the audience to decide on a five-minute period of time that would be most convenient for doing the behavior.

Research strongly suggests that a public commitment to do a behavior will make it more likely that the audience actually will do it. One of our students accomplished that goal in the following way. In a speech urging students to get to know the international students on campus better, this speaker defined several behaviors that could help this happen. During the conclusion of the speech, he asked the class members to turn to the people next to them and tell them which was the best suggestion for getting to know an international student. Then the speaker said, "Will you tell that same person that you will try that behavior sometime this week?" On checking with the audience later in the week, he was pleased to find out that about 90 percent actually had done one suggested behavior. You have probably watched this technique used in religious revivals and television fund raisers, where people make their commitment publicly. After the third step, you want your audience members to be saying, "I can and *will* do the behavior!"

The fourth and final step is not always used in persuasive speeches. Essentially, you are trying to prepare the audience for counterarguments they might receive to keep them from making the suggested change. Counterarguments are especially likely in debates on public policy. Three substeps help build resistance to counterpersuasion. First, you can *provide* a *handle* or a verbal connection between the suggested behavior and something within the common experience of the audience. Each time audience members have that common experience, they will recall the support for the attitude and the behavior. For example, you might tell your classmates, "Each time you enter the student union, remind yourself that getting and staying in shape will keep you from becoming an unknown." Another handle could be, "Each time you walk into the union and notice the tables where the international students sit, remember your commitment to do the behavior you told your neighbor you would try to do." Second, you can preview and *refute* the major *counterarguments* the audience is likely to hear. For example you could warn your class, "Your roommate may try to tell you that exercise . . . But research and experience show that . . . ." You might accomplish the second substep of previewing and refuting counterarguments early in the speech, when you provide support for the cognitive part of the attitude. And, finally, *summarize* the *support* for the attitudes and behavior you are suggesting because repetition helps the audience remember until it is time to do the behavior. After the fourth step, you want audience members to say, "I will continue to do the behavior."

Let's look at the outline of the body of the speech in which the student succeeded in having her classmates sign a petition to encourage better protection of students on campus. The marginal notes show how the steps in developing a persuasive speech were used.

(Motivation to Change—Safety)	I. You (or someone close to you) could be one of the sixty victims a month of crime in our area.	
	A. We all want to feel safe while attending classes.	(Current Need)
(Current Situation Is Undesirable)	B. Current information reveals that sixty criminal reports are filed each month on campus.	
	1. Increased crime costs students money.	
	2. Increased crime hurts enrollment.	
	3. Increased crime hurts students physically.	
(Attitude Reflects a Workable Solution)	II. More patrol officers and better lighting will reduce the crime rate.	
	A. Research from other campuses shows these methods work.	(Reasoning for Cognitive Part)
(Emotional Appeals for Affective Part)	B. These methods will lower the chances that you will have an experience similar to mine.	
	C. These methods will demonstrate that hurting innocent people does not pay.	(Attaching Attitude to Audience Value)
(Urging a Feasible Behavior)	III. Urging our governor and state legislators to take action will help us lower the crime rate.	
	A. The campus will be safer for you if your urging leads to state action.	(Relating Behavior to Satisfaction of Audience Needs)
(Overcoming Barriers)	B. I have prepared a petition to the governor that will allow you to help without taking your time and money.	
(Providing a Concrete Plan and An Immediate Behavior)	C. After my speech, I'll pass the petition around for you to sign.	
(Helping Continuance of Change)	IV. You can urge others to take similar action.	
	A. Each time you pass the large unlighted parking lot near our speech building, tell whomever you're with about the importance of contacting a state legislator.	(Providing a Handle)
(Preview Counterarguments)	B. You may receive arguments that nothing's ever done by the state.	
	C. There is strong evidence that action from the state through funding is the best way to solve this problem.	(Refute Counterargument By Summarizing Support for Attitude)

How Can I Tell If I've Succeeded?

It is important to check for success both during and after a persuasive speech. The most important check in a behavior-change speech is whether or not the audience does the suggested behavior. For attitude-change speeches, the usual check of results is a shift-of-opinion ballot. For your class speeches, you would be able to check with the audience later to determine if the behavior you suggested was done or if its attitude changed. The other important check is whether your audience is with you as you move through the steps of your persuasive speech. Each suggested step has an implied goal in terms of the expected audience response you desire when you have completed it. By preparing and using feedforward contingency messages you will be able to keep your audience with you by accomplishing each step in sequence.[15]

LEARNING BY UNDERSTANDING

1. Reasoning is used to develop the _____ part of the desired attitude; emotional appeals are used to develop the _____ part.

2. List three barriers that might keep an audience of businessmen from a small rural community from doing the behavior of financially sponsoring the high school band's trip to the state capital.

3. Give an example of a handle which you could provide to encourage an audience to continue doing the behavior of wearing seat belts while in a car.

4. State one way you can tell if you accomplished your persuasive goal in changing your audience's attitude and one way to see if its behavior changed.

5. At the 1985 National Individual Events Tournament, Mary Nielsen was a finalist with her persuasive speech "The World Caste System" (see Appendix B). At such tournaments speakers often do not urge their audience (which is usually made up of judges and other contestants) to do a specific behavior. Work with this speech to identify the specific steps of a persuasive speech. Suggest a specific behavior which an audience of college students could do. This behavior should increase attitude change.

ANSWERS:

1. Cognitive; affective
2. Possible barriers include money; not wanting to set a precedent; embarrassment at giving less than another business.
3. An example might be, "Every time you shut the car door behind you, put on your seat belt right away."
4. Shift-of-opinion ballot; ask audience members later or observe their behavior
5. Check your answers with classmates.

LEARNING BY INTERACTING

Work in small groups on a mutually agreed-on persuasive goal. Each group will plan for and develop a persuasive speech to accomplish the same chosen goal for your speech class. Summarize in writing your accomplishment of each of the steps of planning and preparing so you can share your thinking with the other groups.

When all groups have completed their speech outlines, compare the results. Decide which approach would be most successful for your class as a whole.

LEARNING BY SPEAKING

Prepare a six- to eight-minute persuasive speech to urge classmates to change their attitudes or behavior. If you choose to work toward an attitude change, determine a specific behavior your classmates can do to reflect their attitude change and reinforce it.

Prepare a sentence outline and feedforward planning for your speech. In the margin of your outline, indicate where you have accomplished each of the following: providing a motivation to change, indicating a current need, showing undesirability of current situation, developing the appropriate parts of the chosen attitude(s), attaching the attitude to an audience value, urging the behavior, relating the behavior to satisfaction of needs, overcoming barriers, providing a handle, previewing and refuting counterarguments, and summarizing support for change.

REVIEW

The purpose of a persuasive speech is to bring about a change in audience attitudes and/or behavior. This is a difficult goal to accomplish for several reasons. People associate with others who reinforce current attitudes and behaviors. New information will be filtered through their interconnected current frame of reference. Situational constraints limit their change. And, finally, the necessary cognitive or affective parts of the attitude may not be well developed. Attitudes are the vehicle by which a persuasive speaker works toward change. You will work to develop the thinking, or cognitive, part of an attitude and the feeling, or affective, part in order to encourage the desired behavior. There are definite steps to follow in planning and developing a persuasive message. Using these will help you accomplish your purpose.

NOTES

1. Joel Cooper and Robert T. Croyle, "Attitudes and Attitude Change," *Annual Review of Psychology* 35(1984):395.

2. Linda Heun and Richard Heun, *Developing Skills for Human Interaction*, 2d ed. (Columbus, Ohio: Chas. E. Merrill, 1978), 303.

3. Ibid.

4. S. J. Sherman et al., "Smoking Intentions in Adolescents: Direct Experience and Predictability," *Personality and Social Psychology Bulletin* 8(1982):376.

5. R. P. Bagozzi, "Attitudes, Intentions, and Behavior: A Test of Some Key Hypotheses," *Journal of Personality and Social Psychology* 41(October 1981):607.

6. Cooper and Croyle, "Attitudes and Attitude Change," 397.

7. Heun and Heun, *Developing Skills*, 302.

8. Irving S. Shapiro, "Today's Executive: Private Steward and Public Servant," *Harvard Business Review* 56(March–April 1978):95.

9. Stewart L. Tubbs, "Explicit Versus Implicit Conclusions and Audience Commitment," *Speech Monographs* 35(March 1968):14.

10. R. E. Petty and J. T. Cacioppo, *Attitudes and Persuasion: Classic and Contemporary Approaches* (Dubuque, Iowa: W. C. Brown, 1981).

11. Heun and Heun, *Developing Skills*, 317.

12. M. H. Birnbaum and B. A. Mellers, "Bayesian Inference: Combining Base Rates with Opinions of Sources Who Vary in Credibility," *American Journal of Psychology*. In press.

13. R. E. Petty et al., "Personal Involvement as a Determinant of Argument Based Persuasion," *Journal of Personality and Social Psychology* 41(November 1981):846.

14. S. Chaiken and A. H. Eagly, "Communication Modality as a Determinant of Persuasion: The Role of Communicator Salience," *Journal of Personality and Social Psychology* 45(August 1983):241.

15. J. T. Cacioppo and R. E. Petty, "Attitudes and Cognitive Response: An Electrophysiological Approach," *Journal of Personality and Social Psychology* 37(December 1979):2181.

14

HANDLING SPECIAL SPEECH OCCASIONS AND SITUATIONS

In this chapter, you'll be . . .

LEARNING BY UNDERSTANDING

- Basic types of speeches to honor an individual
- Basic types of speeches to commemorate an occasion
- Expectations for each of the basic special-occasion speeches
- The most important skills for special-occasion speeches
- Guidelines for using the media effectively
- How to give an impromptu speech
- How to answer sincere questions
- How to answer insincere questions
- How to give a speech to entertain

LEARNING BY INTERACTING

- Coping with difficult questions

LEARNING BY SPEAKING

- A two- to three-minute special-occasion speech and introduction of another class member
- A two- to three-minute speech to entertain which gives a new perspective to a common experience
- A three-minute radio or television presentation

CHAPTER OUTLINE

I. Public speeches are the most common vehicle for commemorating special occasions and have as their major goal the reinforcement of shared values.
  A. Special-occasion speeches can honor individuals.
    1. Speeches of introduction establish the credibility of the guest speaker and stimulate interest in the speech content.
    2. Welcoming speeches associate the values of the welcoming group with the values of those being welcomed.
    3. Inauguration speeches are given by people taking over the leadership of a group, to note the accomplishments of the speaker's predecessor, highlight the values and accomplishments of the organization, and indicate the direction the new administration will take.
    4. Presentation speeches highlight the values the award represents by describing the award, indicating the values it attempts to reward, and showing how the personal qualifications of the recipient reflect those values.
    5. Acceptance speeches are given by people receiving awards to show appreciation for the honor and to acknowledge any people who were helpful in the accomplishment.
    6. Farewell and appreciation speeches are given when people leave a job or location to note the contributions the person has made and to wish the person well in his or her new situation.
    7. Eulogies are given after a person has completed his or her life to note the values of the person being honored and to indicate how the audience can benefit by remembering the attributes of this individual.
  B. Special-occasion speeches can commemorate an occasion.
    1. Dedication speeches highlight the meaning of a new creation by indicating the values the object represents and inspiring the audience to live up to the values.
    2. Commencement speeches honor a graduate by indicating the challenges accomplished and the challenges ahead.
    3. Keynote speeches open organizational meetings by referring to the goals of the organization, indicating the focus of the meeting, and reinforcing the audience's presence.
    4. Public relations speeches establish a good image by defining the goals of the organization, tying organizational goals with audience values, and indicating the benefits of the organization for the audience.

II. There are four special situations for speaking.
  A. Using the media is the first special situation for speaking.
    1. Using the media is a challenging speaking situation.
      a. The audience is in greater control of the media.
      b. The audience will have a variety of interests.
      c. The speaker will have a definite time limit.
    2. Practice will help you prepare to use the media.
      a. Visit the radio or television station to see the facilities.
      b. Practice responding to the signals given by the station technicians.
      c. Practice the exact timing of your speech.
  B. Impromptu speaking is the second special situation for speaking.
    1. Be brief and develop only one or two points.
    2. Use this formula: Stall with a generalization, give several *because* statements, state your conclusion, and stop.
  C. Answering questions is the third special situation for speaking.
    1. Respond to sincere answer-seeking questions by using the impromptu speaking formula.
    2. Message questions should be summarized and followed with an inquiry about the intended questions.
    3. "Getcha" questions should be received openly, acknowledged, and followed with a summary of your point.
  D. Speaking to entertain is the final special situation for speaking.
    1. Entertaining speeches should be light, original, and appropriate.
    2. The steps for developing an entertaining speech are the same as for other speeches.

14

HANDLING SPECIAL SPEECH OCCASIONS AND SITUATIONS

. . . we have gathered here not merely to pay tribute—but to refresh our spirits and stir our hearts for the tasks which lie ahead.   —John F. Kennedy

PREVIEW

One of the traditions and strengths of American culture is the recognition and celebration of individuals and occasions. People active in their communities and/or professions often are called on to use public speaking skills to commemorate special occasions. We celebrate, through public speeches, the birthdays of famous presidents, the completion of new buildings, school graduations, and many other important events. Most special-occasion speeches fall into two general categories—those honoring individuals and those commemorating special occasions. Examples of the former include the presentation and acceptance of awards, welcomes and farewells, inaugurations, introductions, and eulogies. Examples of speeches commemorating occasions include keynote addresses, commencement speeches, dedications, and public relations (good will) speeches. All these speeches involve the recognition of values that are important to society. A speaker should recognize the expectations of the special situation and choose the appropriate skills of style, memory, and delivery.

In addition to special speech occasions are four special situations that demand unusual public speaking skills. These situations are using the media, delivering impromptu speeches, answering questions, and speaking to entertain.

▨ *Why Do We Celebrate Special Occasions with Speeches?*

The commemoration of special occasions serves two basic purposes. It directly or indirectly reinforces the contributions of individuals to our society. And it allows us to reinforce the values we feel are important. By *value* we mean the concepts that people see as very important. These can be quite general like the *freedom to pursue happiness* or more specific like *the right to bear arms*.

Both these purposes are important to a democratic society. Public speeches are the most common vehicle for commemorating these occasions because they use a symbol system that clearly expresses ideas and feelings and because public recognition is vital to the accomplishment of both basic purposes. Material tokens, such as money, a gold watch, a cap and gown, or the key to a city, might accomplish the first purpose—reinforcing the individual. But they would only accomplish the second—reinforcing values—superficially. As we discussed in Chapter 12, people attach their own meanings to the symbols they use. By using carefully chosen words in a public setting, we can help people recognize the special occasion clearly and vividly and help them recommit themselves, *cognitively* and *affectively*, to the values the occasion represents.

Why Do Some Special-Occasion Speeches Seem More Like Brief Announcements?

True, these speeches are likely to be much briefer and involve little of the reasoning and organization choices basic to most other speeches you have worked on. We have all heard introductions that only say, "Without further comment, I give you . . ." and acceptances that only say, "Thank you, I'm honored." But usually such brief responses do not meet the expectations of those gathered to commemorate a special occasion. If you know the expectations of each audience gathered to hear a special-occasion speech, you will be able to start developing your skills in handling these situations. The ability to handle special situations in a skillful way is a plus that will add to your status (and promotability in the business world) and may reap important personal benefits for you later in life.[1]

What Speaking Skills Are Most Important for Special-Occasion Speeches?

The main goal of special-occasion speeches is to commemorate shared values. Therefore, these speeches are intended to be inspirational rather than informative, persuasive, or entertaining. The most important speaking skills for accomplishing this goal are style, memory, and delivery.

Vivid language will help you express your thoughts about whom or what is being honored or commemorated. Your language also should reflect the level of seriousness and formality of the occasion. Typically, special-occasion speeches are more serious and formal than others. Consider the following excerpts from a special-occasion speech given by President John F. Kennedy. Note the carefully chosen language and also the reference to shared values:

A visit to Hyde Park is both a pilgrimage and a challenge. We journey here to pay tribute to one of America's most honored leaders. And we find here a challenge to renew the march toward those high goals of peace, and freedom, and a decent life for all men, to which he dedicated his life.

We are here at Hyde Park today—not merely to commemorate the cornerstone—but to help complete the edifice. It is fitting that we celebrate this anniversary. It is essential from time to time that we pay tribute to past greatness and historic achievement. But we would betray the very cause we honor if we did not now look to the future as well.[2]

With a special-occasion speech, it is appropriate to memorize brief portions in order to add impact to your delivery. A key feature of special-occasion speech delivery is sincerity, and a speech that is read may be perceived as less sincere. Consider, for example, if Kennedy had looked down and read, ''. . . those high goals of peace, and freedom, and a decent life for all men, to which he dedicated his life. . . .'' We think you will agree that this would have lessened the impact.

The skills of invention and organization are somewhat less important in special-occasion speeches because there are clear expectations of what general pattern your ideas should follow. By following the clear expectations for the content of each type, you will be able to use your creativity in choosing language that will most vividly inspire recommitment to the values the special occasion represents.

SPEECHES TO HONOR AN INDIVIDUAL

Speeches of Introduction

The most typical speech honoring an individual is the introduction of a guest speaker. The two major goals of the person who introduces a speaker are establishing the credibility of the speaker and raising interest for the speech content. As an introducer consider the aspects of credibility building you could assist the speaker in developing. You should consider those components of credibility that are important and expected in this situation and that are not already established for this speaker. The Credibility Analysis Form recommended on page 166 will help you make these choices. It is important not to overpraise; this could embarrass the speaker and set up a standard that is difficult for the speaker to meet. Specifically, avoid praising the speaker's speaking abilities; instead, let the speaker establish the dynamism component of credibility. Someone once told Robert G. Ingersoll, an outstanding speaker in American history, that he intended to introduce him as the ''world's greatest orator.'' Ingersoll supposedly said that he would rather be introduced as an atheist than as an orator. A speaker wants the attention focused on ideas, not on speaking style.

Speeches of introduction usually last from thirty seconds to two minutes, depending on how well the speaker is known and how long he or she will speak. If the speaker is already well known, your introduction would be shorter and would be limited to arousing interest for the topic. Some time ago we were introduced to the audience at a workshop on individualizing instruction as ''the only two people who are more concerned about this topic than you are.'' The introduction directly focused the workshop participants on our common interests.

You will be able to use the skills you developed for introducing your own speeches to arouse interest for others' speeches. It is usually helpful to check with the speaker about which things should be previewed and highlighted so that you can set the stage for the speech.

Welcoming Speeches

People take many opportunities to welcome others. We welcome them into new professional responsibilities (becoming a new professor at the college) and new personal relationships (pledging a social group). The main goal of a speaker for a welcoming speech is to associate the values of the welcoming group with those of the person being welcomed. In a real sense, you are highlighting the reasons for and benefits of bringing new people into the group.

Inauguration Speeches

The inauguration speech is given by a person who is taking over as head of an organization or country. Perhaps the most well-known inauguration speech to us is the speech given by the incoming president of the United States. Other examples of inauguration speeches include those delivered by the incoming president of a sorority or president of the League of Women Voters. During these somewhat formal occasions, we expect the incoming person to reaffirm the values of the group he or she is about to head and to preview the goals he or she will attempt to accomplish while in that position. In such a speech, it is usually customary to: (1) note the accomplishments of the last person in that position; (2) highlight the values and accomplishments of the organization; and (3) indicate the direction the new administration will take.

Presentation Speeches

Society takes many opportunities to present awards for the special accomplishments of individuals. A typical example is the awards assembly at the end of each school year. The group, organization, or society doing the presenting highlights the values the award represents. As a presentation speaker, you would: (1) describe the award; (2) indicate the values it attempts to reward; and (3) show how the personal qualifications of the recipient reflect those values. Again, it is important not to overpraise and embarrass the recipient.

Acceptance Speeches

After a presentation is made, the recipient often makes a brief speech of acceptance. If you are the recipient of an award and unsure of the expectations for a response, ask one of the people involved in presenting the award. Usually such a speech, like after winning an Academy Award, shows appreciation for the honor and acknowledges any persons who were helpful in accomplishing that which led to the award. This speech may be as brief as twenty seconds and usually would not be longer than one or two minutes, unless there are clear expectations that the award would be the introduction to a major speech.

Farewell/Appreciation Speeches

Farewell speeches are more common today, in our mobile society, than they were in the past. Young professionals change jobs and locations often. If the person making the move has been active in a profession or community, she or he may well be honored before leaving. This type of speech is also a common part of retirement ceremonies conducted by business, political, and educational institutions. If you are giving a speech to honor someone who is leaving, you would pay tribute to the individual by noting the contributions the person has made and wishing him or her well in a new situation. If you are asked to make comments on the occasion of your leaving, you could mention some of the outstanding experiences you shared with the people there and indicate how these experiences have contributed to your growth and/or pleasure.

Speeches of Eulogy

Speeches of eulogy are most often given after a person has died. Frequently, they are delivered during civil and religious memorial services. Audiences hearing eulogies expect to be comforted and uplifted. You could pay tribute by noting the values of the deceased and by indicating how remembering this person and his or her attributes could benefit the audience.

LEARNING BY UNDERSTANDING

1. Speeches to honor an individual often reaffirm the _____ the person made.

2. Which type of speech to honor a person does each goal represent?
   a. Show appreciation for award.
   b. Indicate new goals and directions.
   c. Indicate how remembering the person can benefit the audience.
   d. Show how recipient reflects values.
   e. Describe shared values.
   f. Describe person's contributions.
   g. Raise interest in the speech content.

ANSWERS:

1. Contributions
2. **a.** acceptance, **b.** inauguration, **c.** eulogy, **d.** award presentation, **e.** welcoming, **f.** farewell/appreciation, **g.** speaker introduction

SPEECHES TO COMMEMORATE AN OCCASION

Dedication Speeches

Dedication speeches usually highlight the meaning of a new creation or the beginning of a major endeavor. These speeches should focus attention on the goals which the creation or endeavor represents. A speech to begin the annual United Way drive and a speech to dedicate a new building or a major artwork are examples. In such a speech, you would indicate the values the object of dedication represents and inspire the audience to live up to these values.

Commencement Speeches

This situation honors a person as much as an occasion. Speeches of commencement are usually associated with graduating from schools. In such a speech, you would indicate the nature of the challenges the group has met so far, congratulate the people who reflect these values, and indicate the nature of the challenges ahead. Commencement means a beginning, so you would also want to inspire the audience to meet these new challenges. "Success is Not a Trivial Pursuit" in Appendix B is a fine example.

Keynote Speeches

A meeting of a large organization usually begins with a keynote address designed to reflect the values of the organization and to provide a common orientation toward the convention. The speaker is usually an outstanding member or officer of the organization or a person from outside the organization who has high credibility with the audience. In such a speech, you would refer to the goals and importance of the organization, indicate the focus and importance of this meeting, and reinforce the audience's presence and active participation.

Public Relations Speeches

This type of speech has become an increasingly important means of communication between the business community and the public. As businesses get bigger, they are more inclined to include public relations efforts as a means of maintaining positive contact with the public and communicating a positive image. According to Carl Terzian, a consultant in executive speech training,

> A growing number of executives not only are enthusiastically acknowledging lecture requests but are actually seeking them out. Influencing others is very rewarding. Some employ the platform to champion the cause of industry; to create a healthier business climate; to generate sales; to proclaim ambitious corporate goals; to promote an image; for self-development, or merely to satisfy

a restless ego. . . . Many corporations retain experts to concentrate on researching and cataloguing material, writing manuscripts, screening and soliciting invitations and coaching executives on speech discipline and techniques.[3]

Government, service, and educational institutions also recognize the necessity of communicating a positive public image by means of public relations speeches.

The public relations speech is essentially persuasive. But rather than selling a specific product or service, it is designed to sell a positive image of an organization. In such a speech, the speaker usually defines the general goals of the organization, ties the organization's goals to the values of the audience, and indicates how the organization can benefit the audience.

LEARNING BY UNDERSTANDING

1. The main goal of special-occasion speeches is to _____ .
2. Which type of speech to commemorate an occasion does each goal represent?
    a. Sell a positive image
    b. Provide a common orientation toward a convention
    c. Highlight the beginning of a major project
    d. Indicate the challenges ahead
3. What three skills areas are most important for special-occasion speeches?

ANSWERS:

3. Style, memory, and delivery
2. a. public relations, b. keynote, c. dedication, d. commencement
1. Reinforce shared values

SPECIAL SPEECH SITUATIONS

Besides the many special occasions when you may be called on to speak, you may also find yourself in situations that demand additional skills. You will work here on developing skills for four such special situations—using the media, handling impromptu speaking, answering questions, and speaking to entertain.

Using the Media

Radio, television, and the print media are the main sources of information and influence for most people in our society. Tony Swartz, author of *Media: The Second God*, asserts that in the area of political thought,

> the media have replaced political parties as the main channel of communication to the electorate and the vehicle for organizing people and getting them to the polls. . . . The media, rather than a political party or club, now inform and form our political views and behavior.[4]

Swartz further asserts that the media have the same influence on our consumer and religious behaviors.[5] It is probably that you will use the media at some time to gain a larger audience. When speaking through the media, it is important to remember that they tend to highlight some speaking skills over others. For example, when you are quoted in written media you lose much of the nonverbal impact of your speaking behaviors, while on radio and television those nonverbal skills can become overly important. Speaking of the impact of radio and television on political public speaking, Swartz suggests that

> radio, and then television, drew our attention away from issues and caused us to focus on the more personal qualities of the candidate, his ability to speak, and his style of presentation.[6]

This emphasis on different communication skills when using the media is due both to the greater control which the audience has in a mediated situation and to the time limits and technical nature of the media.

Audience members receiving your message through a mediated channel will not only choose when and where they will receive your message, but also how long they will receive it. Think of all the other things you do and the interruptions you have when you watch television or listen to the radio. Rarely will your listeners be focusing their entire attention on you. If the message does not meet their needs, expectations, or attention span, they can easily change the station or turn the page. Audience members probably will decide during the first fifteen seconds or two sentences if they will stay with you. Because your media audience will possess a great variety of interests, adaptation will be more difficult.

Further, the limitations of time and space make media speaking a greater challenge. There will not be time to clarify your original statement if it was fuzzy. You might be expected to make a point or summarize in a short time. If you are using the print media or if your program is being taped for later showing, someone may edit or delete your comments without your approval.

The guidelines in Table 14-1 will help you take advantage of the media and cope with their limitations in terms of the audience and time frame.

There are also special delivery skills for handling the specific media requirements of radio and television speaking. The physical format and equipment required for these situations often distract and intimidate people who are new to

TABLE 14-1 SPEAKING THROUGH THE MEDIA

Limitations	Guidelines
Audience Has More Control	1. Use best first to get and keep audience attention. 2. Use vivid language to keep audience attention. 3. Use short sentences to aid understanding. 4. Use repetition to aid understanding and adapt to changing attention. 5. Use personal language and singular pronouns.
Audience Is More Varied in Knowledge, Needs, Attitudes, and Interests	1. Analyze audience of the medium. 2. Appeal to a variety of specific interests.
Time or Space Is Limited	1. Plan phrasing of main points. 2. Give important material first; entire sequence may not appear. 3. Practice timing, especially for conclusion. 4. Watch director's cues and leave time for planned conclusion.

these media. We would suggest that you visit your campus or local radio and/or television station to become familiar with the setup.

For both radio and television speaking, you will have to learn to use the microphone effectively. Radio stations usually use a table mike, and television stations use a small mike that is hung around the speaker's neck. Both mikes are very sensitive and will pick up any extraneous noises; a sensitive mike will even pick up your breathing. By using some of the relaxation methods suggested in Chapter 2, you will be able to breathe regularly and avoid the distracting sound of deep breathing on the air. The station manager will explain how to use the mike and then will ask you to say something into the mike to get a sound level of your voice. Try out your conclusion or one of the points you would like to make.

Radio and television station staff use specific signals for communicating with speakers at the time of the broadcast. For example, bringing down an arm with the index finger pointed at you indicates that you are on the air or that the taping has begun. And drawing the index finger across the throat indicates that you are off the air. Most technicians will also indicate when you have one minute to go by holding up one finger. Practice ahead of time to use that minute effectively. For example, give yourself about ten seconds to make a transition and plan for a forty-five second conclusion. Usually, there is a large clock with a second hand in sight. We recommend that you be several seconds short rather than run overtime; although dead air is bad, being cut off without finishing your summary/conclusion is worse because you may not be able to accomplish your purpose. One final suggestion: When you receive the finger-across-the-throat signal, stop and remain

Speaking on broadcast media requires special delivery skills and extensive practice.

silent for several seconds until you are sure you are off the air. You have probably heard statements made by people on the air who thought they were not.

There are some important distinctions between radio and television speaking. With radio speaking, you only have to be concerned with the oral message. Because of this and the close timing, it is advisable to write out and read your speech instead of using the *extemporaneous* approach we have suggested for most of your speeches. Practice alone in a small room. And practice to include appropriate variety in your voice. You will want to *sound* spontaneous, and your voice will be the main nonverbal means you have to add interest to your speech. We recommend that you mark the text of your radio speech exactly where you expect to be at the end of each minute. This will enable you to determine if you are going too fast or too slow and enable you to make a small adjustment early to get back on the correct schedule.

Television speaking, on the other hand, requires that you are also aware of your other nonverbal behaviors. If you want to use visual aids on television, ask ahead of time how large they should be and tell the camera personnel how and when you will use the aids. Choose clothing that will feel comfortable and look appropriate; solid colors or larger prints are more appropriate than clothes with fine detail. Avoid jerky hand and body movements, especially those that might take you out of the range of the camera. Instead, move slowly and purposefully.

If you will be speaking directly into a camera, practice doing this, using some physical object to represent the camera lens. While this will be challenging, people trust sustained eye contact, so it will be worth your effort. The station personnel will tell you ahead of time if they will be switching cameras during your speech. There will be a red light on the top of each camera and the camera that is on will have the red light lit. Again, hold eye contact for several seconds with the last camera you were on after the speech is over.

Because of these special skills required for radio and television speaking, it is important to prepare and practice carefully. As with other speaking situations, practice in circumstances similar to the actual media experience. Therefore, use of a cassette recorder in preparing for radio speaking and a video camera for television speaking will be valuable.

You may give a public speech where representatives of the print media are present. A reporter might quote excerpts from your speech in a newspaper or magazine article. If this material will be used in a feature article, the writer may also comment on what you have said. If it appears in commercial print media, the quotes and comments will be influenced by what sells. If accuracy of your comments is important, provide a copy of your speech to reporters ahead of time. This will reduce the chances of your being misquoted.

In summary, effective use of the media involves adapting your speaking skills to the aspects of audience control and variation, the time (and space) limits imposed by the media, and the technical aspects of the media. Just as public speaking teachers became important in ancient Greece when people argued their own cases in court, now media communication consultants are becoming a vital profession as media grow in importance. You may work with, or become, a media consultant in academic, political, governmental, business, religious, or community settings.

LEARNING BY UNDERSTANDING

1. What could you do to overcome each of the following limitations of media use?
   a. Audience control
   b. Time limits
   c. Audience varied

2. Describe three situations within the next week where you may be asked to give an impromptu speech or answer a question.

3. Number the suggested steps for handling impromptu speaking situations in the order you would use them for both induction and deduction.
   _____ Give several *because* statements.
   _____ Stall with a generalization.
   _____ Stop.
   _____ State your conclusion.

ANSWERS:

3. 2, 1, 4, 3 (for induction) 3, 1, 4, 2 (for deduction)
2. We imagine you have come up with a variety of answers. They may be situations in classes, on the job, or a variety of other places.
1. a. best first, use personal language; b. plan phrasing of main points, practice timing; c. analyze medium's audience, appeal to many interests

Impromptu Speaking

You might find yourself being asked to make a statement or short speech with no advance warning. In these situations, you will call upon your memory of basic organizational and audience adaptation principles and your ability to think quickly. While an impromptu speech is one that is done with no *specific* advanced preparation, it is not necessarily one for which you have no preparation. Mark Twain once said, "It usually takes me more than three weeks to prepare a good impromptu speech." In a similar vein, Henry Ward Beecher commented, after a seemingly impromptu speech, that he had been preparing for it for forty years.

Normally, you can anticipate when you might be called on to make a statement. For example, if you are about to attend an awards ceremony and you have a chance to win an award, you could think about what you would say if you win. If you are running for an office, you might appear at an event where you are asked to make a statement even though you were not scheduled to talk. And, finally, if you are assigned a major reading to be discussed in class, you might anticipate being called on to summarize your reactions.

In fact, many speaking situations in your everyday life could be considered impromptu. Consider, for example, that you are attending a small party where people are discussing a local school bond issue. Several people know that you were active in getting the issue on the ballot. A friend turns to you and says, "Well, why do you think it should be passed?" Everyone stops talking and looks at you expectantly. If you consider how often you are called on to make an impromptu statement, you will realize the many opportunities you have to practice and develop your speaking skills. Probably you will be asked to make statements only about

Many occasions arise in which you could be asked to explain your point of view.

subjects in which you have some background. When you think ahead and anticipate the request, you can mentally pull together some of your background and organize one or two main ideas to be developed.

In impromptu speaking situations, your listeners expect you to be brief. We suggest that you think quickly of one main point and two or three supporting points that you would like to make and an appropriate organization plan. Do not begin to speak until you have made those decisions. Then make your planned points and stop. If your listeners want more development, clarification, or support, they will ask. Their questions will also give you more information about their background and thinking, allowing you to adapt more specifically to them in later statements.

Here is a simple format for practicing the skills of impromptu speaking.[7] We think you will be able to use this approach comfortably in your everyday impromptu situations:

FORMAT FOR IMPROMPTU SPEAKING

1. Stall with a generalization (one with which both you and your audience agree) to give you time to think.

2. Give several *because* statements, or reasons leading to your conclusion or main point.

3. State your conclusion or main point.

4. Stop.

First, you stall with a generalization to give yourself time to select your conclusion and your support for it. You might say, for example, "That's an important issue to consider" or "I've been doing a lot of thinking about that lately" or "That issue really concerns people, doesn't it?" If you use an inductive format, which is more typical of a casual oral style, your listeners will be able to move with you to your main point. Next, you state any reasons or subpoints that provide the basis for your main point. For example, you might say, *because* added revenues would allow higher teachers' salaries, *because* we could offer more extracurricular activities for students, and *because* it is the least expensive way to get these revenues. . . ." Then you could state your conclusion: *"I believe that people should vote for the school bond issue."* Avoid the temptation to repeat, give more examples, or restate your point. Just stop. Your listeners will ask if they need or want more information.

This brings up an important point. While the four-step format we have recommended is especially well designed for supporting conclusions, it could easily be used for developing or clarifying ideas also. Your development of impromptu speaking skills will not only be valuable for your professional advancement, it will also lead to better personal conversational skills.

Answering Questions

The third speaking situation you may find yourself in is that of answering questions. A question-and-answer period following a speech or an interview or a surprise question asked by a teacher in class are examples of this situation, which closely resembles impromptu speaking. Probably you will be prepared in the content area about which you will be questioned. But since you do not know the specific questions, you will not have a prepared answer. The general recommendations of thinking before you talk and being brief apply here. When you receive a sincere request for information or an opinion, make sure that you understand the question and then follow the guidelines for an impromptu speech. You might repeat the question so that everyone in the audience hears it, or paraphrase it in your own words if you are not sure what is being asked. For example, an audience member might ask, "What will happen if the school bond issue doesn't pass?" You might rephrase the question and ask, "Are you interested in knowing what effect I think failure of the bond will have on the community?" This will focus the question and save time. Most audience members are not skilled at asking questions that reflect their areas of concern; by paraphrasing, you can help them focus their questions.

Do All Questions Expect Answers?

The truth is, not all questions are sincere requests for information. In fact, Paul Edwards, a public affairs counselor, suggests that only 10 percent of all questions are asked by people really seeking answers. In an article, "Nine Out of Ten Questions Don't Need an Answer," Edwards says that based on what motivates questioners, questions can be classified into three categories: "Message" questions, "getcha" questions, and "answer-seeking" questions.[8] Obviously, *answer-seeking questions* are asked by people who really want an answer. *Message questions* are asked when the questioner wants to make a point or state an opinion. *Getcha questions* are intended to discredit the idea you are discussing. People often ask these questions in order to express strong feelings on an issue. Incidentally, the questions you are asked after your speeches in this class probably will be sincere requests for information.

Table 14-2 will help you identify and cope with message, getcha, and answer-seeking questions. In dealing with both message and getcha questions, it is important to be calm and reasonable in both your verbal and nonverbal responses in order to maintain your credibility. If you can handle these two types of questions effectively, you will be able to help the questioner channel his or her concern into a meaningful question you can answer.

If you suspect that no one in your audience will ask questions, you might want to encourage questions during your speech by saying, "Some of you might like to ask me more about that later" or "I could give you several examples later

TABLE 14-2 TYPES OF QUESTIONS

Type of Question	Verbal Indicators	Nonverbal Indicators	Coping Strategies
Message question	"Don't you think . . . ?" "I think. . . ." "My research clearly shows that. . . ."	Voice tone does not go up at end. Eye contact is with audience, not you.	Allow brief statement; paraphrase statement; agree with all or part if possible. Tactfully ask what question is.
Getcha question	"Do you really mean . . . ?" "You can't be serious about. . . ." "Why did you avoid . . . ?"	Sarcastic tone of voice. Tense facial expression. Eye contact moves to the audience after beginning.	Paraphrase the question with unbiased language. Communicate openness by calm tone of voice and direct eye contact. Acknowledge any part of the criticism that is accurate. Summarize your point.
Answer-seeking question	"How would you . . . ?" "What is the next . . . ?" "What would happen if . . . ?"	Voice tone goes up at the end of questions. Eye contact with you.	Repeat question if whole audience did not hear. Paraphrase the question if you are not sure of its meaning. State important part of answer first. Use impromptu speech procedures.

if you like." Attorney Floyd Abrams used the following comments to encourage questions in a speech to the College of Communications at Boston University:

> Much of the pleasure I have in being here is the anticipation of our question/answer/discussion period to follow. To allow sufficient time for that, I will try to say just about enough to address some issues without saying so much that no one is able to rouse himself or herself enough to comment.[9]

But it is more likely that you will have too many questions. Sometimes, one person in the audience wants to dominate and ask lots of questions, but it is better to avoid having a dialogue with this person. Be sure you answer the question to the entire audience and include everyone with your language. You might even have to say, "I'd really like to hear what some of the rest of you think about this" and turn your attention to another part of the room. Unless there is a moderator, it is the speaker's responsibility to stop the questioning. It is better to stop at the peak of interest than to continue until everyone is tired. To wrap things up, you might say, "I'll take one more question" or "We'll go another minute before we have to stop."

Speaking to Entertain

Speeches to entertain often are called after-dinner speeches because many organizations use speeches as the entertainment after a regular dinner meeting. The essential difference between an entertaining speaker and a comedian is that the audience expects an entertaining speech to have some common thread or focus. The key qualities of an effective entertaining speech are lightness, originality, and appropriateness. *Lightness* suggests that this speech does not have to be taken seriously. Instead, the audience should be able to relax, smile, and leave feeling good. *Originality* means that the speaker is expected to present something he or she has created and developed. While you may borrow humor from other sources for parts of your speech, you should create most of it yourself. Finally, an effective entertaining speech should be *appropriate*. Nothing in the speech should make the audience uncomfortable or embarrassed. And remember, a joke directed toward yourself is one of the most effective types of humor.[10] John Deeth's after-dinner speech in Appendix B provides fine examples of each principle. Note especially his joke on himself regarding the spelling of his last name.

How Do I Develop a Speech to Entertain?

The steps for developing a speech to entertain are similar to those for speeches to inform or persuade. Let's review those steps, with an emphasis on entertainment.

STEPS IN DEVELOPING A SPEECH TO ENTERTAIN

1. Decide on a general topic area.
2. Decide on a specific humorous approach to the topic area.

3. Choose an organizational plan adapted to your approach.

4. Develop (or select) light, appropriate, and original materials.

5. Place materials within your organizational plan.

6. Choose appropriate and vivid language.

7. Plan feedforward contingencies.

8. Practice your message, emphasizing memory of key parts and timing.

The best topics for a speech to entertain are those with which you and the audience are familiar. By choosing a familiar area, you will be able to create or research materials that lend humor to that topic. Brainstorming will provide many topics that can be treated humorously. Commonplace experiences seen from a new perspective are great sources of humor. For example, in a speech to entertain your class, you might talk about taking tests, job interviews, family relationships, or campus social life.

The second step is deciding what particular humorous approach to take. Several basic humorous approaches to topic areas and examples for each appear in Figure 14-1.

The next step is choosing the organizational plan that will help you develop the humor of your topic. Any of the plans suggested in Chapter 7 could be used. For example, you might take the topic area of dealing with parents and use a chronological development ("The Day My Parents Grew Up") or a problem-solution development ("How I Cured My Parents' Worst Habit").

The fourth and fifth steps, developing (or selecting) materials and placing them in your organizational plan, will be handled much as they were with informative and persuasive speeches. Figure 14-1 will help you develop materials with a light, humorous touch. In addition, there are many existing sources of humorous materials; one of the most well-known sources, *The New Speaker's Treasury of Wit and Wisdom* by Herbert V. Prochnow (New York: Harper & Row, 1958), will be in your library.

Figure 14-1 Approaches to Humor

Approach	Example
OVERSTATEMENT (making more of something than there is)	*". . . the meals on the rubber chicken circuit"* (exaggerating the chewiness of the chicken served at many banquets)
UNDERSTATEMENT (making less of something than there is)	*"I thought they had forgotten my quarter-pound hamburger* (pause) *until I found it* under *my pickle."* (belittling the size of the meat)
PUNS (creating humor by using language in a different way)	*"There may be* poultry *fees on the public speaking circuit."* (poultry as a pun for "paltry")
UNEXPECTED RESULTS (when something comes to a different conclusion than expected)	*"It is a sad fact of life that square banquets* (pause) *make* round *people."* (one shape leads to a different shape)

The sixth step is choosing language. The emphasis here is on vividness rather than clarity. Keep in mind the qualities of lightness and appropriateness as you choose your language. After making your language choices, you may want to memorize several key portions. Reading a punchline or an especially humorous conclusion will have less impact than delivering it while maintaining eye contact with your audience. G. J. Tankersley's speech in Appendix B contains good examples of vivid language choices.

Delivery skills are also important in speeches to entertain. In fact, a sense of timing is often considered the most important skill in using humor. Knowing where to pause and give emphasis in a joke tells the audience when to smile. If there is laughter, wait until it has almost subsided before you go on. Practice your speech at least four or five times. Your feedforward planning should help you anticipate where laughter will occur.

What If They Don't Laugh When I Expect Them to?

Most people judge the success of a speech to entertain by how much laughter they get. But laughter may not be the desired response for many parts of your speech. As we indicated earlier, the speech to entertain is designed to relax audience members, to make them smile and feel better after it is over. Your feedforward preparation should include anticipating nonverbals that would indicate enjoyment and relaxation as well as actual amusement. Plan feedforward contingencies in case you do not get the desired response, and remember that your audience will be on your side.

LEARNING BY UNDERSTANDING

1. Name the three kinds of questions you might be asked. Which of these sincerely demands an answer?

2. Which type of question goes with each of these nonverbal indicators?
   a. Voice goes up at end; eye contact with you
   b. Voice tone not up at end; eye contact with audience
   c. Sarcasm and tense facial expression

3. What coping procedures would you use for each of the three types of questions?

4. List the three qualities of an entertaining speech.

5. Order the following steps for preparing an entertaining speech.
   _____ Plan feedforward.
   _____ Develop light, appropriate, and original materials.
   _____ Decide on a general topic area.
   _____ Choose appropriate and vivid language.
   _____ Decide on a specific approach to the topic area.
   _____ Practice your message, with emphasis on memorizing key parts and timing.
   _____ Place materials within your organizational plan.
   _____ Choose an organizational plan adapted to your approach.

ANSWERS:

1. Message, getcha, answer-seeking; the last is a sincere request.
2. **a.** answer seeking, **b.** message, **c.** getcha
3. Several answers would be appropriate. See Table 14-2.
4. Light, original, appropriate
5. 7, 3, 1, 6, 2, 8, 5, 4

LEARNING BY INTERACTING

Break into groups of three or four. Each person should choose and describe a topic about which she or he would feel comfortable answering questions. Each person will then answer questions, using the suggestions in this chapter. The other group members should ask the three types of questions—message, getcha, answer-seeking—to give the responder practice in using all the skills.

LEARNING BY SPEAKING

You have worked on skills for a variety of speech types in this chapter. If there is time, you may be able to prepare a speech for several of the types. Following are suggestions for several short speeches you might give.

1. Prepare a two- to three-minute special-occasion speech. Choose an occasion for which you are likely to give a speech in the future. Plan to accomplish each of the goals for the speech occasion you choose. Prepare a sentence outline for your practice and either a word or phrase outline for use during the presentation.

2. Prepare an introduction for the special-occasion speech of one other person in this class. Talk with the person you will introduce so that you may give an effective thirty-second introduction before the person speaks.

3. Prepare a two- to three-minute speech to entertain your audience. Take a situation, occasion, or topic which is familiar to both you and your audience and provide a new perspective which lends humor to the topic. Prepare feedforward for important parts of your message to handle audience reactions.

4. Prepare a three-minute speech for either radio or television presentation following the guidelines suggested in the text for that medium. If you are able to actually use the appropriate facilities, prepare your speech ahead of time and have it taped (either audio or audiovisual). Present your tape during your class presentation time.

5. Plan a two-minute summary of one of the speeches you gave earlier in the term. Summarize your specific purpose, main points, and supporting material. Allow two to three minutes for audience questioning. Review the suggestions for answering questions and get feedback from your audience on how well you coped. Your teacher may assign class members to ask message and getcha questions as well as answer seeking to give you an opportunity to practice your coping behaviors.

REVIEW

Special-occasion speeches are used to honor individuals and to commemorate special occasions. They are a major way that our culture reinforces its values and traditions. Each special-occasion speech has expectations for the points it will cover which usually include identifying and reinforcing the values which the special occasion represents. Special-occasion speeches rely primarily on the speaking skills of style, memory, and delivery.

In this chapter you also worked on four special speech situations which call for additional skills. Media speaking requires adaptation to the facilities of a radio or television studio; while impromptu speaking and answering questions share the need for thinking quickly and responding briefly. Speaking to entertain focuses on lightness, originality, and appropriateness.

These special speech types are used often by people with an active professional orientation.

NOTES

1. Richard D. McCormick, "Business Loves English," *Vital Speeches of the Day* 51 (November 1, 1984):52.

2. Gerald Gardner, ed., *The Quotable Mr. Kennedy* (New York: Popular Library, 1963), 17–18.

3. Carl R. Terzian, "Going to Communicate: Try Speaking!" *Public Relations Journal* (May 1976):16.

4. Tony Swartz, *Media: The Second God* (Garden City, N.Y.: Anchor Books, 1983), 113.

5. Ibid., chaps. 7 and 12.

6. Ibid., 114.

7. Janet Stone and Jane Bachner, *Speaking Up* (New York: McGraw-Hill, 1977), 141.

8. Paul R. Edwards, "Nine Out of Ten Questions Don't Need an Answer," *Public Relations Journal* 32(July 1976):16.

9. Floyd Abrams, "Will the First Amendment Survive the 1980's?" *Vital Speeches of the Day* 51 (April 15, 1985):410.

10. Charles R. Gruner, "Advice to the Beginning Speaker on Using Humor—What the Research Tells Us," *Communication Education* 34(April 1985):142.

SAMPLE CRITIQUE FORMS

Informative Speech Critique Form

Speaker's Name _____

Speaker's Specific Topic _____

The speaker's specific purpose was _____

_____

The speaker's main points were:

1. _____

2. _____

3. _____

4. _____

5. _____

SPEAKER'S CHOICES OF:	ASSESSMENT OF QUALITY:						
	(not very effective)					(very effective)	
Specific topic	1	2	3	4	5	6	7
Specific purpose (or central idea)	1	2	3	4	5	6	7
Research	1	2	3	4	5	6	7
Developing, clarifying, and supporting materials	1	2	3	4	5	6	7
Pattern of organization	1	2	3	4	5	6	7
Introduction	1	2	3	4	5	6	7
Body	1	2	3	4	5	6	7
Conclusion	1	2	3	4	5	6	7
Listening guides	1	2	3	4	5	6	7
Credibility appeals	1	2	3	4	5	6	7
Emotional appeals	1	2	3	4	5	6	7
Reasoning	1	2	3	4	5	6	7
Language	1	2	3	4	5	6	7
Delivery	1	2	3	4	5	6	7
OVERALL EFFECTIVENESS	1	2	3	4	5	6	7
	(very little)					(a lot)	
I learned something new by listening to this speech:	1	2	3	4	5	6	7

STROKE:

SUGGESTION: Listener's Name _____
                                     (optional)

Persuasive Speech Critique Form

Speaker's Name _____

Speaker's Specific Topic _____

The speaker's specific purpose was _____

_____

The speaker's main points were:

1. _____

2. _____

3. _____

4. _____

5. _____

SPEAKER'S CHOICES OF:	ASSESSMENT OF QUALITY:						
	(not very effective)					(very effective)	
Specific topic	1	2	3	4	5	6	7
Specific purpose (or central idea)	1	2	3	4	5	6	7
Research	1	2	3	4	5	6	7
Developing, clarifying, and supporting materials	1	2	3	4	5	6	7
Pattern of organization	1	2	3	4	5	6	7
Introduction	1	2	3	4	5	6	7
Body	1	2	3	4	5	6	7
Conclusion	1	2	3	4	5	6	7
Listening guides	1	2	3	4	5	6	7
Credibility appeals	1	2	3	4	5	6	7
Emotional appeals	1	2	3	4	5	6	7
Reasoning	1	2	3	4	5	6	7
Language	1	2	3	4	5	6	7
Delivery	1	2	3	4	5	6	7
OVERALL EFFECTIVENESS	1	2	3	4	5	6	7
	(very little)					(a lot)	
I changed my attitude(s) as a result of this speech:	1	2	3	4	5	6	7

A behavior I will adopt as a result of this speech is: _____

STROKE:

SUGGESTION:

Listener's Name _____
(optional)

Entertaining/Special Occasion Speech Critique Form

Speaker's Name _____

Speaker's Specific Topic _____

The speaker's specific purpose was _____

_____

The speaker's main points were:

1. _____

2. _____

3. _____

4. _____

5. _____

SPEAKER'S CHOICES OF:	ASSESSMENT OF QUALITY:						
	(not very effective)					(very effective)	
Specific topic	1	2	3	4	5	6	7
Specific purpose (or central idea)	1	2	3	4	5	6	7
Research	1	2	3	4	5	6	7
Developing, clarifying, and supporting materials	1	2	3	4	5	6	7
Pattern of organization	1	2	3	4	5	6	7
Introduction	1	2	3	4	5	6	7
Body	1	2	3	4	5	6	7
Conclusion	1	2	3	4	5	6	7
Listening guides	1	2	3	4	5	6	7
Credibility appeals	1	2	3	4	5	6	7
Emotional appeals	1	2	3	4	5	6	7
Reasoning	1	2	3	4	5	6	7
Language	1	2	3	4	5	6	7
Delivery	1	2	3	4	5	6	7
OVERALL EFFECTIVENESS	1	2	3	4	5	6	7
	(very little)					(a lot)	
I enjoyed this speech:	1	2	3	4	5	6	7

STROKE:

SUGGESTION: Listener's Name _____
                               (optional)

APPENDIX B

SAMPLE SPEECHES

HUG A BAT—NO WAY

MARY NIELSEN, Northern Illinois University

An informative speech delivered at the American Forensic Association's National Individual Events Tournament, Towson State University, Towson, Maryland, April, 1985.

On a typical, warm, summer evening at the outdoor theatre in Door County, Wisconsin, the audience sits in rapt anticipation as Juliet says, "Wherefore art thou Romeo?" Before Romeo can step out of the shadows beneath the balcony, there are shrieks of terror as a black shape goes swooping by, attracted by the bright lights. It's only a bat—this creature that makes the audiences in Door County cover their hair with their hands and shudder and children scream. These flying mammals are legendary—for centuries bats have stood for supernatural horror and demonic death. In the classic film *Dracula*, Bella Lugosi's hideous transformation into a vampire bat turns the blood ice-cold. Surprisingly enough, most people have never even seen a bat except in silouettes. So why are they afraid of them? Ignorance. To make you better acquainted with this mysterious creature, I will present some general information on bats including the kinship of bats and man; I will attempt to allay your fears of bats by refuting the myths and misconceptions of bats; and I will focus on the natural and scientific benefits of bats.

Bats are mammals—the only mammal that can fly. As mammals, their progeny are born live, and they nurse their young. Man is also a mammal whose offspring are born live and who nurse their infants. There is a great deal of similarity between the anatomy of a bat and the anatomy of man. Both have well-developed brains, spinal cords, four limbs, two ears, two eyes, a nose, and teeth. This is the arm. [VA: STUFFED BAT] This is the leg and foot. Bats have hand-like structures at the end of the arm. The bones of the fingers are elongated and joined by a double membrane of skin. This forms the wing, and here is the thumb. Bats are found all over the world except in extreme desert and polar regions. Charles Mohr in *The World of the Bat*, published in 1976, tells us there are 847 known species of bats worldwide—40 of these in the United States. By far the largest population of bats is found in the tropics. In a spectacularly illustrated article appearing in *Discover* magazine, May, 1984, Merlin Tuttle, one of the world's leading authorities on bats, states that bats range in size from the miniature Kitty's Hog-Nosed bat which is no bigger than a bumblebee and weighs less than a penny, to fruit-eating bats such as those whose wings can span several feet and weigh four to five pounds. [VA: PHOTOGRAPH] The photographs in this article are both repugnant and exquisitely beautiful. Although one little Brown bat in America has been documented as living 24 years, the average lifespan of a bat in the wild is ten years. Bats are considered slow reproducers because in most species they have only one offspring a year. In temperate climates, such as America, bats hibernate in the winter, usually in caves or old buildings. But tropical bats seem to be active all year around. Bats are nocturnal creatures and adroitly locate objects in the dark by using a complex neuromotor system scientists call echolocation. In simple terms, the bat emits a sound and listens for its echo. The echo tells the bat exactly where the object is. In this way they can intercept insect prey in midair or detect and avoid wires as thin as a human hair in total darkness. In his book *The World of Bats*, Alvin Novick states that bats are unique. There are no other living mammals like them.

It is their very uniqueness that have made them the subject of legends and the victims of misconceptions. Many of the legends going back to the fables of Aesop around 600 B.C. center around the duality of the bat—whether it is a bird or whether it is an animal. This ambiguity can be found in tales among some of the North American Indians. In China, the bat has long been a symbol of good luck and happiness, but according to Clover Morrill Allen in the book *Bats*, in most cultures the bat has been pictured as something evil and supernatural—the possession of the soul or the body by the devil represented as a bat. The ugly, little bat with his wings like a cape, his pointed ears, beady eyes, and sharp claws is an apt symbol of Lucifer and wickedness. The movies and literature of the present day go on to perpetuate these legends as in *Dracula* and, more recently, *Indiana Jones*. There are two informative articles that point out the misconceptions people hold about bats. The first, by Bob Strohm, appeared in *National Wildlife* June 1982 and the second, by Merlin Tuttle, in *International Wildlife* in 1983. Some of the more prevalent myths concerning bats are that they are vicious, filthy, aggressive, and transmitters of diseases. In fact, according to these two authors, such stories are greatly exaggerated. Bats are very gentle creatures, and they are meticulously clean. Merlin Tuttle has even trained bats to come to his hand where he feeds them bananas. The bats' wings are its major means of locomotion. Therefore, they are continually grooming and cleaning them and other parts of their bodies. Vivid imaginations based on a modicum of truth have portrayed bats as blood-sucking attackers and carriers of disease. There *are* three species of bats found in Central and South America according to M. Brock Fenton in his book *Just Bats* that do feed on the blood of living animals. These are not huge bats as presented in horror movies that drain the blood of the victim, but rather they are half the size of a man's hand and consume about a tablespoon of blood. They attack sleeping victims, usually cattle and other domestic animals. Very seldom do they attack man. As for most bats, the only time they have ever been known to bite humans is if someone tries to pick them up when they are injured or wounded as any hurt animal would do. Only ten people in the United States and Canada have died of disease from bats in over thirty years. More than ten people die *annually* from stray dogs and other wild animal bites such as raccoons and skunks. And bats are not the reservoir of rabies as once believed. New scientific evidence shows that while an occasional bat may have rabies, the virus that they carry, once thought to be a rabies virus, is actually a *rio bravo* virus—not harmful to bats or people. In addition, bats have been accused of spreading two kinds of respiratory diseases—tuberculosis and histoplasmosis—through their droppings. According to Strohm, there is no evidence to suggest that bats ever transmitted tuberculosis to man. And histoplasmosis, which is a fungal disease, is mostly contacted from bird droppings, not bat droppings. The few cases caused by bat droppings occurred in exposure in caves where there was a great buildup of droppings, or "guano." Parasites that feed on bats are very specialized—they do not transmit infections to people and rarely pose any problems to humans.

This misunderstood creature has a very important part to play in nature's scheme of things—ecology. But man seems determined to interfere—often exterminating whole colonies of bats in his mistaken belief that bats are harmful and dangerous. Some bats are natural insecticides and pesticides. A single Grey bat may eat 3,000 or more insects during a night's feeding, without the toxic side effects associated with commercial insecticides and pesticides. Grocery stores would not be the same without bats. The fruit-eating species disperse seeds and nectar. Bats pollinate more than 130 kinds of tropical trees and shrubs. Some of the common products that might disappear from stores if bats were exterminated are peaches, bananas, mangos, avocados, and even cashews. Just think, we wouldn't have any chewing gum if it weren't for a bat pollinating the sappadilla tree that provides chicle used in gum. Bat guano, which contains nitrogen, is a major source of fertilizer in underdeveloped countries in Southeast Asia. An article in *Smithsonian*, January, 1984, tells us that one monastery in Thailand owns a cave inhabited by bats that supplies over $52,000 a year by mining guano. The mining provides a livelihood for local people, and the profits from guano sales are used to support a monastery and a grade school. The students are taught to defend and respect bats. These bats are protected by law, but still they are threatened. Poachers net them in huge quantities and sell the meat to restaurants. The bat meat is believed to greatly increase sexual performance, and the bat's blood is mixed with whiskey and used as an aphrodesiac. Bats are extremely valuable in scientific research. Because they are exceptionally long-lived, disease resistant, and are mammals similar to man, they are becoming increasingly important. Research on bats has contributed to the development of new vaccines, artificial inseminations and birth control methods, drug testing, and to studies of aging and space biology. By studying the highly sophisticated sonal system of the bat—echolocation—scientists have come up with ingenious navigational aids for the blind such as an electronic cane that emits sounds that a trained blind person can interpret. And the Polaroid 600 Land Camera has an automatic device called a *transducer* that emits sound waves and receives the echo in a split second, calculating the distance between the camera and the subject—instant focusing.

This, then, is the bat. This ugly creature whose appearance makes it very easy to hate. This creature that belongs to the same biological class as man. A much maligned creature who has been used by storytellers and entertainers to inspire fear and horror in their audiences for centuries. A creature that has been the victim of half-truths and exaggerations. Now, however, scientists are beginning to understand the worth of this creature—its place in nature and in the laboratory. Perhaps nobody will put a bumper sticker on their car stating, "Have you hugged a bat today?" but maybe now we can learn to understand them.

I CAN SEE CLEARLY NOW

MICHAEL D. STOLTS, University of Wisconsin—Eau Claire

An informative speech delivered at the American Forensic Association's National Individual Events Tournament, Towson State University, Towson, Maryland, April, 1985.

I finally realized that I was nearsighted when I was in the eighth grade. I couldn't see the blackboard at the front of the room, even from the front row of desks. I convinced my parents of how bad my eyes were shortly afterward, when, on a plane taxiing up to the ramp, I asked what the big red mark was on the tail of the jet right next to us. Their answer: TWA.

Within two months, I had glasses. I could see much better, but for a teenage boy, glasses can be something of a nuisance. Two years ago, I switched to contact lenses. They're better than the glasses, but have their drawbacks as well. The perfect solution would be to get rid of my contacts altogether, but keep the 20/20 vision they give me.

If you feel the same way, you'll be glad to know that, for the price of about five sets of contact lenses, you can undergo corrective eye surgery. Two revolutionary new procedures: radial keratotomy, also known as RK and myopic keratomileusis, or MKM, actually re-shape the cornea to correct myopia. Even if you aren't nearsighted, you may benefit from these procedures as they have paved the way for other surgical and non-surgical procedures that can correct hyperopia, or farsightedness, cataracts, and glaucoma.

In order to see how RK and MKM work, however, it will first be necessary to clear up myopia by examining the functioning of a normal eye, a myopic eye and a hyperopic eye. Then each procedure will be looked into in depth, and finally we will focus on some of the problems each faces.

Myopia, or nearsightedness, is a condition that, according to ABC TV's "20/20 Magazine" on April 4, 1985, affects nearly 25 percent of all Americans. Normally, when light enters the eye, the rays are bent by the cornea, the transparent outer coat of the eye, and again by the lens, and focus on the retina which then transmits the image to the vision center of the brain which interprets what is being seen. Simple. The myopic eye, however, is in a sense too long. The incoming rays are refracted by the cornea and lens, but come into focus before reaching the retina. As a result, the image that finally reaches the retina is out of focus and blurry. Hyperopia is just the opposite. The eyes are too short, causing the rays to reach the retina before they come into focus. Radial keratotomy can correct only myopia, whereas myopic keratomileusis has spawned a similar procedure to treat hyperopia.

Of the two procedures, radial keratotomy is the older and more widely practiced. The technique was perfected in Russia by Svyatyslav Fyodorov in 1974. By 1982, Fyodorov had performed more than 3,000 RK's with a success rate of better than 90 percent, according to *Time* magazine, November 15, 1982.

In 1976, Phoenix eye surgeon Dr. Leo Bores went to Moscow and learned the operation from Fyodorov. He brought the technique to the U.S. and has been its major proponent ever since.

The operation itself is quick, relatively simple and painless. The eye is anesthetized with eye drops and the cornea is carefully and precisely cut several times with a diamond-edged knife. (Don't try this at home.) These incisions are relatively deep, cutting 70 to 90 percent into the one-half-millimeter thickness of the cornea. "The slits radiate, like spokes of a wheel, from the center area of the eye to the cornea's outer edge," explains the *New York Times Magazine*. Hence, the name "radial" keratotomy. The slits weaken the tissue of the cornea, allowing the natural internal pressure of the eye to make the outer edges of the cornea bulge out slightly, causing the central area of the cornea to become more flat. The resulting change in curvature changes the angle of refraction and helps bring light rays into focus on the retina instead of in front of it.

Originally as many as 16 slits were made in RK, but as the technique improved, that number may be as small as six, with an average being eight. This improvement is beneficial in many ways. It carries less danger of infection or perforation, reduces scarring, and leaves room for additional cuts, if necessary. The entire procedure takes only 15–30 minutes for one eye, and the eye is sufficiently healed to be exposed to light within 24 hours, usually with immediate and noted improvements in sight.

Indeed, the improvements are sometimes extraordinary. Joseph Leonte, a New York architect, started with 20/400 vision. He couldn't even see the big E at the top of the eye chart. After his RK, his vision improved to 20/50, not perfect, but at least good enough to drive in most states. Drs. William Meyers and John Cowden conducted a study of 223 RK patients and reported "substantial reduction of myopia resulted immediately in all cases."

With such promising prospects, RK business is booming. *Time* in November 1982 claimed, "American surgeons have performed the procedure more than 20,000 times." *Facts On File* in November 1984 updated that number to 63,000, and it is likely to rise dramatically in the near future.

Radial keratotomy is not for everyone, however. It is recommended that young people avoid the procedure because the white part of their eyes is still very flexible and may cause the cornea not to flatten out properly. Also, for the profoundly nearsighted, RK will simply not work well enough. Fortunately, those individuals can find help in MKM, myopic keratomileusis.

MKM is the brainchild of Dr. Jose Barraquer, an opthamologist from Bogota, Columbia. He spent 20 years developing the tools and techniques to make MKM workable. Dr. Lee Norden learned from Barraquer and introduced MKM to the United States in 1983.

MKM is somewhat more complex than RK. *New York* magazine from April 1984 explains that, "the technique involves slicing off about 60 to 70 percent of the central portion of the cornea with a cutting tool known as a microkeratome." The corneal tissue is then frozen and ground like a contact lens on a machine called a cryolathe. This is an extremely delicate procedure as there is no room for mistakes. Once the cornea is cut, there is nothing left for a second try. Fortunately, the cryolathe is computerized. Dr. Robert Rubman explains, "All I have to do is feed in the patient's corneal curvature, the thickness of the section, and how much we want to correct. Everything else is taken care of." The frozen carved cornea is then thawed and sewn back onto the eye like a living contact lens. The entire 54-step procedure takes 90 minutes, is done under local anesthetic, and produces results within 72 hours.

Again, as in RK, the result is a flattening of the cornea and a correction of the focus on incoming rays. For Diana Stokke, this was "the answer to a dream." Before her MKM, Diana had 20/4,000 vision. That meant that she could only see at 20 feet what normally sighted people could see at 4,000 feet. In other words, if you were to ask Diana, "Do you see that bird in that tree?" she might respond, "What tree?" Immediately after her MKM, however, her vision improved to 20/50, and in the following weeks, improved steadily beyond that. Because the operation is so new in the U.S., there have been no extended studies to report general effectivenes, but Drs. Norden and Rubman are optimistic.

Lest you form the opinion that RK and MKM are the perfect solution to the problem of myopia, allow me to explain some of the drawbacks. First of all, with RK, the results are unpredictable. Some people experience almost total correction of vision, but others under exactly the same circumstances see only partial improvement. A large percentage also suffer partial regression, necessitating repetition of the procedure. About half also experience a phenomenon known as night glare, but few lose the ability to drive at night. In all, Dr. Tim Johnson explained on "20/20" that severe problems are rare and most side effects minor and temporary.

MKM cannot be used to correct presbyopia—nearsightedness of the elderly. It also will not work with diseased or damaged corneas, but spin-off procedures are closing in on that problem. Finally, neither procedure can do any better than contact lenses or glasses. Dr. Rubman explains, "If your potential (with contact lenses or glasses) was only 20/50 before the operation, you will only be able to see 20/50 afterwards. But if the potential is there for 20/20, there is an excellent chance that you will see in the 20/20 range afterwards."

Cost is perhaps the greatest drawback, however. A radial keratotomy costs between $1,000 and $2,000 per eye. MKM costs approximately $3,500 per eye. Insurance companies are hesitant to help pay for the operations because of their experimental nature.

Obviously, at this stage of development, RK and MKM are not operations one would undergo on a whim. They're primarily for those individuals who are so profoundly nearsighted that conventional means—contact lenses or glasses—are inadequate. Still, if you find yourself so inclined, you can join ranks with Joseph Leonte, Diana Stokke and the thousands of others who have undergone radial keratotomies and myopic keratomilesuses. Even if these specific operations are of no personal use, you or a loved one may benefit from the several spin-off procedures, some involving corneas you can donate simply by signing the back of your driver's license, that can treat cataracts, glaucoma and other optic diseases. As for me, I'm neither brave nor blind enough to put myself "under the knife." Besides, now I know what a TWA jet looks like. How can I convince my parents to pay for the operation?

LASER SURGERY

RANDY LARSEN, Humboldt State University

An informative speech delivered at the American Forensic Association's National Individual Events Tournament, Towson State University, Towson, Maryland, April, 1985.

Born with clusters of growths called papillimas on his vocal cords, two year old Robert has never made a sound. Viewing the growths through a microscope, Dr. Herbert Dedo targets one, then fires a carbon dioxide laser. The CO_2 laser beam is itself invisible, so Dr. Dedo sweeps a red guide light over Robert's throat. Each split second pulse vaporizes papillimas tissue in a puff of smoke. As he sees the healthy tissue emerge Dr. Dedo says, "When you think of the power and precision of this tool it seems more like *Star Wars* than anything else."

When Robert awoke in the recovery room he cried softly. His mother said, "It was the most beautiful sound I had ever heard."

Fortunately for Robert and many other people it's no longer necessary to go to a *Star Wars* galaxy far, far away to benefit from laser technology. The laser's potential as a science fiction weapon receives more media attention, but in medicine it's already a ray of life and hope. Dr. Janos Varos of the Laser Research Foundation in New Orleans feels that "By the year 2050 almost all surgery in all areas will be performed with the laser."

It seems, then, that this medical weapon deserves some attention of its own.

In order to understand the lasers medical applications it would be helpful to understand what a laser is and how it works. Therefore, we'll look at, first, the laser's burning beginnings as well as, second, a universe of medical uses and, third, the future of the surgical force.

The actual laser process is relatively simple; in fact, many experts do not rule out the possibility of lasers being utilized by ancient civilizations.

The word "laser" is an acronymn formed from the first letters of the words *l*ight *a*mplification by *s*timulated *e*mission of *r*adiation. Of these five components, stimulated emission, a concept theorized by Albert Einstein way back in 1917, is the cornerstone of the laser's production. Stimulated emission is the actual process by which a cylinder filled with a pure substance, for example neon or argon, has its contents funneled into a coherent, nondefracting beam of light. The resulting beam is of pure color and according to Alan Mauer's 1982 book, *Lasers*, may be three times hotter than the surface of the sun.

The type of laser varies depending on the element placed in the cylinder as each beam has a unique set of characteristics. For example, a CO_2 laser beam is totally absorbed by water and considering that the human body is nearly 90 percent water, it acts as an effective scalpel. The red beam of the ruby red laser, on the other hand, is absorbed only by dark blue colors. Consequently, if I was to take a ruby red laser and fire it at this set of balloons (a dark blue balloon inside a clear balloon) the inside balloon would be popped but the outside balloon would remain unaffected. So, if there is something undesirable in you, perhaps a tonsil or an appendix, the surgeon may dye the tissue and then have it vaporized with the laser.

There seems to be a universe of medical uses for the laser. Until recently, they were limited to a handful of procedures such as repairing detached retinas in the eye. But as Alan Mauer states, "(Today) the list of medical uses for this almost unbelieveable tool goes on and on." Lasers have been used for everything from removing birthmarks to acupuncture. Little boys have been circumcised with the laser and doctors are using them to stop internal bleeding. Three of the more interesting areas are: gynecology, ear surgery, and cardiology.

First, with the use of the laser, gynecologists have been able to do more for women than previously seemed practical or even possible. Many gynecological surgeries are not considered life-saving, for example fertility enhancement, and are therefore termed "elective procedures." Most doctors are reluctant to perform gynecological elective procedures because of the high risk to the patient due to lengthy operating time. Says Dr. Joseph Bellina of the Laser Research Institute, "You just can't keep a patient under a general anesthetic that long for an elective process." But lasers can help. As the laser cuts, it seals tiny capillaries keeping bleeding to a minimum. This can cut operating time in half, by eliminating the need for sponges, clamps and surgical incisions. Consequently, many doctors are not as reluctant to perform these gynecological elective procedures.

The laser is also being used to treat chronic uncontrollable menstrual bleeding, a condition which forces approximately 150,000 women each year to undergo hysterectomies. In addition, it's being used to vaporize cervical cancers. Says Dr. Bellina, "Using a scalpel instead of a laser to remove a genital cancer is like using an elephant gun when a BB gun is needed."

As well as being used for gynecology, the laser is now entering an even smaller human cavity: the ear. Dr. Rodney Perkins of Palo Alto, California, has, with one type of laser microsurgery, been able to restore hearing to over twenty patients. The patients were suffering from a hearing defect caused by an abnormally boney growth in the inner ear. It's known as ottosclerocis. Perkins treats the patients by vaporizing defective stape bones in the inner ear. The stape is a bone that transmits vibrations; and hardening, causing the stape to lock in place, can severely impair hearing. Previously, doctors actually used tiny picks and chisels to unlock the stape bone but this procedure itself could cause permanent hearing loss and prolonged dizziness.

At Stanford University, Dr. Richard Goode is utilizing the laser for another type of ear surgery. It seems that in many young children a sticky swamp of fluid collects in the inner ear. The resulting infection can impair hearing and is extremely painful. Conventional methods of draining the ear are themselves extremely painful and usually call for a lengthy stay in the hospital. Dr. Goode's method requires a CO_2 laser and a red guide light. The patients hear only a "pop" as the thin beam vaporizes a tiny hole in the eardrum. This allows the ear to drain and heals in about a month.

One of the brightest uses for lasers is in the area of cardiology. Heart disease is this nation's number one killer, claiming over 750,000 lives each year. In an effort to save lives, over 150,000 coronary bypass surgeries are performed annually. The average cost is over $30,000, recovery time ranges from four to six weeks.

At the University of Stanford, Dr. Richard Ginsberg has an alternative. Ginsberg utilizes the laser to clear clogged arteries carrying blood to the heart. The laser technique requires the insertion of a thin optical wire into a vein in the arm. The laser is then connected to the wire which transmits the light to the blockage, which, in turn, vaporizes the clot. Recovery time for this technique is less than 24 hours.

The possibility of the lasers heat perforating the arterial wall has limited the procedure to only the most severe cases. However, a cooler, highly precise laser, called the eximere, will probably receive FDA approval sometime this summer. The eximere will expand the laser's role in cardiology considerably. According to Ted Koppel of "Nightline," "The eximere may make coronary bypass surgery a thing of the past."

Meanwhile, the future of the surgical force will expand even further. According to Terry Fuller of Detroit's Sinai Hospital, "In the near future, if you do not understand the concept of lasers you'll not be able to understand medicine." Not only that, you might not be able to boast a healthy smile. Dentists are looking into the possibility of laser brushing and laser root canal treatment. Some doctors believe lasers will allow them to control the function of organs and operate on single parts of cells. In Massachusetts, engineers are planning to marry the laser to a computerized control system. This promises unheard of precision in surgery. The problem area will be scanned with a laser light and then appear on a three-dimensional screen. The doctor simply needs to punch in the depth of penetration and allow the computer to do the job of guiding the laser. If the patient moves slightly, the computer tracks it. In the case of a large movement, it shuts down automatically.

Lasers in medicine seem to be the lightwave of the future. But when the future will arrive and the extent to which it will be amplified hinges on several flies in the laser ointment. One of the biggest problems is simple inertia. Doctors are comfortable with existing techniques, and trying to get them to put down the scalpel and turn on the laser is comparable to trying to get the average American to switch to the metric system. Says Dr. Milton Zaret of Scarsdale, New York, "Simply because the laser is an exotic sounding modality of treatment does not necessarily mean it's always the best modality."

But a more substantial reason is cost. Hospital administrators still must see a clear-cut advantage in trading in their scalpels, which run anywhere from three to five dollars, for a laser unit which costs from $30,000 to $150,000. And medical insurers have still not developed a consistent reimbursement policy for laser surgery.

One final problem is the existence of restrictive safety regulations and the prevalence of malpractice suits which have slowed the rate of clinical experimentation considerably. Consequently, the United States is falling far behind Western Europe in the actual application of laser surgery.

But even with these problems, the laser's future seems bright. We hear so much about military "Star Wars" technology; it's encouraging to know the laser has life-saving capacities as well. Dr. Janos Voros believes, "The laser will revolutionize surgery." In some areas, it seems it already has.

DEADLY DISCRIMINATION: TESTICULAR CANCER

JUDITH J. BARTON, University of Iowa

A persuasive speech delivered at the American Forensic Association's National Individual Events Tournament, Towson State University, Towson, Maryland, April, 1985.

We live in an age of equal rights: suffrage, fair housing, Equal Opportunity Employment. We have made advances to wipe out sex discrimination in America, but despite these advances, we have failed to address an issue of sex discrimination which is deeply ingrained in our attitudes and our actions. Women aren't the victims of this discrimination—men are. I say victims because our inaction contributes to America's second leading cause of death in men between the ages of 19 and 35—testicular cancer.

A victim of cancer of the testes may not be your idea of a victim of discrimination. But if we don't take the first steps to control this disease, we are discriminating not against the right to liberty or the pursuit of happiness, but the right to life.

The American Cancer Society, in *Cancer Facts and Figures 1985*, estimates that 5,000 Americans will develop cancer of the testes this year. You may think, "Five thousand. Certainly there are many diseases more significant than this. Why does testicular cancer demand our attention more than them?"

Well first, the incidence appears to be rising dramatically. Since 1978, the number of diagnosed cases has doubled.

Second, the statistic itself may be deceptive. Because testicular cancer spreads so rapidly, many of its victims may appear in other categories, like lung cancer.

Finally, the importance of testicular cancer goes beyond frequency. It targets the young (it is the most common form of solid tumor cancer in men between the ages of 19 and 40); and it usually attacks men who are otherwise healthy and, oddly enough, usually those who are white, upper middle class, and skilled or professionally employed.

But additionally, like all other forms of cancer, testicular cancer is not just a personal tragedy: It also affects countless relationships. Just as the thousands of breast cancer patients depend upon the support and understanding of their friends and family, so will the thousands of testicular cancer patients.

So whether you're male or female, whether you know someone who has been stricken with this disease or have been spared this trauma so far, it is important to understand cancer of the testes. For it's only by understanding testicular cancer that we can take the steps to controlling it.

It is time. We must start down the road of equality by looking first, at the discrimination in our attitudes and our institutions; second, at the importance of moving against this disease; and finally, at the actions we must take to provide equal protection of ourselves and our loved ones from this cancer which threatens half the population, but affects us all.

The first step is to recognize the discrimination in our attitudes and institutions. Dr. Marc B. Garnick, of the Sidney Farber Cancer Institute of Harvard Medical School, states that "No one seems to give a damn about male sexual health. We train girls still in pigtails how to check their breasts. . . . We are ready for men to do something just as important for themselves.''

But so far, men are not being informed about their right to health. Currently, medical institutions do not place enough importance upon male sexual health. Women are encouraged to see a gynecologist every one to two years, but men in the most vulnerable age group for testicular cancer see physicians very rarely, and usually not for uro-genital problems. Therefore, men are rarely examined for testicular cancer, or even told of it. A man who previously heard this speech was surprised to learn that an undescended testicle increases the risk 20 to 40 times. The doctors who perfomed his surgical descension never warned him of his great danger.

Or perhaps his doctors didn't think to sound the warning. Medical schools ignore the need to teach doctors to teach patients. According to the May-June 1984 issue of *Harvard Magazine*, only 1.5 percent of total teaching time in medical schools is allocated to the instruction of preventive techniques.

It may be that even further education is not enough to change doctors' behavior. Dr. George Connolos in *Cancer Medicine* charges that doctors value organs differently—many surgeons say that ''no ovary is too good to leave in and no testis is too bad to take out.'' Because of strong identification with their patients, male physicians may misdiagnose cancerous testicles in favor of diseases which do not threaten the removal of a testicle. So even men who know of the possible problem may be misled by physicians who are chauvinistic.

But so few do know. While those little girls in pigtails are learning their potential hazards, the health risks boys face are ignored. Primary and secondary schools are often afraid to teach sex education. *Health Education*, January-February 1984, reports that only ten percent of America's schools have adequate sex education programs, and that they are more likely to teach 12-year-olds the responsibilities of parenthood than about testicular cancer.

Finally, the media have begun to address sexual concerns, but only those of women. It's no longer taboo for ''Cagney and Lacey'' to spend two hours on breast cancer—and that's great. But there is not even a fifteen-second public service announcement on cancer of the testes.

Because of apathy, fear, and neglect, we haven't learned of this problem from our doctors, teachers, or media. Now, we must overcome these discriminatory attitudes and effect a solution.

We've taken the first step toward equal treatment of this disease: We've seen the impact of discrimination on male sexual health. We must now take a second step: We must understand the importance of our actions.

The cure for this disease is determined by the particular type of testicular cancer as well as how much the cancer has spread. After confirmed diagnosis the diseased tissue is surgically removed, and the treatment is then supplemented with radiation, chemotherapy, or a combination of techniques. But in 1969, only ten percent of those diagnosed as having testicular cancer survived. In 1980, proceedings of a conference on testicular cancer concluded that ''the answer to increased survival rates lies not in more extensive surgery, stronger X-rays, or more effective chemotherapeutic agents, but in earlier diagnosis.'' According to Lawrence Einhorn in *Testicular Tumors: Management and Treatment*, with early diagnosis the survival rates for some forms of testicular cancer may approach one-hundred percent. But some individuals don't report symptoms to their physicians—some delaying as long as 2–4 years. In 1984, physicians' reports to the American Cancer Society indicated that by the time they'd been diagnosed, 88 percent of testicular cancers had spread through the lymph nodes—to the liver, to the lungs, to other organs where the disease launches its final attack on the individual.

Clearly, individuals are not giving themselves a fighting chance. Either they don't know about testicular cancer or they haven't made the commitment to themselves and their loved ones to ensure their health. We must now make the commitment to take action; the action that may lead to early diagnosis and treatment; the treatment that may save a life.

Once we have taken steps to understand the discrimination and to understand the importance of our actions, we must take a third step. We must act.

I'd like to explain a simple technique called the Testicular Self-Examination, or the TSE. In many respects, it is much like the women's breast self-exam, except that most men are not taught how to examine themselves. Every male above age twelve should perform a TSE once a month. It takes about three minutes, doesn't cost a penny, and can be done in the privacy of your own home, without any fear or embarrassment.

The best time to perform a TSE is right after a warm shower or bath, when the scrotal skin is relaxed. Each testicle should be examined separately by rolling it between the thumb and fingers of both hands, checking for any swelling or hard lumps. Although not all lumps are malignant, if one is found it should be reported immediately to a physician, preferably a urologist. Dr. George Prout of Harvard Medical School emphasizes that a one to two month delay can mean the difference between life and death.

The only way to guarantee early detection of testicular cancer is the TSE. Boys should be taught the TSE in their birds and bees lecture. Doctors should include instruction of the TSE in clinical visits and physicals for school or employment. Schools should create educational programs to establish good habits for better health—including male sexual health. Groups should contact the American Cancer Society or their local hospitals for films and presentations. And there are pamphlets. This one is entitled *For Men Only*, but it's not. It's for every man, and for everyone who knows a man—a son or father, brother or husband, friend or lover. I'll make some pamphlets available after the round. *I'd* feel better if everyone would pick one up. *Read* it. *Follow* it. *Share* it. You could even send one to your congressman.

But this knowledge means nothing if individual men and women don't transform knowledge into action.

Do not simply recognize the significance of testicular cancer in your mind, but apply that concern to your life.

Do not merely consign your understanding of male sexual health to your brain, but emancipate that knowledge to teach those you love.

Do not simply leave the importance of early detection in your memory, but remember that action is the key to treating testicular cancer.

And please, do not just *think* about the TSE—*do* it. Men need to do it for themselves. Women need to remind them.

We must not continue to evade this issue, just because "men don't talk about things like that." Men have an equal right to awareness, and equal right to health, and an equal right to life.

THE WORLD CASTE SYSTEM

MARY NIELSEN, Northern Illinois University

A persuasive speech delivered at the American Forensic Association's National Individual Events Tournament, Towson State University, Towson, Maryland, April, 1985.

A midnight blue Lincoln Continental goes streaking down the New York City River Road. In pursuit is a trooper, siren screaming, who has clocked the speeding car at 85 miles per hour. As he nears the car, he suddenly turns off the siren and slows down. He has spotted the DPL license plate and figures what's the use? Just another case of diplomatic immunity. The trooper feels insulted and frustrated, and he is not alone. Once again there is a growing resentment in the United States over the abuses of diplomatic immunity. Let's examine this concept: its history, its current status, the violations here in America, and a viable solution to this continuing indignity.

A simple definition of diplomatic immunity is the exemption from both civil and criminal laws granted to representatives of foreign countries to allow them to conduct the business of their governments in a safe and orderly fashion. The original idea behind diplomatic immunity was and *is* a valid one—protection of the messenger or courier. There can be no communication between governments if their representatives are harmed. Diplomatic immunity depends on reciprocity—We'll protect your diplomats and extend them privileges if you do the same to ours. William Barnes of the State Department outlined the historical development of diplomatic immunity. He cites Cicero around 100 B.C. who expressed the Roman attitude, declaring that ambassadors were sacred and to be protected by both divine and human law. But during the Renaissance in the sixteenth century, there were *two* theories in Europe concerning the doctrine of diplomatic immunity. One theory called upon each nation to extend full diplomatic immunity to the agents of other countries, while the second theory argued that diplomatic agents who broke the rules of the nation where they were stationed should be liable for prosecution.

This second theory was rejected, and since then we have created or allowed to be created one whole section of the population that is above the law. This was not planned, but like Topsy in *Uncle Tom's Cabin*, ''It just growed.'' By the time the United States formally entered into the international diplomatic scene in 1790 many of the present privileges and immunities had already been established. In 1790, this was not such a great concern because governments were not the huge bureaucracies they are now, but after World War II the United States resumed diplomatic relations with most of the countries of the world, and the United Nations was established with permanent headquarters in New York.

Rumblings of dissatisfaction could be heard, and these rumblings did not go unnoticed by the diplomats themselves. So delegates from 123 nations met in Vienna in 1961. This was the Vienna Convention on Diplomatic Relations. The workings of this convention are reprinted in the book *Diplomatic Law* by Eileen Denza. Rules and regulations were set forth to be used as guidelines by the diplomats and the nations where they are stationed, and they did make two concessions—the requirement of liability insurance on diplomatic vehicles and the exclusion of the very lowest echelon, the servants and their families, from full diplomatic immunity. But for the most part, the delegates jealously guarded their own privileges.

These rules were not incorporated into federal law in the United States until 1978 and only then after repeated violations of civil and criminal law. In *Newsweek*, August 8, 1977, there were numerous infractions reported. Three cars registered to Idi Amin's Uganda mission had been issued 1,761 traffic tickets in eleven months, and the most devastating incident happened in 1974 when a cultural attaché at the Panamanian embassy ran a red light and smashed broadside into the car of Dr. Halla Brown, a 62-year-old professor of medicine at George Washington University. The impact severed Dr. Brown's spinal cord and left her a quadriplegic. The attaché was not insured in 1974, even though the Vienna Convention in 1961 had listed liability insurance as a guideline. The Panamanian ambassador, even though Dr. Brown's expenses exceeded $250,000 and she will require around-the-clock nursing care the rest of her life, offered his condolences and nothing else. In addition, *Newsweek* reported that New York City, where the city government was in dire financial straits, was spending more than two million dollars a year to protect foreign diplomats who in return amassed 200,000 traffic tickets annually worth about four million dollars—few of which were paid. No wonder citizens were irate.

Congress finally decided to act, and on August 17, 1978, the Senate passed a bill to supposedly limit diplomatic immunity. In reality, what they had done was to incorporate as law the Vienna Convention of 1961. Less than a month later, September, 1978, *U.S. News and World Report* estimated that more than 40,000 foreigners were *still* enjoying protection that was not given to American citizens. The irate citizens, particularly in New York, started acting out their frustrations against foreign diplomats, especially the delegates to the U.N. The frustrations took the form of threatening telephone calls, broken windshields, and garbage dumped on diplomatic cars. The delegates continually urged the city of New York to inform its officials and its people that the U.N. is an important body, and that the diplomats should get the respect they deserved.

A 1983 issue of *Newsweek* magazine, however, presented the side of the victims. Carol Holmes, of Manhattan, was raped by the nineteen-year-old son of an attaché at Ghana's mission, who was released less than forty-five minutes after his arrest. Kenneth Skeen, of Hiatsville, Maryland, a bouncer at a Washington, D.C. stripjoint, was shot three times by a man who was identified as the son of Brazil's ambassador to the U.S., but no charges were ever brought against him. And the wife of a Soviet diplomat was charged with shoplifting in Paramus, New Jersey, and released. Her husband demanded an apology from the police chief who told him in disgust to, "Go pound salt." These are the cases that hit the headlines, but what really irritates most of us are the widespread violations: non-payment of property taxes, exemption from sales tax, failure to pay for goods and services, and the most flagrant—parking and traffic violations. As Carol Holmes, the rape victim said, "The State Department is protecting foreign diplomats at the expense of the United States citizens."

The United States should take seriously our complaints before the threatening telephone calls and vandalism by the United States citizens turns into downright terrorism. Instead of trying to teach the citizens of New York, Washington, D.C., and the rest of the United States that they have to treat the diplomats and their staffs as sacred cows, it would be much better to educate the diplomats and their entourages. As representatives of their countries, they are important people and to be respected, but they are not above the law. It is becoming almost impossible to convince us, the people of the United States, that allowing a diplomat or his family to break laws or enjoy privileges will improve his efficiency and effectiveness. Where is there any proof that by saving $600 to $1,000 in sales tax on the purchase of a luxury automobile the efficiency of a diplomat is enhanced? Or that by allowing diplomats to renege on grocery or liquor bills they can settle international affairs?

The defenders of diplomatic privileges and immunities rely heavily on precedence. In March, 1985, when White House Deputy Chief of Staff Michael Deaver and three of his associates were challenged as to the propriety of their purchasing nine luxury BMW's at a 25 percent discount while on a visit to West Germany, they quoted "diplomatic privilege and precedence" as justification for their acts. Further investigation shows that this practice of obtaining discounts by using diplomatic passports is so widespread many of the diplomats don't even leave the country. They merely order the car by telephone and send a copy of their diplomatic passport to the company. NO they aren't breaking any laws and YES people have been doing it for years. But White House Counsel Fred Fielding restricted the practice in the future.

Diplomats should realize that times have changed; particularly here in America. We are not illiterate peasants or loyal subjects to kings. We feel that we are just as important as the people that run governments. Many of us or our ancestors came to this country to get away from tyranny, and we do not expect the United States to have two sets of laws—one for us and one for foreign diplomats.

Changing the course of diplomatic immunity will not be an easy one, but the United States will have to act as a leader. Much of diplomatic immunity depends on reciprocity; therefore, George Schultz, Secretary of State, should appoint members of his department to meet with representatives of individual countries and discuss new policies. They should point out the antiquity of the ideas contained in the Vienna Convention—the ideas that go back to Cicero, assuming that ambassadors are divine and sacred. They should assure these nations that the United States will do everything in its power to protect their representatives and their embassies. But just as the representatives of the U.S. in foreign service will be instructed to obey the rules and regulations of the country to which they are assigned, so shall the U.S. expect the representatives of foreign nations to obey the civil and criminal laws that apply to the citizens of the U.S.

This is not a new concept. Remember this is one of the two theories that was advanced back in the Renaissance period. If this concept had been accepted back in the sixteenth century, we would not have the difficulties we are experiencing now. The diplomats will fight to keep their privileges and immunities. But we the people of the United States are serving notice that we no longer will be treated as second-class citizens in our own country. The state trooper will once again be able to arrest anyone speeding on the New York City River Road.

SUCCESS IS NOT A TRIVIAL PURSUIT

G. J. TANKERSLEY, Chairman and Chief Executive Officer, Consolidated Natural Gas Company

A keynote speech delivered at Bethany College's ''American Business in Action'' Lecture Series, as published in Vital Speeches, *Vol. LI, No. 4, December 1, 1984.*

I hope my remarks this afternoon won't sound like a commencement address given at the wrong time in the school year, but I'd like to talk to you today about some very old-fashioned concepts. Things like: making the most of your education; training yourself to work efficiently; recognizing that there is a difference between the school world and the job world; and, especially, about acquiring the character traits and the thinking habits that I believe make it possible to be a success in a job.

I've probably had more occasions than many other businessmen to consider these subjects over the years. That is largely because I've spent a good part of my own ''extracurricular'' time on education.

Currently, I'm co-chairman of a drive to raise funds for Auburn University, which is my alma mater. I'm a member of the Business-Higher Education Forum, a group of about 80 business leaders and college presidents who concern themselves with some of the issues I'm going to discuss today. And I've been working at the University of Pittsburgh, where I'm a Vice Chairman of the Board of Trustees and Chairman of the Board of Visitors at the Business School.

Also, I used to teach. Just after World War II and before I started my career in the gas business, I taught thermodynamics for four years at Auburn's Engineering School.

There are numerous discussions today among both educators and business people about just how students who are contemplating business careers—whether they're enrolled in business courses, in engineering, in the humanities, or whatever—how those students should be preparing themselves for work in the business world.

What subjects should they be studying? What skills should they be developing? What combination of work and study is best for most students? What are businesses looking for in a graduate?

I'd like to give you my thoughts on all that today. But before I do, let's consider some of the common characteristics of people who have pursued exceptionally successful business careers. Let me be a little bit Socratic and pose two questions for you.

First, why are we finding—at Pitt, at the Business-Higher Education Forum, and elsewhere—that the high performers in the classroom are very often not the high performers at the office? Grades in school are important, of course, but strangely enough there is a mass of data that shows that grades are not a very good predictor of who will go far in a career and who won't.

Second, why does the kind of intelligence measured by IQ tests have surprisingly little to do with success in careers? That is a fact. Or at least, it is being accepted as fact by more and more of the psychologists who do research in this area.

An article in the July 31 issue of *The New York Times* summarized this research, quoting social scientists at Penn State, Harvard, and Emory Universities. The article stated that while the best business executives always do at least moderately well on IQ tests, IQ rankings are simply not the factor that distinguishes those who advance in their careers from those who do not.

This lack of correlation between school grades and IQ on the one hand and advancement in business careers on the other hand is an anomaly. It doesn't fit in with the accepted notion of the way things are. So let's take a few minutes to explore this a little further.

As students, you've lived for the last 12 to 16 years in a world of tests. The measure of most of your achievement in school, the measure of most of your scholastic success, so far, has been your ability to answer questions on exams. But what is the biggest difference between examinations and the real world?

Well, among the differences, of course, is that many tests rely primarily on factual recall and not on reasoning ability. Another is that IQ tests and the Scholastic Aptitude Tests, particularly, require types of problem solving that aren't necessarily related to what you actually do on most jobs. There aren't very many places, for instance, that will hire you to solve problems of verbal analogies.

But those are the small differences. The big differences are something more fundamental. There are three characteristics of test problems that make them crucially different from real-world problems: Test questions are well defined and precisely stated; all the information needed to solve test questions is at hand (in your textbook, at least, if not in your memory); and, the most fundamental difference of all, problems on tests have right answers.

All this is especially true of those standardized tests that measure "Scholastic Aptitude" or "IQ." There is almost always just one, specific, absolutely certain, right answer for each question that's posed on a test. Otherwise, machines couldn't score them. That isn't the way it is in the real world.

The distinction is very, very important. The psychologists trying to resolve that anomaly I mentioned earlier about career achievement and IQ tests are finding that one very important characteristic of the superior performer in business is his or her ability to deal with uncertainty.

Uncertainty is the rule in the business world. A business person always plans for the future. But you have no idea what the conditions in the future are going to be. Of course, you base your decisions on the available data. But the available data can never answer entirely your questions about what is going to happen next. Moreover, in the real world vital information doesn't necessarily arrive on a convenient schedule, so you never have all the information you'd like when decision time arrives.

Accordingly, the "right" answer often changes, as you learn more. The answer that's right today may well be wrong if conditions change—even subtly—tomorrow. On top of that, there may be several "right" answers to a business problem, all of them equally acceptable. Or there may be several acceptable "right" answers, but one of them might be just a little bit better than the others.

Most successful businessmen have long recognized this, at least instinctively. Roger Smith, the Chairman of General Motors, puts it this way: "One of the hallmarks of a competent manager is the ability to tolerate ambiguity," he says.

The psychologists are beginning to document this in a systematic way, and, as you might suspect, they have a fancier way of describing it. The best business managers, they say, display "greater cognitive complexity" and engage in "multi-dimensional" decision making. In other words, they are saying that there are different kinds of "smarts" at work in business success than the kind of "smarts" that existing tests measure.

What do they mean by those terms "cognitive complexity" and "multi-dimensional"? Well, according to a prominent researcher at Penn State, the hallmarks of cognitive complexity include: the ability to plan strategically without being rigidly locked into one course of events; the capacity to acquire ample information for decision making without being overwhelmed with data; and the ability to grasp relationships between many rapidly changing events.

The researchers are now able to draw diagrams illustrating the ways different individuals make decisions. They can chart the sequences in which new information is recognized and in which the small decisions leading up to the big decisions occur. The more successful executives, working on sample business problems in a laboratory experiment, are much more aware of the relationships among separate events and different decisions than the less successful executives. The charts of the way they think and make decisions are much more complicated and much less linear than those of the less successful group. They are more "multi-dimensional" in their thinking. As a result, they see farther ahead and make fewer mistakes.

The researchers are trying to devise tests that will show in advance who the multi-dimensional thinkers are. I'll be interested in their results, if they succeed. But we'll leave the problems of test writing to them. For today it's enough to be clear on this point: It's not "school smarts" or "IQ" alone that will make you successful in business or make you successful in a management career in other areas, such as government, education, or health.

Now, of course, I'm not encouraging you to abandon your studies. Don't go out and burn your books and decide you're going to spend the rest of this semester in town at the movies. Far from it. You need to learn everything you can while you're here as an undergraduate. Take full advantage of this opportunity for unfettered study because you won't encounter such a wonderful opportunity once you're out there earning a living.

That brings us to a key question, though, and that's: "How do you develop or nurture this ability to think "multi-dimensionally?" I doubt that it can be taught to you. But I very strongly suspect that you can learn it, and that you have to learn it through experience.

What kind of experience? Well, a job, obviously. But extracurricular activities are another way. Community work another. Anywhere where there would be demands made on you for planning and organizing. These would be good introductions, good practice for you in learning how many variables have to be considered in doing even elementary planning for any sort of organization. Try it. If this sort of learning only comes with experience, then I would say it's one of the best uses you can make right now of your extracurricular time.

I believe that the ability to think multi-dimensionally is at the root of one hard-to-define quality that I look for in the managers at our company—and that's foresight. It's an indispensable quality in a leader. There are other qualities that I personally rate highly in judging managers in my organization. Let's consider three of them. I call them "empathy," "ego drive," and "vision."

Empathy is the ability to share other people's feelings; to see things, even if you don't agree with them, from their point of view. This is important in virtually all phases of business, and extremely important in any large organization. You can't underestimate the need to handle interpersonal relations well, and empathy is the quality that counts most in that.

Ego drive is a very personal thing. You have to want to be somebody special. You have to have some clear personal goals for yourself. And I don't mean by this that you necessarily have to aspire to be chairman of the board. Maybe you want to be a superb accountant or a respected, skilled engineer. But you still must have an idea of what constitutes achievement for yourself and you must have the drive to meet it. Don't be afraid to think big.

On the other hand, I'm not encouraging you to become an egomaniac. A person with ego drive is one who recognizes that he or she can earn high rewards for high achievement. An egomaniac is a bore who no one wants around.

You will find that most career counselors urge people at any stage of their careers to have a set of written personal and business goals. It doesn't matter if you revise these goals every six months. Or every year. Indeed, you should be reevaluating them regularly. But as a practice exercise, maybe you ought to try this tonight. Sit down and write what you want to be in five years and the things you have to do to get there.

There's a great scene in *Alice in Wonderland* where Alice asks the Cheshire Cat, "Would you tell me please, which way I ought to go from here?" "That," the grinning cat replies, "depends a good deal on where you want to get to." If you don't know where you want to go, how can you expect to get there? At Consolidated, we ask each of our managers annually to tell us in writing exactly where he or she wants to be five years hence. It's a formal part of our Manpower Development Program.

The third item I wanted to mention is vision. This is different from planning ability or foresight. It is not at all the same thing. Many more executives have good planning and problem-solving instincts than have vision. Vision is creativity. This is the executive or the entrepreneur dreaming of something entirely new. Something nobody has ever tried before. You could almost call it "entrepreneurial vision."

Someday, after the psychologists master the mysteries of multi-dimensional decision making, they should start studying vision. It is probably the most important characteristic that any individual can bring to the business world. Indeed, this is the ability that makes successful business people so often look "lucky." The two young men who founded Apple Computer had a vision—a "personal" computer. One that an individual could have at his desk or in his home. Lee Iacocca had a vision—a sound and healthy Chrysler Corporation. And he had the planning skills and ego drive to bring his vision about.

I said at the outset that I would give you some of my thoughts on what you should be studying in anticipation of a business career. My advice in this area is pretty basic: I'm going to suggest that above all, while you're here, learn to read and write well.

Please don't be offended by such elementary advice. Faculties have been finding at virtually every business school in the country that a sizable minority of the students beginning graduate business studies just don't write at an acceptable level. The students are shaky in grammar and vocabulary, and their writing is confused. They haven't figured out yet how to say what they mean in clear, simple, and forceful ways. Don't let yourself become part of that group.

You don't want to spend time in graduate school—or on your first job—doing remedial work in English. It's easier to work on your writing here. And there's no secret to learning to write well. No special formula. The one and only way to learn to write is to practice writing. It's like learning to play the saxophone: You've got to do it regularly if you're going to do it well. And a good teacher will make the job a whole lot easier, so enlist the faculty's help in this.

Don't shy away from those courses here that require a lot of writing during the term. Indeed, you might seek out a few such courses for the practice it will give you. And write something every day. Even if it's only a letter home, which I'm sure your folks would find welcome. But take care in writing it. Finely honed communication skills—listening, reading, writing and speaking—are key capabilities of the very best managers.

Another bit of advice I'll give you is probably commonplace these days. And that's to learn something about computers. But I'm not going to advise you to go take a course in how to program a computer. Programming, though it is a highly useful skill, may in fact be the least necessary skill to learn. In many departments at our company right now, there are more personal computers in use than typewriters! All of our analytical people—in rates, in marketing, in our gas operations department, in financial planning, in cash management, in strategic planning—they're all using computers in their work daily. But few of them are computer programmers and many of them don't know very much about programming at all. But they have learned how to use the ready-made, and increasingly user-friendly programs that are on the market. The key to it all is that they can multiply their time and their skills because of the computer's ability to do "drudge" work quickly.

So, before you get out of college, acquire at least a nodding familiarity with how a spread sheet program works, how a data base management program works, and how a word processing program works. You're unlikely to use in a job the specific program you'd learn now, but the concepts will stay with you. Also, learn to type. People who know their way around a keyboard can work computers a lot faster than those who don't.

Finally, don't neglect the humanities while you're here. You want to form now the habits of reading, of research, of turning to history for information, and to literature for insight, that will mark you as an educated man or woman for the rest of your life. Learn how to learn while you're here. Instill in yourself the enthusiasm for self-learning. It will hold you in good stead as a business person, if that's the career you choose.

I might mention that many companies are coming to value training in the humanities as a good preparation for a business career. They note that liberal arts graduates, at least, often can write and communicate better than many business graduates and that they have a broader outlook on problem solving. So while you are here, make sure that you are at least touched by the humanities. You can't divorce effective education in business management from a solid, broad-based liberal arts education.

For those of you who are contemplating business careers, let me give you another bit of advice. While we strongly endorse the pursuit of MBAs, you need not go to graduate school and earn an MBA before you take your first job. A lot of companies, my own included, like to grow our talent at home. We like to see people working on advanced degrees while they're working full time. And we reimburse the total cost of graduate study pursued while working.

A fundamental shortcoming in business school curricula is that the functional business skills such as accounting, finance, marketing, human resource management, and quantitative analysis frequently are taught as if these skills will be implemented in a self-contained, vacuum-like environment. From a practical point of view, nothing could be further from the truth. Every business decision requires the coordination and blending of all of these functional skills. On-the-job experience gives the individual the opportunity to participate in this coordinating and blending process. In addition, work experience enhances the student's capacity to judge the relevance of the classroom materials and to view the subjects with greater insight.

You might be interested to know that some trend-setting business schools, such as Harvard and Stanford, now virtually require that MBA candidates have a few years of work experience. Only 3 percent of the MBA candidates at Harvard came there directly from undergraduate school. At Stanford, the number is 5 percent.

I have talked a great deal about business today, because that's what I know best. But I want to emphasize that most of my remarks also apply to those of you who will pursue careers outside of business. Management and planning skills, empathy and vision, good writing habits and computer skills, after all, are needed in the profession, in education, in health care, and in government, too. You can prepare yourself for one type of career in much the same way that you prepare yourself for the other. The person with the skills I mentioned will have a competitive advantage in any field.

Nevertheless, let me close with one thought about business and business careers. I personally believe that business is the most effective, positive agent for change in our society. In this sense, it is the most radical element in our society, and the most self-renewing. I believe it does the most good for the most number of people. In contrast to some others, I see the products of American business—whether you're talking about steel or breakfast cereals, personal cars or personal computers—I see these products as key determinants of the considerable personal freedoms that we enjoy now and will enjoy in the future.

Consequently, I believe strongly that students contemplating business careers should prepare themselves carefully and thoroughly. They have a serious mission ahead. Frankly, the students now coming into business will have to be some of the best business leaders our country has ever had. We're now facing the most challenging problems of foreign competition that we've ever seen. Not only in basic industries, but in high-technology areas too.

Challenge presents opportunity. And opportunity attracts leaders. I, personally, look forward to the emergence of leaders from among students at colleges such as Bethany. As I suggested with the title of this talk, business and success at business is not a trivial pursuit. It's not trivial in what it means to the individual. It's not trivial for the nation as a whole.

HAVING A BAD SPELL?

JOHN C. DEETH, University of Wisconsin—Eau Claire

An after-dinner speech delivered at the American Forensic Association's National Individual Events Tournament, Towson State University, Towson, Maryland, April, 1985.

You're looking at the only survivor of the third grade ever to get eleven out of 10 wrong on a spelling test. So how did I do that? Well, I spelled my name this way [VA: JOHN DEITH], which is wrong. It's really spelled *this* way [VA: JOHN DEETH], D-double-E-T-H. Now be sure you get that right. I mean it! It seems people are always spelling my name wrong, even when it's literally right in front of their faces. When I spell it for people like I just did for you—D-double-E-T-H—it invariably comes back D-W-E-T-H. [VA: DWETH]. But the one that really kills me is when people spell my name this way. [VA: DEATH] DEATH! What, do I look warmed over to you? It sounds like I could start my own punk rock group! "Here's Johnny Death and his angry Samoans."

So maybe I'm getting a little bit carried away. But when my cousin's wedding was announced in the paper, that's how they spelled his name. The newspapers can't seem to agree on how to spell this name either. [VA: QADDAFI/KHADAFY/GADDAFFI] These are only three of the 13 different spellings major news organizations have given to the Libyan leader's name. Now do you know why editors get ulcers?

Like a lot of people, I've got some problems with my spelling. There's no reason for me to be ashamed of this. Tests conclusively prove that spelling ability and intelligence are not directly related. But when we think about it, there really are a lot of reasons why people have problems with their spelling. So why doesn't everyone sit back for a spel- . . . *while*, while we first look at the way the media obeys spelling rules to the letter. Next we'll see how regular and standardized our spelling is. And finally we'll look at some of our simple spelling rules. Uh-huh.

As in many areas of our lives, the mass media exerts a big influence over our spelling habits. And, as in other areas where the mass media has a big influence over us, it tends to be a bad influence. Yes, friends, today there's big money in copyrighted misspelling. Don't you wish you had thought of it first?

Our problem begins at the breakfast table, as we sit down for a bowl of Kix, Trix, Froot Loops, or Rice Krispies. [VA: KIX/TRIX/FROOT LOOPS/RICE KRISPIES] We can wash these down with a glass of Kool-Aid or Quik, [VA: KOOL-AID/QUIK] or with a six pak of Lite beer. [VA: 6 PAK OF LITE BEER]

But if we dig deeper we can see that the problem goes far beyond this. With spelling habits like these, is it any wonder that even our dogs can't spell? [VA: KAL KAN/KEN-L-RATION/BONZ]

Advertising executives aren't the only people who think up these copyrighted witticisms. Heavy metal musicians—uh, well, people in heavy metal bands, anyway—also do. These people have been accused of casting spells of another kind, but that's not what my speech is about. The only spells I can see are mis-spells, as in the names of these popular bands. [VA: DEF LEPPARD/ MOTLEY CRÜE/ RATT] Def Leppard? Motley Crüe—does English have umlauts? I forget. And

Ratt—these guys can't even get three letters right. [VA: Hold up four fingers and then realize mistake.] After taking a look at these—or even worse, listening to any of these groups for more than five minutes—it becomes obvious that Mama, weer all crazee now. [VA: MAMA, WEER ALL CRAZEE NOW]

Media misspelling has even entered the world of forensics. Take, for example, this trophy from a tournament called, for some reason, the Gopher Gambit. But wait. It says *Gropher* Gambit. I guess that just goes to show that you get what you pay for. [VA: obviously broken trophy]

Finally, media misspelling has entered the political arena. What more would you expect from a society that spells relief R-O-L-A-I-D-S? It's possible to say a great deal about your political opponent with one carefully misspelled word. Just ask anyone who's seen the President's name spelled this way. [VA: RAYGUN] I'm sorry, but you just can't do that to Mon—Dale? [VA: MON-DULL]

While media misspelling is creative, it can get confusing, especially when such misspellings become accepted practice. And in the unregulated, unstandardized private sector, spelling is just as creative. As another former president, Andrew Jackson, once said, "It's a damn poor mind that can only think of one way to spell a word." True, Old Hickory used to fight duels at the drop of an empty whiskey keg, for his time he was right. There were no standards in English spelling until 1828, when Noah Webster published his first dictionary. This event gave millions of Americans a better answer to "How do you spell 'onomatopoeia'?" than "Sound it out."

We've all got friends who can't spell. Aren't they wonderful to be around when they're writing letters? Resumes? Doctoral dissertations? Or, worst of all, papers for English professors whose only system of grading is counting the spelling errors. These friends like to call you late at night and ask you how to spell words like "baby," thinking it ends in I-E.

But thanks to Noah Webster, you can tell your friends to go look it up in the dictionary, rather than telling them to go someplace else. But what if you can't spell a word like, say, "psychology," and you don't even know the first letter? Why, it's possible to lose an entire university department, all because Noah Webster thought "psychology" looked cute with a silent "p" at the beginning!

Actually, the silent "p" comes to us from the ancient Greeks. Unlike many other languages, English grows by absorbing words from other cultures. Wonderful, right? Well, not really. You see, we do this so rapidly and voraciously that no one bothers to check the spelling or pronunciation. And the words we adopt tend to be real killers. [VA: ASSASSIN/MOLOTOV/GUERILLA] For example, we get "Assassin" from Arabic, "Molotov cocktail" from Russian and "guerilla" from Spanish. While you might like to shoot anyone who makes you spell these words, you must admit they've revolutionized our language. Well, I guess that joke bombed.

Unlike Arabic, Russian, and Spanish, all of which have completely phonetic spelling, English has the most bizarre, unstandardized spelling of any major world language. Take for an example this word. [VA: GHOTI] According to George Bernard Shaw, if you were to pronounce the "G-H" as in "enough," the "O" as in "women," and the T-I as in "action," this word could be pronounced "fish." Smells pretty rotten to me. What really stinks is when we tell children who are first learning how to read to "sound it out."

Now that you've seen how unstandardized our spelling is, you're probably feeling a bit like that child—rather confused, and with good reason. Well, don't worry. Order is about to return to your life in the form of—SPELLING RULES! [Derisive laughter at this concept.] Spelling rules? Isn't that like calling a 50-megaton warhead a "Peacekeeper?"

We've all been taught spelling rules. The most familiar one to most of us is "I before E except after C, unless pronounced A as in neighbor and weigh, but if the moon is full, use the infield fly rule." Simple! Logical? Easy to use and understand on an everyday basis, right? But most people tell us our spelling is weird. [VA: ~~WIERD~~ Weird]

The "I before E" poem is an example of something known as mnemonics. That's M-N-E-I—I forgot. Noah Webster had a nasty sense of humor. Another mnemonic helps us remember "we are weird," helping us remember the exception to the I before E rule.

I thought this mnemonics stuff was really neat, so I thought up one of my own for the word "graffiti." I remember that graffiti has two f's mostly because most words in graffiti tend to start with that letter. No one ever seems to screw that one up.

To every rule there is an exception, and spelling is no exception to that rule. To every spelling rule there is an exception. And to every exception, there are three more rules, four guidelines, six federal standards, and about nine bills pending in Congress.

Here's an example of a rule I personally know and use on an everyday basis— whether to end a word in E-F-Y or I-F-Y. I'm sure you know this one, too. The rule says to use I-F-Y, and that there are four exceptions. Or was that IRS and two exemptions? Anyway, the bottom line is that there are about eight words in the entire language which end in either E-F-Y or I-F-Y. It's pretty iffy to me as to whether you can call that a rule or not.

So there you have it. You've seen the way the media abuses spelling, the lack of standards, and rules that you can barely call that. By now, you're probably thinking that spelling is a lot like . . . third world politics. ANARCHY RULES! And the sad thing is that you're right. And like third world politics, spelling is often very confusing and complicated, even though it is potentially important. But don't worry or be ashamed. Most people have as much trouble telling Angola from Uganda as they do spelling my name. Tomorrow, somebody might ask you how to spell "Bophuthatswana." You probably won't know. But just remember, that doesn't have to be the Deeth of you.

INDEX